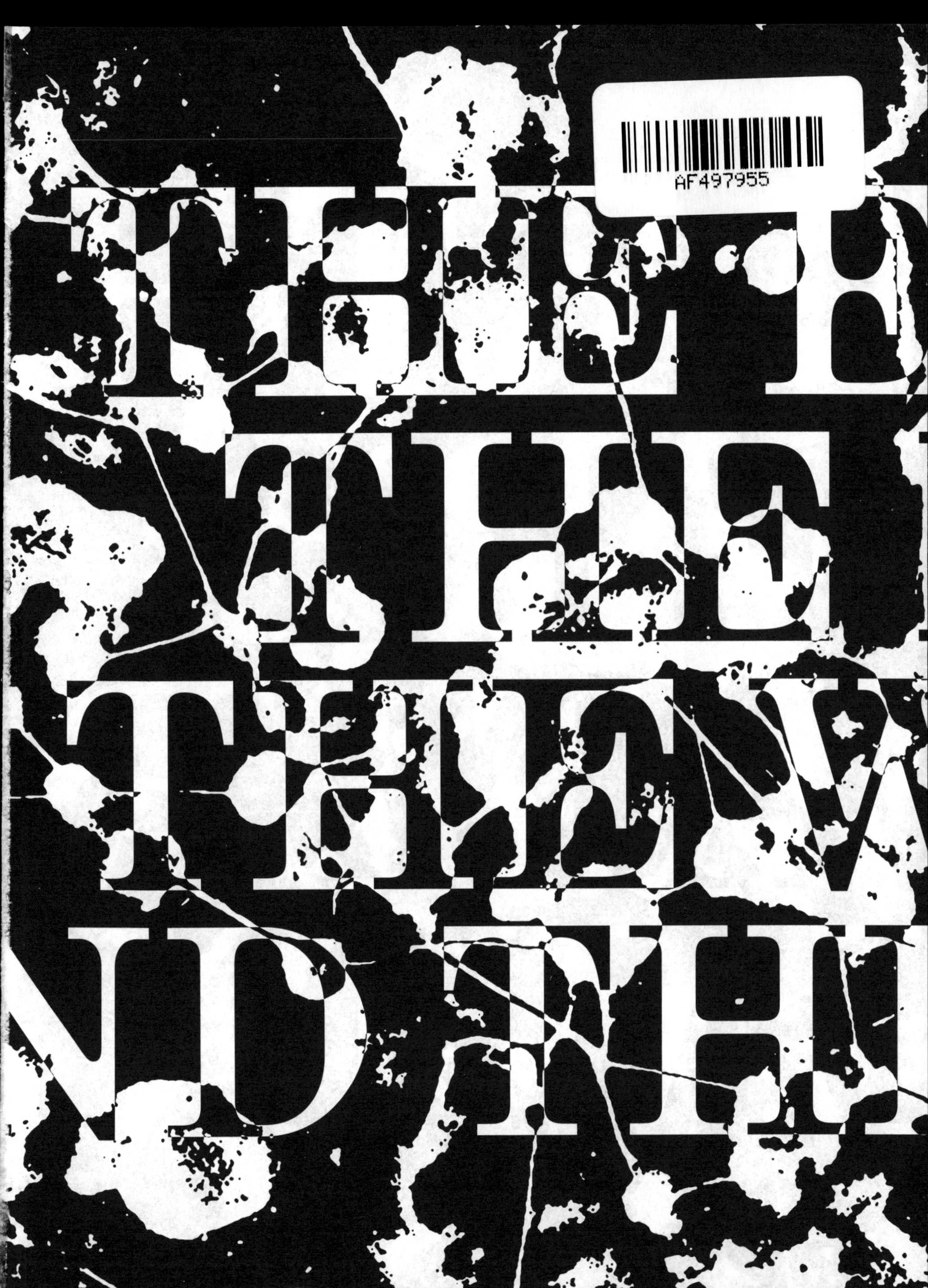
AF497955

EARTH
FIRE
WATER
WIND

Ministério da Cultura, Nubank
and Instituto Tomie Ohtake present

THE EARTH
THE FIRE
THE WATER
AND THE WINDS

For a Museum of Errantry with Edouard Glissant

INSTITUTO
TOMIE OHTAKE

CARA

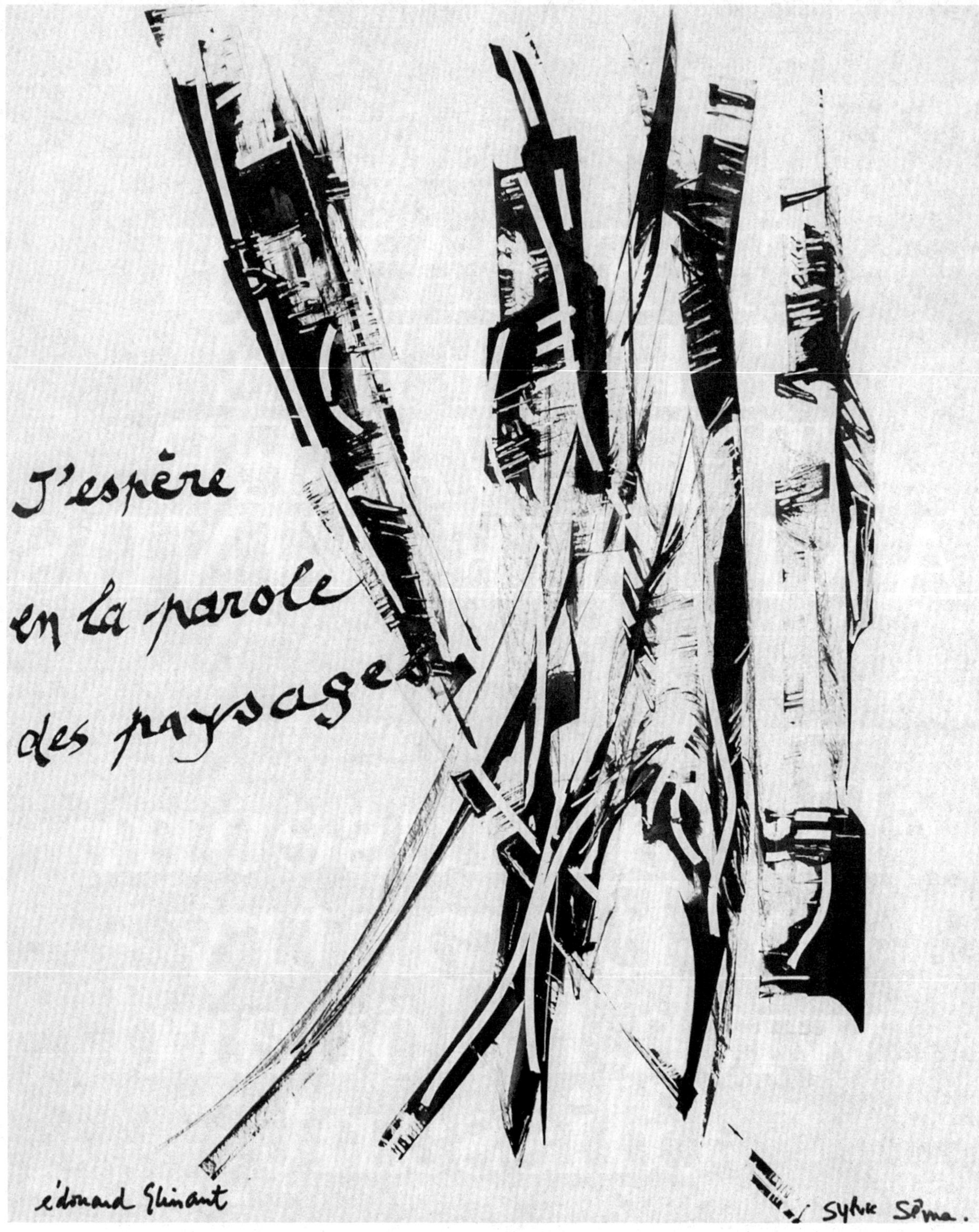

J'espère
en la parole
des paysages

I wait
within the words
of landscapes

Édouard Glissant and Sylvie Séma Glissant. *Untitled*, 2003. Ink on paper. Private Collection.
Translated by Sebastião Nascimento.

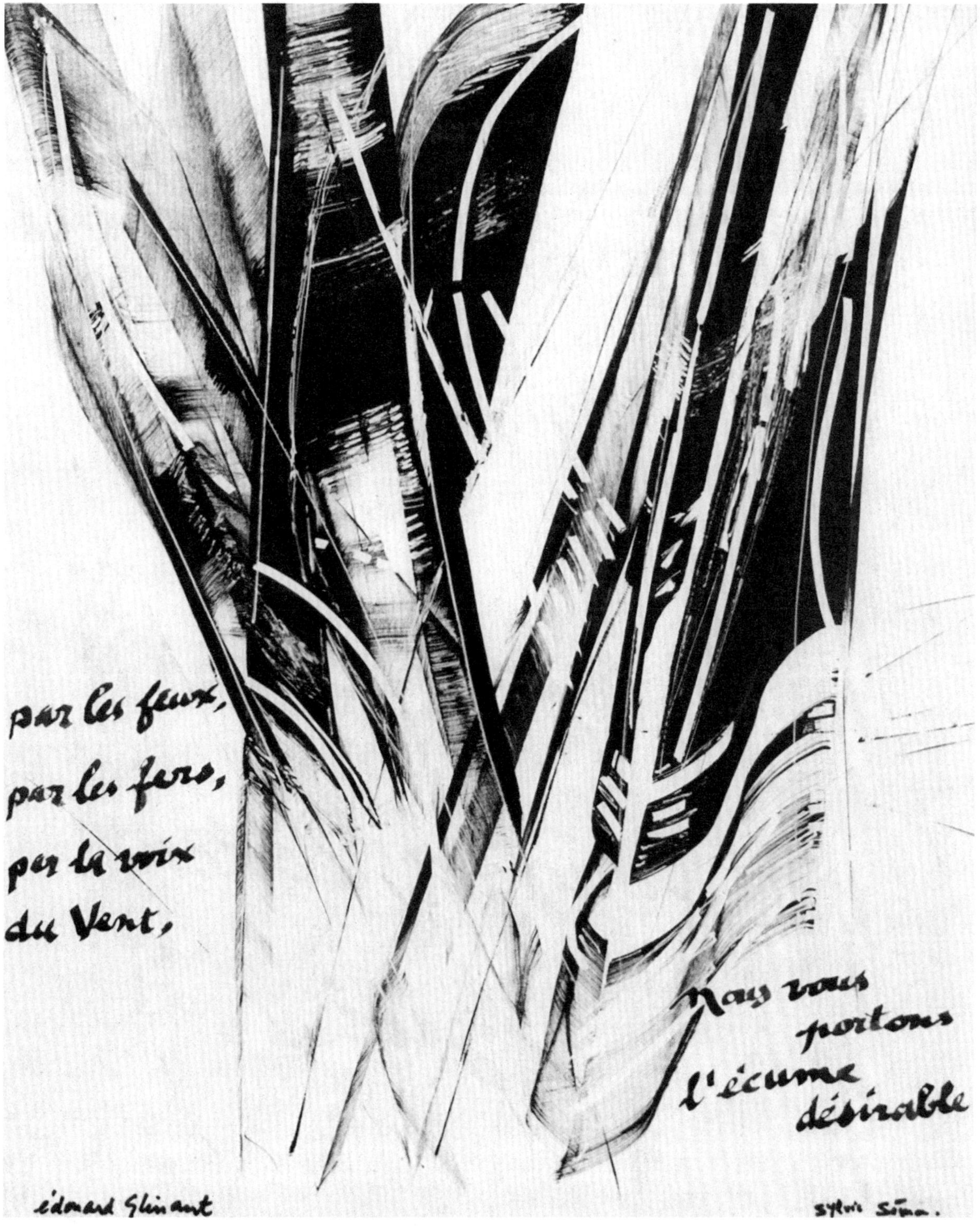

par les feux,	for the flames,
par les fers,	for the chains,
par la voix	for the voice
du Vent,	of the Wind,
nous vous portons	here we deliver
l'écume désirable	the coveted foam

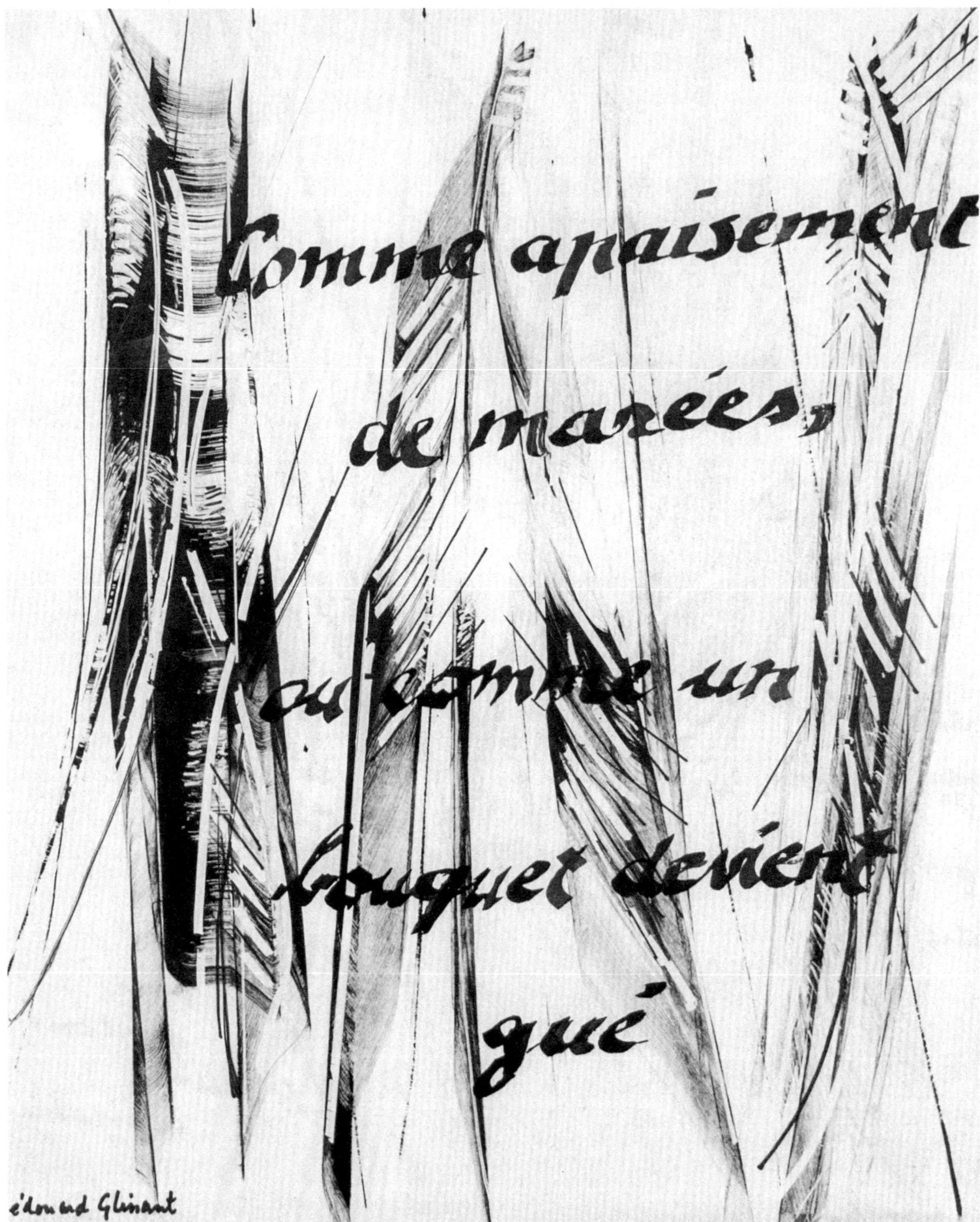

Comme apaisement
de marées,
ou comme un
bouquet devient
gué

As a soothing
of tides,
or as a
branch turns
ford

Édouard Glissant and Sylvie Séma Glissant. *Untitled*, 2003. Ink on paper. Private Collection.
Translated by Sebastião Nascimento.

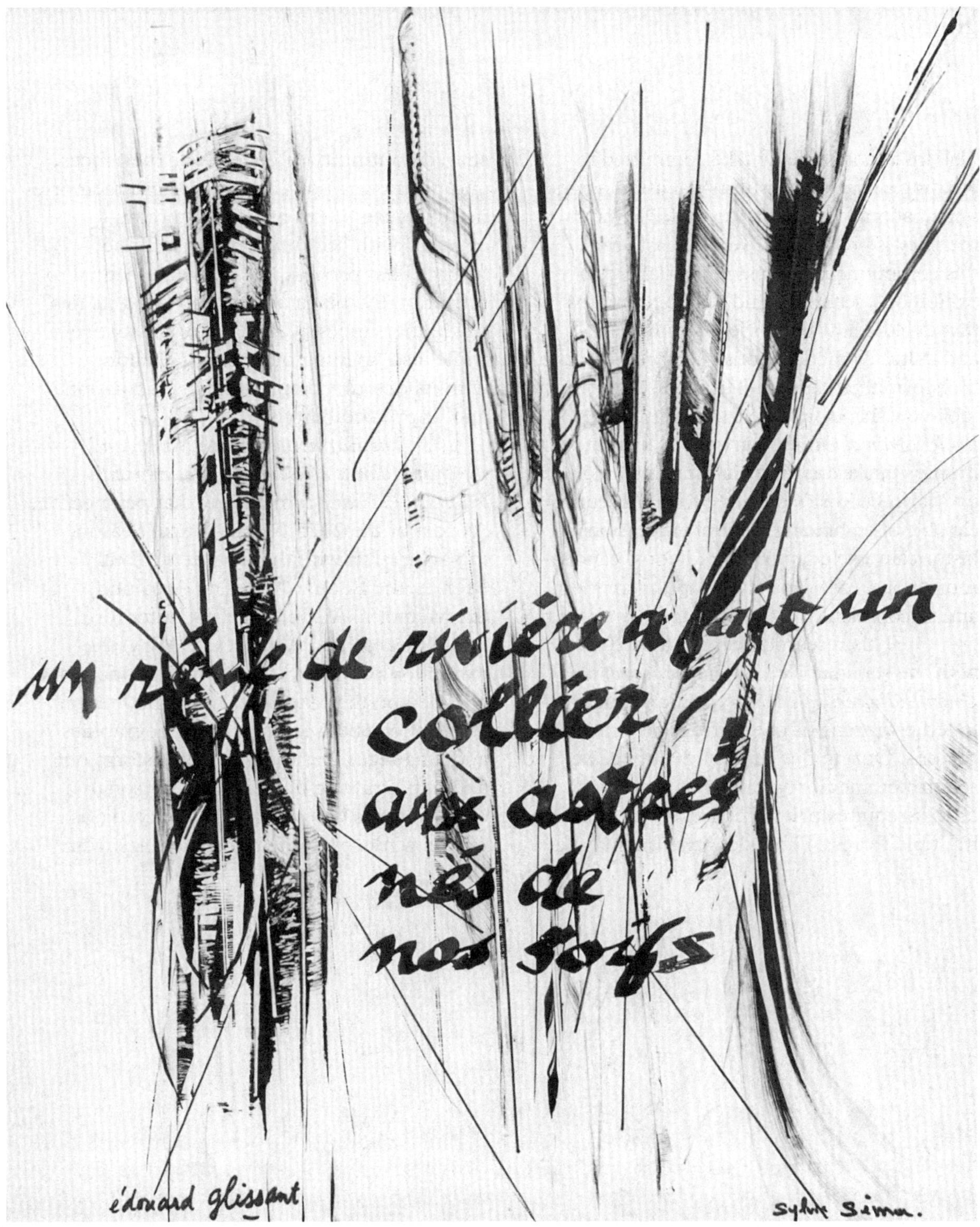

un rêve de rivière a fait un	a dream of river wove a
collier	flowing wreath
aux astres	for the stars
nés de	that thirsted
nos soifs	into being

The Instituto Tomie Ohtake committed to building a space for institutional listening and imagination, focused on the multiple ways memory is produced. Over the past years, this commitment has been materialized in exhibitions, seminars, and public programs that explore how territories, communities, and cultural practices construct, preserve, and transform their heritages. In 2023, this trajectory took new shape with the exhibition *Towards the Museum of Origins*, on view in Instituto Tomie Ohtake and Itaú Cultural, inspired by Mário Pedrosa's proposal for a museum capable of embracing cultural expressions historically excluded from traditional canons—Indigenous, Afro-Brazilian, popular, modern, and unconscious.

This research deepened in 2024 with the seminar *Towards the Museum of Origins: Politics of Memory*, which brought together dozens of guests from all Brazilian regions. During five days of dialogue, we reaffirmed memory-making as a political task: it requires prioritizing care, recognizing multiple forms of knowledge, ensuring the shared continuity of collective experiences, and promoting conditions for those memories not to freeze but to remain in motion—engaged with both the present and the future. That process has made it essential to reflect on the place of heritage—and its ties to identity, ancestry, and historical justice—while also opening ourselves to errantry, with its detours, displacements, fabulation, and unpredictability.

The Earth, the Fire, the Water, and the Winds: For a Museum of Errantry with Édouard Glissant comes from that perspective. As part of the 2025 France–Brazil Season, in partnership with the Institut du Tout-Monde, the Édouard Glissant Art Fund, the Mémorial ACTe, and the Center for Art, Research and Alliances (CARA) the exhibition proposes a museum in motion: not founded on the fixation of an origin, but on the relations between histories, geographies and languages that touch and transform one another. Drawing on Glissant's personal collection, his writings and oral records, as well as works by contemporary artists from the Americas, the Caribbean, Africa, and Europe, the exhibition activates the concepts of creolization, archipelago, opacity, and tremor as foundations for a poetic politics of memory. Between heritages and errantries, we continue to seek ways of imagining the museum (and cultural institutions) as sensitive, collective, and unpredictable spaces—where thought is born from the encounter between worlds.

The Instituto Tomie Ohtake thanks the Ministry of Culture, through the Federal Law for Cultural Incentives (Lei Rouanet), for making the exhibition.

We are grateful to Nubank, institutional sponsor of Instituto Tomie Ohtake; to SKY, bronze-level supporter; and to the Norma and Leo Werthein Foundation, supporting sponsor, for their contributions to this project.

Our recognition goes to the Institut Français and the Instituto Guimarães Rosa (Itamaraty) for leading the 2025 France–Brazil Season, of which this exhibition is part, and to the companies that make up the initiative's support committee: Engie, LVMH, ADEO, JCDecaux, Sanofi, Airbus, CMA CGM, CNP Seguradora, L'Oréal, TotalEnergies, Vinci, BNP Paribas, Carrefour, VICAT, and SCOR.

We extend our thanks to the co-organizers Mémorial ACTe, the Édouard Glissant Art Fund, and the Institut du Tout-Monde; to CARA for its partnership; and to the Institut Français for its institutional support.

We also thank the individuals who generously contributed to the realization of this exhibition and the development of its educational and public programs: Alexandra Mollof, Cleusa Garfinkel, Ivani and Jorge Yunes Collection, Laura Ning, and Sarina Tang.

We express our heartfelt thanks to all contributing artists, to the collectors who generously lent us their pieces, and to the curatorial, technical, educational, administrative, and production teams who worked tirelessly to bring this project to life.

We celebrate the longstanding dialogue with Sylvie Séma Glissant since the inception of this project. Without her trust and enthusiasm, none of this would have been possible.

The Institut du Tout-Monde (ITM) was founded in 2006 by Édouard Glissant, based on an aesthetic, a philosophy, and a poetic intention that had permeated his work and underpinned his commitment. The ITM has thus become a rhizomatic place of Relation and exchange, a platform for the world imageries and writings to meet, a space where creolization is expressed, an observatory of the unpredictable steps of globality, its accidents, the incidences and metamorphoses of living, a construction site for the utopias of the *Tout-Monde* [Whole-World]. Most of all, Édouard Glissant wished to offer a place for exchange, where people could accompany each other, following the wind lines of the world; where they could meet at its trembling points; what he used to call "a common place," where the thoughts of the world can meet other thoughts of the world; a place that is both real and utopian, opening up to the unpredictable possibilities of Relation and our co-presence at the moment of the encounter; both a crossroad of reflection dedicated to new modes of interculturality and a platform for actions that give concrete expression to otherness. Édouard Glissant never tired of repeating: "I change through exchange with the other without either losing myself or betraying who I am."

The ITM has established its administrative headquarters at La Maison de l'Amérique latine in Paris, its workshops in Aubervilliers in the Île-de-France region, and La Maison Edouard Glissant in Le Diamant, Martinique, at the junction of the Atlantic Ocean and the Caribbean Sea.

ITM holds seminars and multidisciplinary series in the humanities, participates in the circulation of a nomadic museum of the arts of the Americas, founded by Édouard Glissant, and collaborates to the creation of artist residencies with the Édouard Glissant Art Fund. It also organizes international poetry meetings in the form of "baroque archipelagos" (like the "Poetics of Resistance" evenings), and grants two literary prizes—the Carbet Prize for the Caribbean and the Tout-Monde Prize—as well as both the Édouard Glissant Prize and Scholarship. It has lately set up the Éditions de l'Institut du Tout-Monde, and encourages research groups that "reweave, relay and recount" the spaces of thought and poetic voices that "speak" the world. In 2018, the ITM also founded the Édouard Glissant International Center for Studies.

The exhibition *The Earth, the Fire, the Water, and the Winds: For a Museum of Errantry with Édouard Glissant* marks a milestone in the history of the Institut du Tout-Monde, as it brings together Édouard Glissant's personal art collection—a constellation of works that accompanied his life and thought—alongside contemporary creations that resonate with his poetic vision. This show is presented as part of the 2025 France–Brazil Season, and it embodies Glissant's dream of an artistic archipelago: a space of encounter between voices, territories, and imageries that echo and transform one another through Relation.

SYLVIE SÉMA GLISSANT
Director of the Institut du Tout-Monde

Our common project feels somehow less like a beginning than a continuation. This joint undertaking between the Instituto Tomie Ohtake, the Mémorial ACTe, the Édouard Glissant Art Fund, and CARA didn't come out of nowhere. It follows in the footsteps of long-standing, sometimes discreet connections between Brazil and the Caribbean, between artists and thinkers, between those who, like Glissant, choose to wander rather than settle.

This exhibition, *The Earth, the Fire, the Water, and the Winds: For a Museum of Errantry with Édouard Glissant*, invites us into those connections. It brings together fragments of Glissant's world—his personal art collection, unpublished writings, his voice—alongside contemporary works from artists who, each in their own way, confront the questions that inhabited him: What forms of unpredictable beauty rise from the chaos of our intertwined histories?

The title itself comes from a poetic anthology by Glissant, in which the elements—earth, fire, water, and winds—are not metaphors, but presence. They remind us that identity, like landscapes, is shaped by movement, by erosion, by unpredictable encounters; by some sort of alchemy. This project follows those intertwined poetics and aesthetics. It's neither a tribute nor a retrospective, but an unfinished, necessarily open space for Relation; a space that might feature what Glissant would call *le tremblement*: the tremor at the core of all encounters.

It is also, inevitably, a gesture toward one of Glissant's unfinished projects: the M2A2, the Martinican Museum of the Arts of the Americas. A museum he imagined not as a sanctuary for certainties, but rather as a living, moving space where the Caribbean could meet the Americas—and beyond. This exhibition, these collaborations, these residencies at the Maison Édouard Glissant, and these shared spaces of reflection, are our way—modest though persistent—of keeping that idea alive.

We're looking forward to following this path and exploring, together, the unpredictable routes of errantry.

MATHIEU GLISSANT
President of the Édouard Glissant Art Fund

The orientation project of the Mémorial ACTe (MACTe), launched in December 2024 and designed to guide the years to come, is titled: *"The Rhizome is the Matrix of Connection."*

This powerful expression draws from the thought of Édouard Glissant, for whom the rhizome serves as a vibrant metaphor for identity and culture—not fixed, singular, and rooted in a unique essence, but instead fluid, plural, and constantly evolving. In contrast to the single root, which symbolizes a closed and rigid identity, the rhizome spreads in multiple directions, forming a living, unpredictable, and profoundly free network.

The MACTe grounds its scientific, artistic, pedagogical, and cultural orientation in that spirit. The project cherishes a clear ambition: to fully accept the protean nature of the topics it addresses, embracing their complexity, and opening up a space where memories meet imagination, and where knowledge engages in a dialogue with emotion.

Such initiative also stands as a living tribute to Glissant's *Poetics of Relation*—a worldview deeply connected to our institution. The MACTe preserves his private collection, and the ties run deep: in 2007, President Jacques Chirac commissioned Glissant to draft a foundational report on creating a center dedicated to the memory of slavery and its abolition; this vision helped shape what the MACTe would later become.

As the Mémorial ACTe celebrates its 10th anniversary, in 2025, it's only natural the institution has contributed to the exhibition *The Earth, the Fire, the Water, and the Winds: For a Museum of Errantry with Édouard Glissant*, by showcasing Glissant's private collection and collaborating with the Instituto Tomie Ohtake the Édouard Glissant Foundation, the Institut du Tout Monde, Glissant Art Fund and the CARA.

This unique collaboration between Brazil, mainland France, and Guadeloupe perfectly reflects our mission: to keep Glissant's thought alive through the interconnection of cultures, histories, and identities, allowing each generation to creatively reinterpret and reimagine it in the light of its own context.

ISABELLE VESTRIS
Executive Director of the Mémorial ACTe

To take part in *The Earth, the Fire, the Water and the Winds: For a Museum of Errantry with Édouard Glissant* is, for CARA, to take part in a way of thinking that unfolds through companionship, movement, and mutual resonance. Glissant's thinking offers a vision of the world shaped by relation, a weaving of geographies, histories, and temporalities that do not seek uniformity, but live together with intensity and opacity. This publication opens a space of attention and drift, where fragments, traces, and gestures generate thought that moves with the world, not above it.

At CARA we understand art as a field of interdependence, where artistic, textual, and curatorial practices inform and transform one another. Our work grows through context, proximity, and shared time. Each program is rooted in long-standing relationships shaped by exchange, collective rhythm, and mutual listening. This book echoes that ethos. It does not trace a single path but gathers many, offering moments of encounter as a form of knowledge.

Glissant reminds us that thought grows at the edges—in intervals, in crossings, in what escapes categorization. The images, voices, and texts assembled here suggest a way of inhabiting time and language as sensitive, living materials. At CARA, we remain attuned to that sensibility. Our work draws from the coexistence of multiple languages, from embodied practices, and from ways of knowing passed on through gesture, breath, cadence, and relation. We understand curating as a practice shaped by contact and drift, a movement guided less by resolution than by reverberation.

New York sustains this kind of listening. A city shaped by migration, reinvention, and linguistic multiplicity, it holds within it the relational world Glissant described. In its polyphonic streets and overlapping temporalities, the *Tout-Monde* [Whole-World] is not a concept, it is the everyday. CARA is deeply embedded in this terrain, creating space for artistic practices that move across disciplines and for forms of knowledge that arise in conversation with the conditions of the present.

The iteration of the exhibition we will present in New York grows from this context. It is shaped by Glissant's collection, by the urgencies of our time, and by the connections that form when works, people, and ideas share space. This publication is part of that unfolding, a constellation in motion.

Since its founding, CARA has been committed to building a space for collective life through art and language. We understand the museum not as an institution of preservation, but as a living process of care, relation, and imagination.

To walk with Glissant is to believe that thought is not something we hold alone. It moves in rhythm with others, in relation to place, and always toward the possible.

MANUELA MOSCOSO
Executive and Artistic Director of the Center for Art, Research and Alliances, New York

The 2025 France–Brazil Season is an initiative by Presidents Luiz Inácio Lula da Silva and Emmanuel Macron to celebrate the 200th anniversary of diplomatic relations between the two countries and to deepen bilateral cooperation on key themes for our shared future: climate and ecological transition; democracy and the rule of law; cultural diversity and relations with Africa. The Season programming, which was organized by the Institut Français and the Instituto Guimarães Rosa, with the support of the Ministries of Foreign Affairs and Culture and the Embassies of France in Brazil and of Brazil in France, will take place in France from April to September and in Brazil from August to December.

The Season in Brazil aims to create new exchange opportunities between artists, thinkers, curators, and cultural institutions from both countries, as well as to present lesser-known facets of French culture with influences of Africa and the Caribbean. Among them, the cultures of the French territories in the Americas (Martinique, Guadeloupe, French Guiana) hold a special place, due to their historical and aesthetic affinities with the Brazilian culture.

The great Martinican poet and thinker, Édouard Glissant, is one of the most singular voices from that region; a voice that resonates with particular strength in these troubled times. In a world threatened by totalitarianism, nationalism, intolerance, and the use of force, Glissant reminds us that our humanity can only survive through Relation. He tirelessly calls us to "change, by changing with the Other," a phrase that could well serve as the motto of this Season.

I sincerely thank the Instituto Tomie Ohtake for presenting for the first time—as a partnership with the Mémorial ACTe of Guadeloupe, the Institut du Tout-Monde, and the Édouard Glissant Art Fund—Édouard Glissant's personal art collection, enriched by works by contemporary artists in dialogue with his vision. The sensitive, subtle, far-reaching curatorial work of Paulo Miyada and Ana Roman not only introduces the thought and the poetics of Glissant to the Brazilian public, but also fulfills one of his dreams: an artistic archipelago standing as a metaphor for the *Tout-Monde* [Whole-World]. A space to imagine new relations between Brazil and France.

ANNE LOUYOT
General Commissioner of the France-Brazil Season

"Those who meet up *here* always come from an 'over there', from the expanse of the world, and here they are, determined to bring to this 'here' the fragile knowledge that they have taken from over there.

Fragile knowledge is not imperious science. We sense that we are following a trace. So this is my second proposition: That the thought of the *trace*, as opposed to systematic thought, acts as a wandering that guides us. We know that the trace is what puts us, all of us, wherever we come from, in Relation. ¶ And for some people, over there, so far so near, right here, on the hidden face of the earth, the trace was lived as one of the places of survival. For example, for the descendants of the Africans transported into slavery into what would soon be called the New World, it was usually the only possible form of action."

Édouard Glissant, *Treatise on the Whole-World*. Translated by Celia Britton. Liverpool: Liverpool University Press, 2020, p. 9.

196 Journal d'un voyage sur le Nile [Diary of a Journey on the Nile]

Édouard Glissant

The Earth, the Fire, the Water, and the Winds

For a Museum of Errantry with Édouard Glissant

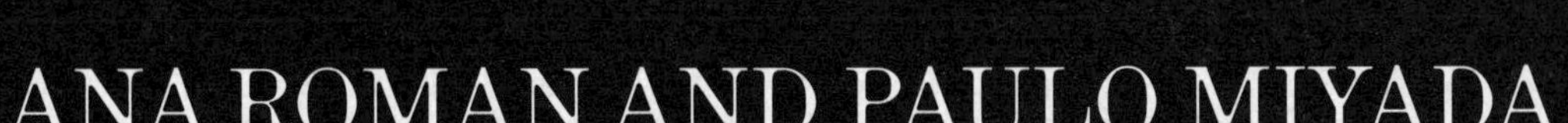
ANA ROMAN AND PAULO MIYADA

Man is not a thinking reed, but,
as Shakespeare said, a walking forest.
Édouard Glissant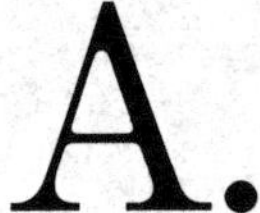

A.

Glissant, Now

It makes sense that Édouard Glissant's writing has become a key reference point for many of the voices questioning the ongoing forms of colonialism that continue to uphold myths of purity, superiority, and control rooted in Eurocentric thought.[2] Without seeking to establish a closed philosophical system, Glissant developed his poetic thinking between Martinique and Paris, with passages through the United States, and an openness to the languages and places of the world. Along the way, he built a sustained critique of single-root thinking and a monumental affirmation of multiplicity, always careful not to reduce countercolonial struggle[3] to the short-term goal of simply replacing one totalizing power structure with another.

We arrived at 2025 still surrounded by evidence of hatred toward otherness—the fuel burning wildly on all sides, not only in wars and genocides, but also in xenophobic migration policies; in efforts to control bodies, sexualities, and forms of affect; in mechanisms for spreading falsehoods; and in the refusal to heed the planet's messages of exhaustion. In such context, turning to Glissant may help

[1]   Édouard Glissant, *Le Discours antillais*. Paris: Gallimard, 1997, p. 447.

[2]   In addition to initiatives directly associated with Glissant and the Institut du Tout-Monde, as discussed below, the relationship between Édouard Glissant's thinking and contemporary art has deepened since the 1990s, especially by listening to curators who are inspired by his work as a conceptual and ethical tool. Hans Ulrich Obrist, whose conversations with Glissant were collected in *The Archipelago Conversations* (2021), was a pioneer in presenting these ideas-creolization, opacity, archipelago-in exhibitions such as *Utopia Station* (Venice Biennale, 2003). More recently, his archival projects, such as *Hans-Ulrich Obrist Archive: Chapter 1 - Édouard Glissant*, exhibited at venues like LUMA Arles (2021) and West Den Haag (2024), have deployed Glissant's videos, writings, and ephemera as spaces of poetic and political exchange. Such inspiration guides shows like *This Language that Is Every Stone* (IMA Brisbane, 2022), co-curated by Obrist, Asad Raza, and Warraba Weatherall, and permeates the 34th Bienal de São Paulo (*Faz escuro mas eu canto* [Though It's Dark, I Sing], 2021), organized by Jacopo Crivelli Visconti, Paulo Miyada, Carla Zaccagnini, Francesco Stocchi, and Ruth Estévez, who implemented the poetics of relation as a curatorial principle. In 2017, the Mémorial ACTe and the Museo del Caribe presented the exhibition *Gabriel García Márquez, Édouard Glissant, La Caraïbe: Solitudes et Relation*, as part of the France-Colombia Crossed Season, showcasing part of Glissant's personal collection. In 2024, Julien Creuzet deepened that legacy in the French pavilion at the Venice Biennale, collaborating with the Édouard Glissant Art Fund and the Maison Édouard Glissant. In the same year, the exhibition *The Trembling Museum*, curated by Dominic Paterson and Andy Mills, with guest curation by Terris Geis and Manthia Diawara, discussed the collection of African art at Glasgow's Hunterian Museum from a Glissantian approach.

[3]   We use the term *countercolonial* to refer to forms of resistance that not only react to colonialism, but also propose autonomous cosmologies and existences. See: Antonio Bispo dos Santos, *A terra dá, a terra quer*. São Paulo: Ubu / Piseagrama, 2023.

reveal that the opposite of this hatred also stirs on all sides, breathing life into the conviction that it is possible that "I can change through exchange with the other without losing or distorting myself."④

When Glissant is quoted in isolated phrases, his convictions can sometimes come across as a vaguely progressive, humanist, or romantic appeal. But that perception is dispelled upon closer reading of his poems, essays, treatises, speeches, plays, and novels. It becomes clear Glissant doesn't ignore the historical violence of colonialism or their present-day forms; quite the opposite: he situates concepts such as Relation, creolization, trace, errantry, *here and elsewhere,* and *Tout-Monde*⑤ (Whole-World)⑥ at the very heart of how the contemporary world is formed. Those concepts function simultaneously as learned forms of resistance and as reactive responses sparked by the global expansion of a control apparatus rooted in the homogenizing monopoly of a single idea of civilization and progress. In other words, it's not a romanticized vision of the past or a mythologization of any particular social group that drives Glissant. Instead, he searches within the conflicts of the present for the embryo of a future that is both desiring and desirable.

Other pathways—among which are poetics, aesthetics, and philosophy—primarily nourish Glissant's gaze, though it was informed by history, sociology, and anthropology. For that reason, one way to build a more attentive engagement with his work is not only through reading his texts,⑦ but through a careful study of his ideas and his dialogue with other thinkers. For that matter, research into his position within the wider network of Caribbean intellectuals is especially important—as is the body of writing by authors from Martinique, an island

④ Édouard Glissant, *Introduction to a Poetics of Diversity*. Translated by Celia Britton. Liverpool: Liverpool University Press, 2020, p. 113.

⑤ In this text, we have chosen to translate *Tout-Monde* as Whole-World, following established and widely recognized translations. However, it is worth noting that an alternative rendering—One World—also resonates with Édouard Glissant's Philosophy of Relation.

⑥ In this essay, we will not thoroughly define all the terms created by Édouard Glissant; many of them are discussed in the transcribed talk between the author and Patrick Chamoiseau, to which we will return later. On the other hand, we will focus on a few key concepts that will make subsequent passages easier to understand.

⑦ Among Édouard Glissant's texts already published in English, the following stand out: *Caribbean Discourse: Selected Essays*. Translated by J. Michael Dash. Charlottesville: University Press of Virginia, 1989; *Poetics of Relation*. Translated by Betsy Wing. Ann Arbor: University of Michigan Press, 1997; *The Fourth Century*. Translated by Betsy Wing. Ann Arbor: University of Michigan Press, 2001; *The Overseer's Cabin*. Translated by Betsy Wing. Lincoln: University of Nebraska Press, 2011; *Sun of Consciousness*. Translated by Nathanaël. New York: Nightboat Books, 2020; *Poetic Intention*. Translated by Nathanaël with Anne Malena. New York: Nightboat Books, 2010; *Treatise on the Whole-World*. Translated by Celia Britton. Liverpool: Liverpool University Press, 2020; *Introduction to a Poetics of Diversity*. Translated by Celia Britton. Liverpool: Liverpool University Press, 2020; *A New Region of the World: Aesthetics I*. Translated by Martin Munro. Liverpool: Liverpool University Press, 2023; *Black Salt: Poems*. Translated by Betsy Wing. Ann Arbor: University of Michigan Press, 1999; *The Collected Poems of Édouard Glissant*. Edited by Jeff Humphries. Translated by Jeff Humphries and Melissa Manolas. Minneapolis: University of Minnesota Press, 2019; and *The Baton Rouge Interviews*. Translated by Katie M. Cooper. Liverpool: Liverpool University Press, 2020.

whose small physical scale is inversely proportional to the magnitude of reflections by Aimé Césaire, Frantz Fanon, Édouard Glissant, and Patrick Chamoiseau. These perspectives are complemented by fertile lines of research that compare and contrast Glissant's view of the African diaspora—its scars from the transatlantic slave trade and the beauty of African American culture—with postcolonial thought shaped by authors from other regions, including Léon-Gontran Damas (French Guiana), Léopold Sédar Senghor (Senegal), Wole Soyinka (Nigeria), Edward Said (Palestine), Maryse Condé (Guadeloupe), Gayatri Chakravorty Spivak (India), Abdias do Nascimento (Brazil), and Paul Gilroy (United Kingdom), among many others. Another valuable line of inquiry is to compare Glissant's approach to thought and language with the writings of French theorists Gilles Deleuze and Félix Guattari—particularly Glissant's concept of the archipelago with their notion of the rhizome—and identifying the key similarities and differences between the two.[8]

The exhibition *The Earth, the Fire, the Water, and the Winds: For a Museum of Errantry with Édouard Glissant*[9] contributes directly to initiatives of that kind by presenting, for the first time, an edited selection from a wide-ranging interview filmed in 2008 between Glissant and the aforementioned Martinican writer, Patrick Chamoiseau.[10] Structured like a conceptual primer, with key ideas organized alphabetically, this glossary-conversation demonstrates Glissant's deep connection to orality. His spoken discourse naturally recalls passages from texts he wrote years or even decades earlier, while at the same time unfolding as a spontaneous narration, a kind of thinking aloud.

The aim of this project, however, extends beyond this sort of material, research, and debate. While examining Glissant's lexicon and comparing it with that of other thinkers is essential, it's equally important to highlight the part of his thought that expands the scope of philosophy and the humanities by drawing vitality from poetics—both literary and visual—and from the landscape.

In order to do so, we need to find other ways of thinking *with* Glissant—which is not the same as thinking *about* Glissant. Thinking *with* means standing before a set of ideas, works, and relationships while also standing alongside a

[8]   See Édouard Glissant, "Rethinking Utopia," *Introduction to a Poetics of Diversity*, Liverpool: Liverpool University Press, 2020, p. 113.

[9]   The exhibition *The Earth, the Fire, the Water, and the Winds: For a Museum of Errantry with Édouard Glissant* is an official part of the 2025 France-Brazil Season. The Season is envisioned in dialogue with the Institut Français and the Ministry of Culture of Brazil. It offers a platform for circulating works, ideas, and knowledge, fostering collaboration across different institutions. In such a context, the Instituto Tomie Ohtake project reinforces partnerships with the Mémorial ACTe, the Institut du Tout-Monde, the Édouard Glissant Art Fund, and CARA, and strengthens dialogues with French institutions such as the Bibliothéque nationale de France and the Maison de l'Amérique Latine.

[10]   The full interview encompasses more than 13 hours of recording, covering dozens of core concept-words in Édouard Glissant's thinking. In the exhibition, six monitors display a total of 17 selected subjects: Alphabet, Archipelago, Creolization, Discourses, Errantry, Extension, Identity, Jazz, Landscape, Language, Matta, Notebook, Tremors, True / Alive, Utopia, and Wifredo Lam. This book presents an edited portion of that material, based on the archives of the Institut du Tout-Monde, with support and permission from Sylvie Séma Glissant and Mathieu Glissant. This is the first time this interview is published in English—and the first edition of this material in printed format in any language.

poetic and philosophical body of work. It involves tracing paths that intertwine with the trajectory of a life, and inhabiting the opacity that is intrinsic to friendships, conflicts, and affinities that exceed what can be captured in archival documentation.

B.

The Winds

In 2010, Glissant published the book *La Terre, le feu, l'eau et les vents: Une anthologie de la poésie du Tout-Monde* [The Earth, the Fire, the Water, and the Winds: A Whole-World Poetry Anthology] through Galaade Éditions.[11] The volume presents fragments of texts drawn from a wide range of sources—spanning from Homer to Chico Science, and including Aimé Césaire, Julio Cortázar, Arthur Rimbaud, William Faulkner, Martin Luther King Jr., Blaise Cendrars, Frankétienne, transcriptions of Amerindian chants, and many others. Rather than categorizing these fragments by language, origin, period, or format, Glissant works as a kind of montage artist, weaving resonances, continuities, and contrasts among the pieces he selected.[12] The result is a framework of poetic references collected over a lifetime (Glissant was born in 1928 and died in 2011, less than a year after the publication of the anthology).[13] Thematic links throughout the text are discoverable, but they don't occur in a didactic way; there are no introductions, commentaries, or topical subdivisions to signal them. As Glissant writes in the book introduction:

> An anthology of poetry of the Whole-World such as this one does not follow any logical or chronological order; rather, it abruptly reveals connections of energy, moments of calm and drowsiness, flashes of the mind, and the heavy, sumptuous wanderings of thought—which the anthology seeks to balance so that reader may perhaps imagine new paths of their own. Storms and bright Tropics! Burning glaciers!... We must reflect, as we always have, on that dismissive notion: "nevermind the weak and the oppressed, upon

[11] Édouard Glissant, *La Terre, le feu, l'eau et les vents: Une anthologie de la poésie du Tout-Monde*. Paris: Galaade / Institut du Tout-Monde / Maison de l'Amérique Latine, 2010.

[12] For more information on Glissant's methodology, see: Édouard Glissant and Hans Ulrich Obrist, *Dans un monde imprévisible, l'utopie est nécessaire*. Paris: Seuil / Arles: LUMA Arles, 2024.

[13] The title of the anthology (*La Terre, le feu, l'eau et les vents*) was directly inspired by the poetic universe of Icelandic writer, Thor Vilhjálmsson, with whom Glissant corresponded, and whose writing intensely evokes the elements of nature as forces in constant crossing and transformation.

whose misfortune such excellence has always been built," and on the "contempt for the history of peoples." Because the Elements conceive of their own duration only in the radiance of justice, justice itself becomes a powerful force in the world order and disorder. It provokes the dark and forced laughter of the long-suffering, makes the snickering of those who are desperate quiver, and causes those who profit from the excellence of this world to shudder with discomfort, their frantic comfort wavering from all sides. Poetry speaks of these tremors. [...]

Let us imagine that the authors [of the selected passages] bring together the brilliance and the echo, the lasting thought and the flow, the poem and the word that carries it forward. From one inspiration to the next—and based on those elements (through which we bear witness) and their shared peculiarities—each reader finds their own way. They allow us to pause on a hillside [*morne*], or by the edge of a lagoon, near an alleyway, or a heavy glass-and-metal factory—the everyday settings of our wanderings—to hear the humble poem, the testimony of childhood, the cries and murmurs. For instance, the adolescence of *Franc Jeu* in the town of Lamentin; then the flash, the true cry, *Tropiques*, a magazine that rose from the sea; and young *Élements*, a magazine that shines only from afar; or *Acoma*, a local journal that is now sprouting again. And finally, middle age: sudden events from all over, the *immigration* no one escapes from, the crossroads, but also the crossing, through this time that is constantly being undone and reshaped. That is how I traced the embankment from which this anthology overflowed. And there are many others, for other possible currents of poems—as long as you take part in the flame and the sweetness of the world. The world, the poem's highest purpose: its trust, its mirror.[14]

This quotation—the longest included in the text—exemplifies the tangled weave at the heart of Glissant's poetic conception, in which poetry, landscape, errantry, and revolt are inseparable. What happens when we unfold this tangle

[14]   Édouard Glissant, *La Terre, le feu, l'eau et les vents: Une anthologie de la poésie du Tout-monde*. Paris: Galaade / Institut du Tout-Monde / Maison de l'Amérique Latine, 2010, pp. 18-19. [Free translation]

within the realm of visual arts and museums? And what if the weave of such vibrant poetics were taken as a political, aesthetic, and ethical principle—a way to navigate the diversity, urgency, and fluctuation of artistic production in a world shaken by tremors, injustices, and looming social, environmental and cognitive collapses?

As we'll see, Glissant articulated fragments of a vision for what a 21st-century museum might be. But the poet was never able to implement that vision in any lasting way. In this gap, we have chosen to borrow both the title and the compositional principle of his poetic anthology as a heterogeneous, heterodox method for fabulating a Glissantian museum—a *Museum of Errantry*, as we have chosen to call it.

Glissant envisions the museum as a space where multiple temporalities overlap; a discontinuous, responsive time in which past, present, and future interrogate one another. More than a repository of works or a visual chronology, the museum appears in his writings as a form of resistance—one that is not only political, but also epistemological and responsive. It becomes a way to seek out memory and to generate memory through its detours, absences, and reinventions. Against a single, dominant history, against the monumentalization of knowledge, Glissant proposes the museum as a site of listening and transformation, capable of reawakening dormant meanings and opening space for what has yet to be named.[15]

In light of this, and drawing on Glissant's poetry anthology as a point of departure, we conceived this exhibition as an essay in montage: interweaving multiple layers and elements from diverse origins without imposing divisions or linear order, instead fostering friction, resonance, and convergence among them. The first of these layers is Glissant's personal collection, assembled over the course of his life and accompanying his writing and displacements. This collection, now housed at the Mémorial ACTe in Pointe-à-Pitre, Guadeloupe, is shown here for the first time as primary exhibition material. It includes works by artists with whom Glissant shared personal ties—most of them from Latin America or the Caribbean, though not exclusively. These are records of relationships that shaped Glissant's way of seeing and thinking about art, while also reflecting his influence on the artists themselves, whether through direct dialogue or in writing.

Presenting this collection therefore also means bringing to light Glissant's proposal for the M2A2 (Musée Martiniquais des Arts des Amériques) [Martinican Museum of the Arts of the Americas]. This was a dream first iteration of which took place in 1999 at the Maison de l'Amérique Latine in Paris, envisioned as a prefiguration of the museum to be established in Martinique within the ruins of a former sugar mill in the Lamentin region. Based on the voluntary donation of artworks by artists from across the Americas, the M2A2 was a project Glissant nurtured until the end of his life—an initiative that continues to inspire the work of the Édouard Glissant Art Fund and the Institut du

[15]   Édouard Glissant talks about his museum project in Édouard Glissant and Hans Ulrich Obrist, "Premier entretien privé," in *Dans un monde imprévisible – L'utopie est nécessaire*; and Édouard Glissant, "Beauty and the Beautiful and the Orientation Towards the New Museums." Transcribed and translated by Manthia Diawara and Terri Geis. Originally published in a video on the Afrodiasporarts platform in 2011.

Tout-Monde, under the direction of Sylvie Séma Glissant.[16] Such initiative also gave rise to a second layer of loans for the exhibition, ranging from works held by the Institut du Tout-Monde to direct loans from artists who knew Glissant and/or contributed works to the M2A2.

A close reading of these two layers requires moving back and forth between Glissant's writings, his trajectory of encounters within the art world, and the poetics of each work selected from the artists' broader production. Within this dynamic, two zones of convergence emerged—what we chose to call the "landscape of the word" and the "word of the landscape." These terms revisit and expand Glissant's formulation of *parole du paysage* [word of the landscape],[17] within the context of his reflections on the convergences between language and landscape. They invite us to consider how words shape and are shaped by cultural imaginaries and narratives—in the broader setting of human and nonhuman relations. To make these convergences more tangible within a platform (the exhibition) that is primarily sensory and immersive, two additional layers were introduced: the invitation to other contemporary artists, extending beyond Glissant's immediate circle, and the selection of fragments from his own speech, writing, and drawing.

The participating contemporary artists are from the Americas (with a particular emphasis on the Caribbean and Brazil), as well as from Europe (mainly France), Africa, and Asia. Spanning multiple generations, the selection considered each artist's displacements, diasporas, territorialities, and diversities—and, above all, the connection between their works (whether commissioned or pre-existing) and the pieces stemming from Glissant's personal relationships. The goal is to expand and update the circle of interlocutors brought into dialogue with Glissant's thought, as a kind of living memorial. It is also to combine languages, scales, and temporalities in order to shape a synesthetic experience shared with the exhibition visitors, who are invited to consider the juxtapositions and chart their own path through a dense aesthetic terrain.

Glissant's presence in the exhibition is inscribed as a text within the text— flashes of insights in which the word emerges as an invitation to enter another temporal dimension of reflection. This unfolds through excerpts of poetry and prose selected from his many books, with particular emphasis on the essays he wrote about the artists with whom he maintained a dialogue. In addition, the exhibition space is punctuated by excerpts from the aforementioned "conceptual

[16] The prefiguration presented at the Maison de l'Amérique Latine from September to October 1999 was organized with the support of curator Hélène Lassalle. The exhibition featured a logo designed by Victor Anicet, and toured Latin America. After its opening, the project received donations from artists close to Glissant, as well as from other artists who worked closely with his approach. The expected support from public agencies in Martinique did not materialize, and M2A2 began to be devised as a nomadic museum. In May 2016, Sylvie Séma Glissant and Hélène Lassalle curated a new show titled *Musée du Tout-Monde & Agora Mundo* [Whole-World Museum & Now World] at the Cité des Arts in Paris, featuring several works given to Glissant's project. At the same time, the French State acquired Glissant's personal collection during the poet's inheritance transfer; it is in the care of the Mémorial ACTe, partially realizing M2A2's premise regarding the presence of a collection of international significance on an island in the Antilles.

[17] The idea of "parole du paysage" emerges at different moments in Glissant's work and is directly linked to his relational notion of identity and aesthetics. This concept will be revisited and deeply discussed in this text.

primer," offering concise reflections on central terms in the show, such as *errantry, landscape,* and *language,* as well as *archipelago, creolization, discourse, utopia,* and others. Finally, the display includes a facsimile copy of an unpublished notebook Glissant wrote during a journey along the Nile River in Egypt in 1988.[18] With its drawings and writings, the travel journal serves as a reflection of his thought in motion, in contact with a landscape and a language that, until then, had been familiar only through images, accounts, and texts. Along this journey, the Nile is revealed not as an exotic or distant landscape, but as a living terrain for poetic and intellectual reconfiguration—a space in which his memory of other places and other languages, already visited or merely imagined, is reworked.

The poetic core of the exhibition thus takes shape through the interplay of collection and notebook, interview and artworks—a constellation of works devoid of hierarchical relationships of precedence or illustration. A note left by Glissant at the bottom of a blank page in his Egyptian journal comes to mind:

> Writings without a plan or form, deceptively episodic, circling around their subject like a felucca drifting about in the morning shadows.[19]

C.

Errantry

Born in 1928 in Sainte-Marie, a small rural town in northern Martinique, Glissant grew up in an environment deeply shaped by the plantation social system, by knowledge passed down through popular oral traditions, and by the lingering traces of slavery—which, in the context of the island, remained palpable in every aspect of its social and territorial structure—still deeply present in Glissant's childhood, long after abolition in 1848. He studied at the Lycée Victor-Schœlcher in Fort-de-France, enmeshed in the tension between his life experience on the island and a French education that ignored the landscape, language, and embodied ways of being that marked his life beyond the school walls. Such dissonance between what was taught and what was lived became one of the driving forces behind his

[18]   Édouard Glissant's manuscripts, his *fonds d'archives,* were acknowledged as a French national treasure in December 2014 and acquired by the Bibliothèque nationale de France (BnF, the National Library of France), where they are preserved and studied. The *Diary of a Journey on the Nile,* 1988, is comprised of 112 pages and is cataloged with code NAF 28894 (67) (NIL). Its description within the archive reads: "Illustrated diary of a trip on a felucca on the Nile with Jean-Jacques Lebel, publisher Inge Feltrinelli, painter Matta and his wife Germana, Sylvie Glissant, and Madame Bélenis. Handwritten diary in preparation for *Les Grands Chaos, Fastes,* and the novel *Tout-Monde.* It contains several unpublished texts and poems." [Free translation]

[19]   Édouard Glissant, *Journal d'un voyage sur le Nile* [Diary of a Journey on the Nile], 1988. Manuscript held in the collection of the BnF. Translated by Sebastião Nascimento, p.26.

search for elements that could help articulate a Caribbean identity resistant to homogenization and attuned to the constitutive power of relations—of power, of exchange, of resistance, and of creolization.

In 1946, Glissant moved to Paris on a scholarship and enrolled at the Sorbonne, where he studied philosophy and literature. He also spent time at the Musée de l'Homme, developing an interest in ethnology and anthropology, fields that helped him begin to articulate a distinction between what he called atavistic cultures and composite cultures. At the same time, he was actively involved in intellectual circles linked to anticolonialism and black thought, contributing regularly to the journal *Présence Africaine* [African Presence] and taking part, in 1956, in the first *Congrès International des Écrivains et Artistes Noirs* [International Congress of Black Writers and Artists], held in the Descartes Amphitheater at the Sorbonne.

Upon returning to Martinique, Glissant deepened his political engagement. In 1961, he founded the Front Antillo-Guyanais pour l'Autonomie (FAGA) [Antillean-Guianan Front for Autonomy], a movement that advocated for the autonomy of the French Antilles. As a consequence of his activism, he came under surveillance by the French State and was subject to travel restrictions until 1965. In 1967, he founded the Institut Martiniquais d'Études (IME), an institution dedicated to critical research on Caribbean societies, integrating local knowledge, history, literature, and political thought. The IME marked a pioneering effort to reimagine education from within the Caribbean, breaking with models of intellectual dependency and privileging critical reflection rooted in the region itself. This initiative was followed by the launch of the *Acoma* (1971–1973) journal, a platform for multidisciplinary debate centered in Martinique. Both the institute and the journal were foundational to the development of his ambitious book *Le Discours antillais* (1981) [*Caribbean Discourse*]. Facing practical limitations on his work in Martinique, he returned to Paris, where he directed the journal *Le Courrier de l'UNESCO* between 1982 and 1988. That same year, he moved to the United States, where he taught at the Louisiana State University, later holding a professorship at the City University of New York (CUNY). Back in Paris once again, he founded the Institut du Tout-Monde in 2006.

This brief biography is enough to underscore that we are dealing with a thinker who reflected on landscape, language, and culture, drawing from a context marked by conflict and shaped by his own life of continuous movement—a life of errantry. It's important to keep that in mind in order to understand the genesis of this project at the Instituto Tomie Ohtake.

In 2023, the Instituto held, in partnership with Itaú Cultural, the exhibition *Ensaios para o Museu das Origens* [Towards the Museum of Origins], which explored the intersections of culture, politics, and memory production in Brazil. The catalyst for that initiative was the proposal for creating the Museum of Origins, put forward by Mário Pedrosa, one of the most engaged voices in the transformation of Brazilian art and society throughout the 20th century. Developed during the efforts to rebuild the Museu de Arte Moderna in Rio de Janeiro after a fire in 1978, Pedrosa's proposal involved bringing together five museums: the Museu de Arte Moderna, the Museu do Índio, and the Museu de Imagens do Inconsciente—which already existed but were facing serious difficulties—along with the Museu do Negro and the Museu de Artes Populares, which were to be created. At the time, in the midst of Brazilian attempts toward redemocratization, Pedrosa's idea was not even taken up for discussion—even as it spoke to the fragility of public policies for museums, challenged the role of the cultural field in political processes, and called into question the dominant narratives about the origins of the country.[20]

Ensaios para o Museu das Origens looked to the collections and founding histories of nearly thirty museums and memory centers of varying scales, durations, and fields of activity. The exhibition sought to reflect on what was at stake in Pedrosa's original proposal, which aimed to connect cultural and symbolic spheres without adopting an encyclopedic approach or glossing over particular agendas and processes, and to consider what continues to persist in institutions operating within the Brazilian political and cultural landscape.

The following year, the institute held a seminar that built directly on this exhibition, *Ensaios para o Museu das Origens – Políticas da memória* [Towards the Museum of Origins: Politics of Memory], which brought together dozens of representatives from the spaces mentioned in the original research, along with other guests who expanded the discussions through transversal themes ranging from archaeology to ecology, including modern art, Afro-Brazilian cultures, Indigenous territories, records of political and social history, contested collections, and initiatives aimed at strengthening local communities.[21] The conclusion of this intense gathering led us to write:

> Making memory is a political act—in the most vital and powerful sense the word "political" may carry. It means setting priorities for determining which aspects of culture should be preserved, defining structures for research and conservation, and sharing the relevance of memory with a range of public segments, while always prioritizing a particular context and community as interlocutors. It also means ensuring both the continuity and the cyclical renewal of this work. That's how we put the principles of citizenship into practice— and, beyond that, how we give lasting, shareable form to collective desires and intentions.[22]

[20] *Ensaios para o Museu das Origens* [Towards the Museum of Origins] was held simultaneously at Instituto Tomie Ohtake and Itaú Cultural from September 2023 to January 2024. The exhibition was curated by Izabela Pucu and Paulo Miyada, with Ana Roman as deputy curator, and Daiara Tukano and Thiago de Paula Souza as guest curators. The paragraphs about the project revisit excerpts from the material produced for the exhibition catalogue. See: Ana Roman, Paulo Miyada, and Izabela Pucu, eds., *Ensaios para o Museu das Origens*. São Paulo: Instituto Tomie Ohtake / Itaú Cultural, 2023.

[21] There were five days of workshops, roundtables, and conferences that hosted more than 2,000 participants and 63 researchers, managers, artists, curators, and guest workers. Recordings available at: https://www.youtube.com/watch?v=PcCUVObs9Lc&list=PLeGwcdaIfnMGUgAIU6R275epGrFnc5uOz

[22] *Carta pública: Seminário Ensaios para o Museu das Origens – Políticas da Memória*, Instituto Tomie Ohtake, São Paulo, November 14, 2024. Available at: https://www.institutotomieohtake.org.br/midiateca/carta-publica-seminario-ensaios-para-o-museu-das-origens-politicas-da-memoria/.

The seminar was a direct outgrowth of the research behind *Ensaios para o Museu das Origens,* and since then the Instituto's program has sought to echo the questions, commitments, alliances, and ideas seeded in the process.[23] Its most far-reaching, complex, and ambitious undertaking is precisely the exhibition *The Earth, the Fire, the Water, and the Winds: For a Museum of Errantry* with Édouard Glissant.

The transition from one research project to another is guided by the understanding that we live surrounded by systems and devices steeped in histories of domination and colonization: language, the economy, democracy, the mirror, the museum. It's up to the historical process, with its dialectical tensions and revolutionary drives, to contest the present and future meaning of these devices, propelled by the insubordination of those whom Frantz Fanon called "the wretched of the earth."[24] In this historical dialectic, inflections contradicting or renewing the function of devices like ships, mirrors, and museums may be mapped through linear processes of reflection and debate; but rarely do such devices shift their character through dialogue alone. Devices saturated with ideology rarely change through dialogue alone. It is the case that real transformation almost always occurs when institutions are driven to a true inflection point by impassioned, obstinate, and/or resilient action led by collectives, communities, and individuals who do not want or cannot wait for the slow reform of the prevailing order.

Extending our inquiry into what a museum can be, it may be more fruitful to orient ourselves not by the genealogical trees of linear chronological time, but by a constellation of flashes, ruptures, and sudden irruptions scattered across time and space. Likewise, it may be more productive to worry less about defining epistemological rules and more about annotations and provocations of relationships between elements from different fields of knowledge. This also means asking whether speaking of museums must always mean speaking of "museums of heritage," or whether we might begin to imagine what "museums of errantry"

[23] The exhibition *Ensaios para o Museu das Origens* [Towards the Museum of Origins] is part of a set of initiatives carried out from 2022 to 2025 by the Instituto Tomie Ohtake aimed at critically reviewing collections, displaying knowledge from multiple origins, and reinventing curatorial practices. Among them, the shows Instituto Tomie Ohtake visita Coleção *Vilma Eid: Em cada canto* [Institudo Tomie Ohtake visits Vilma Eid Collection: In Every Corner] (2025), *Manuel Messias: Sem limites* [Manuel Messias: No Limits] (2025), and *Teatro Experimental do Negro nas fotografias de José Medeiros* [Black Experimental Theater in the Photographs by José Medeiros] (2025) stand out, since they repositioned little-known artistic paths and collections; the publication of the *Cadernos-Ensaio* collection, with the volumes *Barro* [Clay] (2024) and *Palavra* [Word] (2024), the latter linked to the world of slam and orality; the exhibition *Gira da poesia: 15 anos de slam no Brasil* [Poetry Tour: 15 Years of Slam in Brazil] (2024), in the context of the *Poesia em presença* [In-Presence Poetry] festival; the book and show *Mira Schendel: Esperar que a letra se forme* [Mira Schendel: Waiting for the Letter to Form] (2024); and the podcast *A parte pelo todo* [The Part for the Whole] (2025) presented by José Eduardo Ferreira Santos, founder of Acervo da Laje. Those projects, based on feedback practices, counter-archiving, and collective fabulation, propose other ways of curating and envisioning futures for museums.

[24] See: Frantz Fanon, *The Wretched of the Earth.* Translated by Richard Philcox. New York: Grove Press, 2004.

could be. Heritage is a powerful idea—the raw material of memory politics—closely bound up with the right to ancestry, identity, and belonging. Yet heritage is also a device for maintaining structural distributions of power, with their perverse asymmetries and systems of oppression, silencing, alienation, and the production of misery. It is part of what makes museums embodiments of a rigid, systemic, and classificatory mode of thought.

No act of remembrance will abolish heritage, we might say, in an improvised paraphrase. No exercise of the right to memory will render the idea of heritage obsolete. But we must insist that heritage need not remain the inevitable horizon when working with memory—or when conceiving museums. Errantry, as Glissant proposed, engages with memory, origin, land, mother tongue, and ancestry through a dynamic in which each person and each people mobilize, rework, and even produce their roots—not as fixed origins, but as mutable forces transforming giving rise to new formations across time and space.

In a dialectical dynamic, errantry can erode the genealogies of power embedded in heritage as a structuring economic logic, while also dismantling its fatalism—the fatalism that fuels essentialism, exoticization, and sectarianism. For Glissant, errantry is often set in motion by conflict, inequality, and historical violence—as in the diasporas—but the cry of revolt[25] is just one among many of its poetic forms of articulation within the unpredictability of what he calls the Whole-World or Chaos-World.[26]

A Museum of Errantry, thus, does not aim to replace or supersede the heritage museums we know and celebrate—those that informed the proposal for the Museum of Origins—but instead acts as a counterweight and an expansion in response to the urgencies and desires of the present. Drawing on Glissant, its fabulation is linked both to traces[27] of the African diaspora in the Americas and to movements of migration and exile to and from Europe. But not only that:

> Those who meet up *here* always come from an "over there," from the expanse of the world, and here they are, determined to bring to this "here" the fragile knowledge

[25] Glissant frequently invokes the "cry of revolt" throughout his writings. For a more in-depth discussion of the concept, see: Édouard Glissant, *Monsieur Toussaint - scenic version. Préface de la version théâtrale de 1978.* Paris, Éditions du Seuil, 1986; and Édouard Glissant, *Poetics of Relation.*

[26] Although they permeate Édouard Glissant's entire work, the concepts of the Whole-World (*Tout-Monde*) and Chaos-World (*Chaos-Monde*) gain density and clarity in the *Treatise on the Whole-World* (*Traité du Tout-Monde*, 1997). Glissant defines Chaos-World not as confusion or disorder, but as the contemporary condition of the world: multiple, unpredictable, formed by relationships among heterogeneous cultures that coexist without submitting to a single order or a dominant center. Whole-World is the image of a living and unfinished whole, in constant construction, formed by differences in relations, encounters, frictions, and displacements between languages, histories, and imaginaries. See: Édouard Glissant, *Treatise on the Whole-World.* Translated by Celia Britton. Liverpool: Liverpool University Press, 2020.

[27] For Glissant, "The trace is an opaque way of experiencing the branch and the wind: of being oneself, derived from the other." (*Treatise on the Whole-World*, p. 10). By not setting origins, the trail is constantly linked to other places and people; therefore, tracking means following marks that bifurcate, accepting uncertainty, and turning memory into the flows of Relation.

they have taken from over there. [...] That the thought of the trace, as opposed to systematic thought, acts as a wandering that guides us. We know the *trace* is what puts us, all of us, wherever we come from, in Relation.

And for some people, over there, so far so near, right here, on the hidden face of the Earth, the trace was lived as one of the places of survival. For example, for the descendants of the Africans transported into slavery into what would soon be called the New World, it was usually the only possible form of action.[28]

To truly embrace the thought of errantry, the very conception of the museum must undergo an irreversible transformation. It means rethinking the values tied to recognizing art and culture as heritage—including the concept of beauty itself. In November 2024, while this research was underway, the seminar "The Orientation Towards New Museums" took place in Dakar.[29] Shortly before the event, the organizers sent the participants—in order to spark the debate to come—a transcript of a lecture by Glissant, selected and transcribed by Manthia Diawara and Terri Geis.[30] There, Glissant argues that museums were built on an ideal of beauty shaped by the great civilizations (particularly those of Western Europe) as a homogeneous and stable value, aligned with their monolithic view of themselves as sole roots. Beyond the relations of power embedded in that fixed perspective, the result is that "the experience of visiting a traditional museum becomes one of tautological repetition."[31]

In a world where the arc of those so-called great civilizations fails to encompass the complexity and Relational[32] movement of a multitude of cultures, the normative convention of the beautiful falls short of the actual experience of beauty. As the poet writes, "in this inextricable, complex movement of world cultures, we are far more sensitive to the trembling, convulsion, and pulse of beauty, rather than to the conventional representation of the beautiful. The beautiful is not

[28] Glissant, *Treatise on the Whole-World*, p. 9.

[29] The seminar "The Orientation Towards New Museums" was held in Dakar on November 9th and 10th, 2024, during the 15th Dakar Biennale (Dak'Art), as a joint initiative by NYU Abu Dhabi and the Guggenheim Abu Dhabi Project. The seminar was attended by Stephanie Rosenthal, Awam Amkpa, Manthia Diawara, Faustin Linyekula, Terri Geis, Victor Ehikhamenor, Jahman Anikulapo, Jess Castellote, Wole Soyinka, Awa Konate, and Shabbir Hussain Mustafa, among other curators, artists, researchers, and cultural leaders from the Global South.

[30] Glissant, "Beauty and the Beautiful and the Orientation Towards the New Museums."

[31] Ibid.

[32] *Relation* is a key concept of Édouard Glissant, which describes the continuous interdependence among languages, cultures, and territories. Instead of alluding to a single origin, Relation emphasizes the link in motion: identities are formed through contact, exchange, and reciprocal transformation. See: Édouard Glissant, *Poetics of Relation*.

beauty. The beautiful is congealed beauty."[33] A museum that responds to that world, then, must aim toward beauty in its mutability—born from the encounter among multiple perspectives in transformation. To quote Glissant's words once more: "The contemporary museum—the new museum that corresponds to and reflects our times—is no longer a museum of representation, classification, orientation, explanation, of beauty. It is a museum of chance, guesswork, discovery, exploration of unpredictable beauty."[34]

The museum is an archipelago-museum,[35] as Glissant speculated at the end of his 2011 lecture; or a mangrove-museum,[36] as imaginatively proposed by Sylvie Séma Glissant during the Dakar seminar; or, as we propose, a Museum of Errantry. To expand on this conception, we have chosen to look more closely at Glissant's relationship with artists, especially those who made the *here and elsewhere*[37] the site of their poetic expression. This is a story that revolves around the Galerie du Dragon.

D.

Dragon

The Galerie du Dragon opened in 1955 in Paris's 6th arrondissement, at 19 rue du Dragon, founded by Max Clarac-Sérou—a poet, translator, and editor who became a gallerist the encouragement of several artists, including the Chileans Roberto

[33]   Glissant, "Beauty and the Beautiful and the Orientation Towards the New Museums."

[34]   Ibid.

[35]   Regarding archipelagos, Glissant writes, "archipelagos are the sites of things that are not ordered. These areas are not systematic areas, they are spaces of non-systematicity, of things that are not arranged according to a logic that is transparent, spaces where the constitutive elements are in a permanent state of relationality instead of being in a fixed relation" (Glissant, "Beauty and the Beautiful and the Orientation Towards the New Museums."). In this sense, archipelago museums would be autonomous islands in a condition of permanent mobility and dialogue.

[36]   In her participation in the seminar "The Orientation Towards New Museums" (Dakar, 2024), Sylvie Séma Glissant proposed the idea of a "mangrove museum" in dialogue with Glissant's notion of an archipelago museum. The mangrove emerges as a metaphor for a porous institution, rooted in multiple histories and geographies, capable of coexisting with instability, interdependence, and flow. This image suggests a museum entangled in its territory, attentive to the ecologies and frictions of the present. There is no written or audiovisual record of the speech to date; this formulation is based on notes made when Paulo Miyada took part as a representative of the Instituto Tomie Ohtake.

[37]   Here and elsewhere (*ici-là*): for Glissant, the relational condition of those who experience simultaneously the place of origin and the space of wandering. The term merges "here" (rooting) and "elsewhere" (displacement) in the same gesture. By breaking the binary logic of belonging, here and elsewhere conveys the continuous rooting-uprooting of the creolized subject. See: Glissant, *Poetics of Relation*.

Matta and Enrique Zañartu.[38] In addition to its exhibition program, often accompanied by brochures featuring commissioned texts, the gallery published several poetry books illustrated by artists, especially through its editorial line *Instances*. Although it never achieved significant commercial success, it stood out in the Parisian art scene as a sustained site of artistic and literary exchange—for many artists and writers from Latin America and the Caribbean as well—and for dedicating much of its program to artists engaged with figuration, fabulation, the fantastic, and aspects of the surrealist legacy.

At a time when Paris was a stage for disputes between constructive and informal abstraction—and when even French critics acknowledged that the epicenter of the global art system had shifted to New York—the Galerie du Dragon became a safe harbor for those who approached art as part of a journey of displacement, errantry, and invention, maintaining a certain distance from the major forces reshaping the artistic mainstream. Though virtually absent from the historiography of French art, the gallery operated for four decades before closing its doors in 1995. During that time, Venezuelan Cecilia Ayala played an increasingly central role in running the space: first as a supporter, then as an employee, a partner, and finally as its owner,[39] preserving part of its original community while renewing it by welcoming a younger generation of artists.

Édouard Glissant was the gallery's most prolific collaborator, having written critical texts for dozens of its exhibitions, both in its early years with Clarac-Sérou and in its later phase with Cecilia Ayala. The list of artists he wrote about in that context overlaps significantly with the works he collected personally, and coincides with most of the visual artists he referenced in his books and essays—from Victor Brauner to Pancho Quilici, José Gamarra to Gabriela Morawetz, Agustín Cárdenas to Antonio Seguí, Irving Petlin to Eduardo Zamora, along with the aforementioned Matta and Zañartu, among others.[40] Glissant also had several

[38]   Except for details and nuances learned in interviews with artists and their families, most of the information gathered here about the Galerie du Dragon can be found in the article by Aliocha Wald Lasowski in a PhD thesis by Xenia Roque Benito. Additionally, Aliocha Wald Lasowski's book *Sur l'épaule des dieux: Les Arts d'Édouard Glissant* [On the Shoulders of the Gods: The Arts of Édouard Glissant] offers a comprehensive analysis of Glissant's relationships with painters, sculptors, musicians, and performers from the Caribbean and South America, exploring how those partnerships fostered his "chaosthétique" ["chaosthetics"] and the concept of Whole-World. See: Xenia Roque Benito, "Os livros ilustrados por Wifredo Lam: confluências do surrealismo à antilhanidade." PhD diss., Universidade de São Paulo, 2021; Aliocha Wald Lasowski, *Sur l'épaule des dieux: Les Arts d'Édouard Glissant*. Bruxelles: Les Impressions Nouvelles, 2022; and Aliocha Wald Lasowski, "Galerie du Dragon." Édouard Glissant [website], January 27, 2018. Available at: https://edouardglissant.world/lieux/galerie-du-dragon/.

[39]   Ayala and Clarac-Sérou married, and upon their divorce, she opened the Minotauro gallery in Caracas, Venezuela. She later acquired Clarac-Sérou's gallery.

[40]   A testimony to Glissant's impact on the history of the Galerie du Dragon is the 1988 exhibition *Autour d'Édouard Glissant* [Around Édouard Glissant], with works by 21 artists: Wolfgang Paalen, Wifredo Lam, Roberto Matta, Enrique Zañartu, Cesare Peverelli, John Hultberg, Agustín Cárdenas, Irving Petlin, José Gamarra, Antonio Seguí, Louis Lutz, Pancho Quilici, Sandro Somarè, Gabriela Morawetz, Gerardo Chávez, Eva Ho, Ramón Alejandro, Eduardo Zamora, Jacques Chemay, Jean Charasse, and Jacques Le Maréchal.

books published in special editions illustrated by prominent artists from that circle, including: *La Terre inquiète* [Worried Earth] (1955), with Wifredo Lam; *Les Indes* [*The Indies*] (1956), with Enrique Zañartu; and *Le Sel noir* [*Black Salt*] (1959), with Roberto Matta.

These three poetry books, together with *Un Champ d'îles* [A Field of Islands] (1953), mark a formative stage in Glissant's poetic thought. They revolve around ways of invoking the Antillean landscape as a multifaceted presence—character, atmosphere, allegory, trauma—acting intrinsically upon every aspect of the history and processes of becoming that shape its denizens, including those who move away from, while also being reshaped by the languages and modes of expression of the peoples who inhabit it and relate to one another and to the land through unpredictable dynamics. The fact that works from Lam, Zañartu, and Matta accompanied these books stands as further evidence of the impact of the collaborative dynamic between Glissant and the artists from the Galerie du Dragon circle.

Such collaboration between the poet and artists had profound consequences on both sides. For his part, Glissant's thinking was consolidated through multiple impulses: his life in Martinique, the move to Paris, and his later wanderings; a complex literary repertoire spanning from his fellow Martinican Aimé Césaire to William Faulkner, and including many of the authors featured in the anthology *La Terre, le feu, l'eau et les vents*; a blunt, intense dialogue with thinkers of the African diaspora, both in France and in postcolonial criticism; and, finally, his immersion in the visual work of artists from diverse backgrounds with whom he lived and worked from the 1950s onward.

By observing paintings, sculptures, prints, and drawings, Glissant found a special resonance for thinking through landscape and language. In various texts on those artists, he took the opportunity to explore the Baroque:[41] its subversion of classical perspective, its use of repetition and variation, and its notion of *mesura da desmesura* [measure of excess] and of *étendue* [expanse] as a visual mode of thought attuned to the landscapes of the Americas.[42] These writings also gave rise to reflections on the jungle as a totality, on the creation of something new and irreversible through the combination of signs of diverse origin, and on stories as events that open cracks in History.[43] He repeatedly reflected on images of stelae, boats, doors, and totems as recurring signs of the convergence between errantry and territory.[44] The diverse origins of the artists with whom Glissant developed these and other structuring ideas of his poetry and essays were essential to his expanding reflection on landscape and history of the Antilles—first to the broader scope of the African American diaspora and, from there, to the Whole-World and the Chaos-World.

[41]   Glissant uses Baroque as a recurring metaphor for a world in the making: circumvolution, contrast, and proliferation destabilize the classical notion of homogeneous nature, creating an aesthetic of turmoil that sustains creolization. Thus, the "poetics of Relation" takes on a Baroque rhythm that rejects syntheses and embraces drifting identities, configuring Whole-World as an open space. See: Daniel-Henri Pageaux, "Édouard Glissant et l'Amérique 'latine'. Du baroque au Tout-Monde." *Francophonie*, no. 6, Fall 2012, pp. 105-20.

[42]   Particularly when discussing the works of Roberto Matta and Pancho Quilici.

[43]   With Wifredo Lam, Victor Anicet, and José Gamarra, among others.

[44]   There are countless examples, but one can mention his writings on Serge Hélénon, Gabriela Morawetz, Sylvie Séma Glissant, and Agustín Cárdenas.

Glissant's engagement with these artists helped shape many of his core ideas—about landscape, errantry, opacity, and the poetic. In turn, his writings about their work opened new ways of understanding their contributions, allowing for them to be viewed not merely as late extensions of Surrealism but as artists whose practices resonate deeply with the transversal concerns of Glissant's thought. Through his lens, we can perceive connections among them that surpass any surface affinities of nationality, race, or style.

In this light, one could argue that the examples of Victor Brauner, Roberto Matta, and Wifredo Lam—the three oldest artists among Glissant's key interests—have more in common than their repeated presence in Surrealist exhibitions. They are artists in errantry, heirs to diasporic peoples who witnessed violence both in their homelands and in the countries they came to call home; immigrants who rejected tautological approaches to artistic autonomy, and who combined signs drawn from multiple cultures and fields of knowledge. They are artists who embraced opacity as a form of protection while pursuing an expansion of the imagination in response to the world's tremor—combining allegories of terror with evocations of vitality. Artists of errant beauty, whose legacies are intertwined with those of other generations through Glissant's work as an art critic.[45]

With that in mind, we now turn to the unfolding of this new artistic genealogy, which stretches from the work created alongside Glissant to that of contemporary generations. But, before doing so, we should underscore that the circle of artists around him was so coherent that, despite their being overlooked by the official art world—including major institutions and galleries—their sphere of exchange extended well beyond the activities of the Galerie du Dragon itself.

In addition to being repeatedly invited to write about several artists in this circle,[46] Glissant promoted their work through *Courier*, the UNESCO magazine, and strengthened their presence in the programming of the Maison de l'Amérique Latine from the 1990s until his death. To this day, the Maison remains a regular venue for activities organized by the Institut du Tout-Monde.

[45] The issue here is not to deny Surrealism nor to assert that there is something inherently contradictory between its complex history and the points of convergence among Brauner, Matta, and Lam, but rather to highlight that there is a complementary relationship between their works and careers that is not at the heart of the Surrealist circle and its dissents, yet strongly resonates in Glissantian thought.

[46] Galerie Thessa Herold, also in Paris, opened in 1993 and incorporated some of the artists associated with the Galerie du Dragon, including occasional writings by Glissant.

E.

The Word of the Landscape, the Landscape of the Word

For Glissant, language and landscape are interwoven fields—linking past, present, and future, as well as personal experience and collective memory. To underline the central role of landscape in his life, he would often weave fabulations about his early childhood:

My first experience of the landscape of Martinique was when I was barely one month old, when Adrienne took me in her arms and walked down from the heights of Bézaudin to Lamentin. Back then, there were no roads, there was nothing, not even paths. We stumbled through ravines, scrambled through savannahs, and so on. And still! I do not know if it is because she told me about it afterwards or if I reconstructed it myself, through my imagination, but I remember that journey. I remember the apricot trees in the hills of Sainte-Marie, and I remember the chestnut trees, those trees were huge, so huge! The chestnut trees, the apricots, the mangoes, the mango trees! The big blue mango trees, right? And I remember the special shade, and I swear I really recall it! The special shade of those huge trees, the heights that have mostly disappeared. And I remember the moment when we both came out, I was one month old, I was in her arms, on the cultivated plains of Lamentin. They were cultivated plains, but slightly silted up by the marshes. They were neat farmland areas like that, a little silted up by the marshes, and we came out onto the Longvilliers River at the entrance to Lamentin, and I remember that! Or maybe I reconstructed it and made up a memory based on stories that Adrienne may have told me. [47]

[47] Édouard Glissant, *Abécédaire d'Édouard Glissant*, interview by Patrick Chamoiseau, January 2008. Rights: Dorlis / Édouard Glissant Art Fund / Institut du Tout-Monde. Translated by Sebastião Nascimento.

Glissant's interest in landscape can be traced back to the Atlantic crossing of his enslaved ancestors: those for whom separation from their native landscape was compounded by a severing from both history and language in a rupture beyond repair. The ocean as tomb and as womb, leading to a new maternity in the Caribbean landscape. Within the disorientation and violence of the diaspora, the land-as-country and imposed language of the colonizer provide the life context in which creolization emerges: the unpredictable, uncontrollable mixing of languages in Relation—and the realization that spurs the cry of revolt. Glissant saw such visceral and raw cry as a necessary but insufficient stage for the community development. It's necessary to shape the word and attain the level of discourse and poetry, which exist in a new, living temporal flow—in a new *duration*.

Such duration, in turn, stands in a reciprocal relationship with both language and landscape—phenomena continually renewed through life experience, weaving together collective imaginaries and the deep-seated powers of each living being. The *word of the landscape* takes shape between subject and environment; not as incorporation or dialectic, but as a profound intimacy. The subject forges the word in a body-to-body encounter with earth, fire, water, and the winds that shimmer, churn, and erupt across this vibrant temporal expanse of the landscape.

The notion of the "word of the landscape" runs through much of the Édouard Glissant collection. In examining this body of work, we propose a complementary concept: the "landscape of the word." In the former notion, territory seeps into speech; in the latter, language is cast outward into space, transforming signs, letters, and codes into terrain, weather, or current. Among the selected pieces, we find visual musical scores snaking across walls like mountain ranges; videos with text lines dissolving into sea foam; sound installations turning poems into air and vibration. The text ceases to be merely a bearer of meaning; it gains geographic thickness, it folds, erodes, echoes, allowing the visitor to move through it as one might traverse a stretch of land. That dual movement deepens Glissant's ongoing dialogue between language and place: language can well up from the ground just as the ground can be reshaped by language. By setting "word of the landscape" alongside "landscape of the word," the exhibition creates a web of intersecting readings in which each work functions at once as map and narrative, inviting the public to experience, sensorially, the idiom of things and the materiality of discourse.

Thus, we interwove works by artists connected to Glissant with others by contemporary artists in an exhibition layout that echoes the ideas of *word of the landscape* and *landscape of the word* through visual and synesthetic relations. There is a historiographical argument at play that, when brought into the present, acts as a flashpoint, a spark. But it's the sensitive interplay among the works—their shared presence—that makes it possible to hope that words, sentences, and poetic discourses might begin to take form within the exhibition through "relations of energy, lulls and slumberings, flashes of spirit and the heavy, sumptuous paths of thought."[48]

This would not have been possible without the trust of the artists and their enthusiasm in response to Glissant's ideas. Nor would it have been possible without the boundless generosity of Sylvie Séma Glissant, who not only paved the way for the partnership with the Institut du Tout-Monde and the Édouard Glissant Art Fund (in collaboration with Mathieu Glissant and Ronan Grossiat),

[48]   Glissant, *La Terre, le feu, l'eau et les vents*. [Free translation]

and fostered the connection with the Mémorial ACTe and the BnF, but also decisively engaged in a long, intense dialogue with us about the ideas and life work of Édouard Glissant.

The development of this conversation is, by nature, partial and tentative. It is a utopian fabulation addressed to the moment we are now living—when errantry and migration are once again being cast as threats to be silenced and contained by the rigid, centralized structures that have inherited the old forms of power. The exhibition has been updated with a traveling iteration at the Center for Art, Research and Alliances (CARA) in New York,[49] featuring a selection of works from Glissant's personal collection.

Moreover, the project activates a parallel trajectory that extends its geographic and temporal reach. Zé di Cabeça (José Eduardo Ferreira Santos) —cofounder of Acervo da Laje, a community-led initiative in the Subúrbio Ferroviário of Salvador—and Rayana Rayo—a Recife-born artist whose work interweaves the body, writing, and maritime imaginaries—were invited to develop new projects in two complementary stages. The first involves an immersion in the African Art Collection of the Museu Oscar Niemeyer in Curitiba, where they will engage with ritual objects, textiles, and sculptures through the perspective of Atlantic circulations that also shape their own practices. The second stage will take place at Maison du Diamant,[50] an artist residency in Martinique tied to Glissant's legacy. There, the artists will bring this recontextualized African archive into contact with the Caribbean landscape, testing new layers of errantry across the Northeast, the South, and the Antilles. The aim is not merely to produce autonomous works, but to foster a continuous flow of exchanges—drawings, journals, sound recordings, and musical scores/objects—that will be woven into future renditions of the exhibition as it travels to other venues.

At its core, *The Earth, the Fire, the Water, and the Winds: For a Museum of Errantry with Édouard Glissant* is an exercise in unlikely and unpredictable encounters. A way of making an exhibition—and dreaming of a museum— grounded in movement and encounter as both principle and purpose.

[49]   The exhibition will be held from February to May 2026.

[50]   This initiative is a result of partnerships among the Instituto Tomie Ohtake, the Ivani and Jorge Yunes Collection, the Museu Oscar Niemeyer, the France-Brazil Season, and the Édouard Glissant Art Fund.

Abécédaire [Alphabet book]

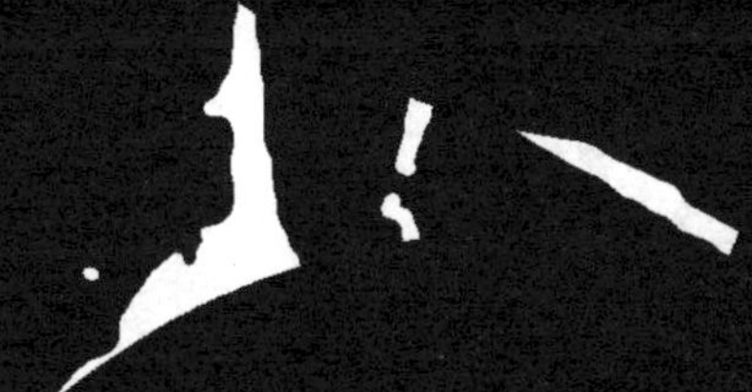

Édouard Glissant in conversation with Patrick Chamoiseau

Recorded in January, 2008

Édouard Glissant, *Abécédaire d'Édouard Glissant*, interview by Patrick Chamoiseau, January 2008.
Rights: Dorlis / Édouard Glissant Art Fund / Institut du Tout-Monde.
Edited by Instituto Tomie Ohtake / Ana Roman and Paulo Miyada. Translated by Sebastião Nascimento.

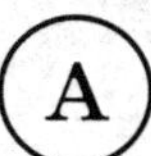

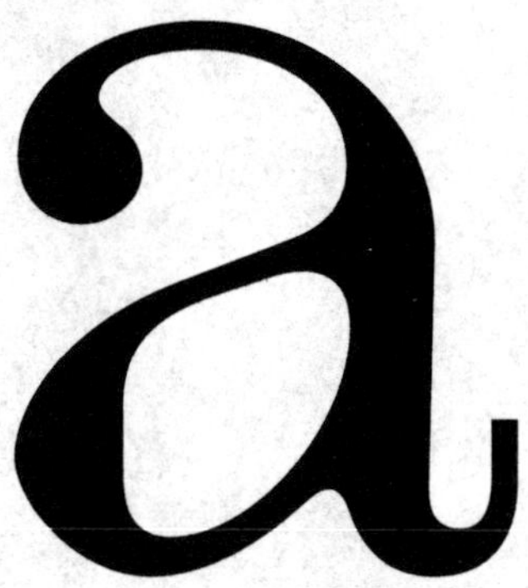

alphabet

Patrick Chamoiseau The first question that comes to mind, you know, is that in Creole, the alphabet is called *"be a ba joubaré."* I've heard it a thousand times. So, before we start this journey through the letters of the alphabet, I'd like you to tell me: Can you remember your first encounter with the alphabet? How did it happen? Do the letters "A, B, C, D," mean anything special to you, and did they mark the beginning of something special in your writing?

Édouard Glissant Yes. First of all, what you just said brought back memories of something very distant, far removed from us. Namely, the songbooks of medieval European troubadours. And those songbooks are made up of "Vidas," accounts of the troubadours' lives, and "razos," the reasons behind their poetry… What makes those collections unique is the fact they are biographies, and they're extraordinary mostly because the poem dictates the biography. In other words, the poem drives the troubadour's life; his life is ruled by the poem he writes himself. I've always been sensitive to this aspect: the moment when poetry is not yet detached from existence. Later, there will be detachments. But here, there is no detachment yet. I think the troubadours of the European Middle Ages are a bit like African griots, a bit like Creole storytellers. There is no real separation between the griot's tale or chant and his concrete life. And I may have always tried, in fact, to be like or in step with the griot or the storyteller, that is to say, to always "poemize" existence, and always give the poem the support and foundation of life, of biography. The other memory, the other dimension that came to mind, is about the landscape in which a poet evolves. But what is a landscape? It's the country, covered with its historical continuum. In other words, in a landscape there is life, the country itself, and then there is the "razos," the reason for life, the poem. And the landscape is the country's poem.

And what is this poem? It's the country's historical continuum. A landscape is what connects, through a historical continuum, the country's past to its future. The poet does that. He strives for that. What do we do when we delve into, or attempt to delve into, pasts that are more or less turbulent, more or less unknown, more or less concealed, more or less erased? We try to restore a historical continuum, a sort of biography of the community, don't we? Most of the time, this is really hard to tackle, really hard to grasp, really hard to retain, and we try to make this historical continuum meaningful to us. If not for others, at least for ourselves. It means the biographical element is crucial, whether it's the collective biography or the biography of the individual, of the particular, of the poet. That is, the urge to exist throbbing within and around us—we strive to bring it all together.

americas

I never lost sight of it, because right from the start there was that huge trauma of the demise of the Inca, Aztec, and Mayan civilizations and the extermination of the Native Americans of North America. It was a historical continuum that needed to be recovered, rediscovered. There are people who never lost that awareness. In my case, at least, I had to reclaim awareness of that massacre, of that eradication, you know?

When we reflect on the history of those civilizations and cultures, which is by no means ideal or perfect, but often horrific and savage, we realize there is a cosmic connection to the Earth that we must recreate.

The Incas, for instance, used volcanic stones at the top of their mountains to draw lightning, which struck the stones and protected the crops and cultures around them. Along the slopes (these were not volcanoes, but mountains), the mountains' foothills. They had a unique connection to the forces of nature. There is evidence the Incas had a calendar that was accurate to within two-tenths of a second over thousands of years, rivaling the most sophisticated calculations of modern science. The Inca priesthood…

In fact, the Inca priests took advantage of that, because they knew the dates of eclipses aligning Moon, Earth, and Sun, and they used them to terrorize the people and assert their power and dominion. But there was a fantastic connection to the elements that we must draw upon. For example, deep in our unconscious minds, as Caribbean people—Martinicans, Guadeloupeans, Barbadians, etc.—there lurks the massacre of the Tainos and the Caribs, perpetuated by the invading colonists. We carry it in our unconscious minds. We may not be aware of it, but it lies deep within us.

I remember when we learned that the last remaining Carib people leaped to their deaths from the cliffs in northern Martinique to refuse surrender. It is the kind of event that takes hold of us on every level: as remorse, as relief, as a point of pride, as a source of sorrow, as a tragedy. And we must realize that the Americas are not merely comprised of those who have arrived, and God knows how diverse they are, but also of everyone who was already there and didn't have the luck or the means to survive and tell the tale. They were either slaughtered, like the Native Americans of the North, or reduced to the bare essentials of subsistence, like the Quechuas of the Andes (who live in conditions of sheer destitution). But we have inherited the drive, the urgency, and the balancing act of it all.

Therefore, there is no America, there are the Americas: the America of those who came, the America of those who had been there all along but did not live to meet us. America… In line with other researchers such as Rex Nettleford from Jamaica, Darcy Ribeiro from Brazil, and scholars from Mexico such as Bonfil Batalla, I believe there is European America, that of Canada and the United States, and there is Mesoamerica, which is the original America of the Indigenous peoples, now called Native Americans in the United States. And then there is Neoamerica, which is the America of colonization, the America of melting pots. It's the America of the Caribbean, the America of Brazil, the America of the Caribbean coast of Latin America, the America of the Caribbean coast of Central America, and to a great extent of Mexico too, because there is a Creole Mexico that is really important, alongside a Meso-Mexico, which is the Mexico of Chiapas and its Indigenous people. And those three Americas are intertwined in an archipelago.

In Peru, Mesoamerica is slaughtered. So, all of it overlaps. And then, like tectonic plates, there's movement, interpenetration. As a result, we can't talk about a single America. It's multiple Americas. There's not just North America, Central America, and South America, there are several Americas. Or, rather, an American archipelago.

The only continental part would be the Midwest of the United States. Incidentally, the fascists in the United States, the Nazis in the United States—deranged as they are, headlong into a death plunge—say, "We want a State in the heart of the United States, and we will leave the rest to all those Blacks, Hispanics, etc." But they are insanely deluded! Because they are going to suffocate to death.

There are, however, multiple Americas, and I thought it was important to mention that those Americas were populated by migratory movements that had nothing to do with each other.

First, we have what I call the armed migrants who arrived on the Mayflower, the first ship. They were equipped with their cannons and technologies. They nearly perished during the first year because they didn't have enough provisions before the crops were harvested. They narrowly escaped death from cold and starvation but managed to survive. That group laid the foundation for American capitalism, first industrial and then financial.

Then there were the domestic migrants, meaning family migrants. The Chinese, the Italians, the poor part of Europe, Ireland, Scotland, Italy, who gave rise to what I call domestic migration, by which I mean familial. They came with their knick-knacks, their pots and pans, and portraits of their grandfathers and grandmothers. And that gave rise to commercial capitalism in the Americas. In Latin America, this commercial capitalism has developed in the background and under the wing of industrial and financial capitalism, which took root in the United States.

And then there was a third type of migrant, which I call the naked migrant, that is, those who were rounded up in Africa and deported to the Americas by way of the Middle Passage, the slave trade, bringing nothing with them because everything was consumed in the belly of the slave ship: their gods, their understanding of commonly used tools, their languages… metaphysics, worldviews, songs. All was lost. And only traces remained. All the efforts of those peoples who spread across the Caribbean, Brazil, the Caribbean coast of Latin America and Central America, and so on, all of their efforts were to retrieve from traces the meaning and content of their ancient cultures.

The significance of the incredible endeavor to recover memories through traces means that what we find becomes meaningful for everyone. Not just for ourselves, but for everyone. That's why jazz, which is how that effort finds expression in music, is meaningful for everyone. That's why reggae has such a big influence around the world. It's not just the kind of music that Rastas perform as part of their ritual ceremonies; it's music for everyone, because it has been recomposed through a phenomenon that sources itself therein: the phenomenon of traces.

Consequently, those three types of migration, once acknowledged and correlated, enable us to articulate a new poetics of the Americas. One that is neither a historical, nor an anthropological, nor a sociological recapitulation, but rather an intuition and understanding of what connects phenomena that intersect, converge, and sometimes contradict each other, yet contribute to a shared view of culture and perhaps even of civilization.

For example, I would argue that painting in the Americas is fundamentally different from European painting because it does not rely on exceptional skill and intuition or an extraordinary command of perspective. All I want to try and show is that art in the Americas relies on layering, accumulation, filling the canvas, flatness; there is no perspective, no depth. There is an endless expanse that even tends to overflow the canvas frame.

The same happens with literature, whether in French, English, Spanish, or Creole. The techniques of the Americas, particularly of Neoamerica, or the America of creolization, feature layering, accumulation, and the vertigo of repetitions, assonances, and brutal mutations that resolve into a smoother flow. And it has nothing to do with the literature of the United States, or Euro-America. Nothing to do with it. Nevertheless, all those literatures, whether Euro, Neo, or Meso, have something in common that is absent in Europe, namely the landscape as a character.

Therefore, if our intuition fails to grasp all those imageries, we miss a piece of reality.

archipelago

When I hear you say "archipelago," I think of the contrast between continental and archipelagic poetics. Because that is the natural setting for our stories. I shall start with continental poetics. I see it as an irresistible force, a sumptuous but also systematic and imposing emanation. Systematic because continental poetics, essentially European in those days, projected onto the world all the great systems of thought they had given birth to. Empiricism, Rationalism, Cartesianism, Hegelianism, dialectics, socialism, communism, even the conception and analysis of capitalism. It may seem obvious to us, but it really isn't. It's part of the power of continental thought to summarize modes of existence and modes of thought into systems. But the system has its limits and disadvantages. Why? Because continental thought, which is one of exploration and conquest, is opposed to what I call archipelagic thought. Archipelagos have

never explored the world. Undoubtedly because archipelagos exist within difference and don't need to seek difference elsewhere. Continental thought seeks difference in other places; it needs to explore the world. This, of course, was at the origin of exploration, but also at the origin of colonialism. Archipelagos are diffracted thoughts, not systematic ones. Archipelagos yield diffracted thoughts.

In ancient Greece, for example, the Ionian archipelago gave rise to what is essentially pre-Socratic thought. That is to say, an idea of the multiplicity of the world. Regardless of the philosophical poets of the time, it was a conception of the world's multiplicity. In the Western example, particularly in Europe, archipelagic thought is contrarily a disseminated form of thought.

It's a way of thinking that avoids the fixity of Truth with a capital T. All archipelagic thought is dialectical, but spontaneously dialectical. It does not theorize dialectics, as Hegel did. Hegel theorized diversity, but he summarized it in a body of thought that is systematic and not diversified. Whereas archipelagic thoughts are teeming and directly in contact with the world. Perhaps not with the reality of the world, but with the world, that is to say, with the passion, the imagination, the palpitation of the world.

This is one of the interesting things Césaire says in *Le Cahier du retour au pays natal* [*Notebook of a Return to the Native Land*]: it pulsates from the very pulse, the very palpitation of the world, it trembles from the trembling of the world…① This is

---

①   In the interview, the passage is paraphrased as "Ce qui palpite, du palpitement, de la palpitation même du monde, ce qui tremble du tremblement du monde…," whereas the original verse reads "chair de la chair du monde palpitant du mouvement même du monde!," translated as "flesh of the flesh of the world pumping with the very movement of the world," in *Return to My Native Land*. Translated by Anna Bostock and John Berger. Middlesex: Penguin, 1969, p. 75; and into "flesh of the world's flesh pulsating with the very motion of the world!," in *The Original 1939 Notebook of a Return to the Native Land*. Bilingual Edition. Translated by Albert James Arnold and Clayton Eshleman. Middletown: Wesleyan University Press, 2013, p. 41. [TN]

archipelagic thought, which is not systematic thought, which is not continental thought. But archipelagic thoughts tend to remain in the place where they are generated. They are not conquering thoughts, whereas systematic thoughts are conquering. And I think that today, when the world has been realized as a totality, archipelagic thoughts are starting to spread across the world as a whole. They consider the worldwide totality as a vast archipelago. Not as a vast continent, but as a vast archipelago. The oceans are elements of this archipelago. We are developing a different poetics from the Atlantic Ocean, the Pacific Ocean, and the Caribbean. I have drawn a parallel between the Mediterranean and the Caribbean to show that the Mediterranean confines and reduces to the singular, while the Caribbean diffracts and rejoins the plural. The point is, therefore, not to say that continental thought should be banned; quite the contrary. It's about reforming it into a kind of "geopoetics" that unburdens it from its vocation as an imperious system that crushes everything, introducing it to the reality of archipelagic thought, which is one of the ways of thinking that can save the world.

What I mean is archipelagic thought, until now overshadowed by systematic continental thought, may be able to help continental thought break free from its systematic mindset and spirit of conquest. When we think of all the archipelagos in the Pacific, the Americas, and Europe, we see they are now visible. Whereas, before, they were not visible at all! What did we use to say? We used to say, "The Earth consists of five continents: Europe, Asia, Africa, America, and Oceania." But Oceania is not a continent, it is an archipelago! In America too, there is the continent, but also many archipelagos. And all the archipelagos that were thus cast into oblivion—there were only five continents, there were no archipelagos—are now resurfacing,

and there are current efforts to represent the Earth with the oceanic archipelagos at its center, and the continents pushed to the edge. Usually, the representation of the Earth is Europe, with Africa as its tail, and then North America with South America as its tail, a small piece of Asia, and that's it. The rest is not visible. And so, today, in reaction to that, a new vision of the globe is emerging, with the archipelagos of Oceania and Asia at the center, and the continents appearing as a kind of ornament, an embellishment to this archipelagic reality. What I further believe is we need a rotating representation of the Earth. I mean, a world map, yes, but one that rotates constantly so that the view of the Earth is utterly diverse, so that there is no longer a center and a periphery, and everything becomes center, and everything becomes periphery.

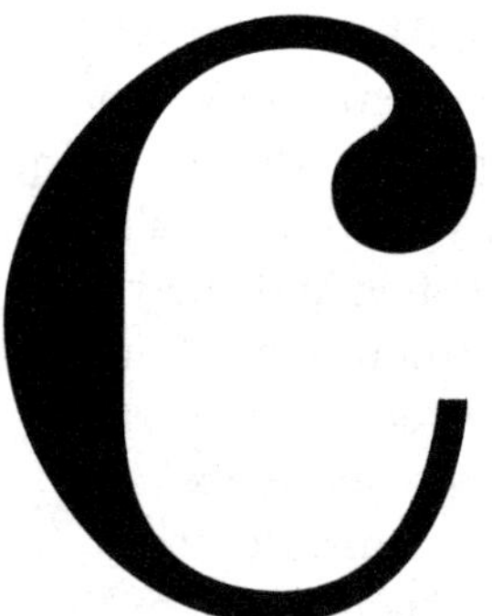

creolization

PC We are moving on to the letter C, to a word that is key. I don't know what to call it. You tell me. It is the word "creolization." Even before you explain what you include in that term, explain what gave you the idea of creolization. Is it because you worked with the Creole language, is it because you were interested in hybridization or the construction of the Creole language, because it is after all a hybrid language? Did you derive the term creolization from the conditions under which the Creole language was formed?

EG It's not that clear-cut. I first had a certain understanding of the Creole language that was perhaps not shared by Creolists. I initially conceived of Creole as an unexpected result of mutually heterogeneous linguistic elements brought together. For example, I often heard Jamaican friends talking about Jamaican Creole. And I would say no, Jamaican Creole is not a Creole language. It is a brilliant, aggressive, almost propaedeutic deformation of the English language, for example in its use by dub poets such as Michael (aka Mikey) Smith or Linton Kwesi Johnson. But its lexicon is a distortion of a French or English lexicon, even if you add Caribbean or African words. It's an aggressive distortion of the lexicon. The syntax is an aggressive distortion of English syntax. Aggressive and brilliant. But all of it takes place within the being-in-the-world of the English language.

In Creole languages, on the other hand, linguistic elements are drawn from radically different places. The lexicon of French-based Creoles, Dutch-based Creoles, or Portuguese-based Creoles like those of Cape Verde, all hail from a very specific place, from a very specific being-in-the-world, namely the being-in-the-Western-world. Despite the input of African words and terms.

The will to live expressed in this lexicon is the will to live expressed, for instance, by Norman or Breton sailors, or by the French language in its formative stages. As for syntax, I don't think anyone has undertaken any specific studies yet, but it's common knowledge that it is a kind of compound of Sub-Saharan and West African syntaxes at work in African languages. From such a starting point, the elements are juxtaposed, and yield unexpected results. And certainly not in any rigid way. The outcome takes hold in a rather tight time frame, which is another of the Creoles' hallmarks, formed as they are within a very short span of time, or even instantly. They start out as a *Petinègue* and very quickly evolve into a system, before becoming a language.②

And I believe those features are elements drawn from areas significantly dissimilar to one another over an extremely brief period of time. It contrasts with the formation of languages in Europe, which take shape over long time spans. At least two, three, four centuries, while Creole languages barely need 50 years to develop an incipient level of organization. And it struck me as a fitting model for cultural phenomena operating in the world. In other words, creolization occurs when there is, instead of synthesis, an adjustment of cultural zones that are heterogeneous to each other, and when, in a very short time, those elements combine and produce unexpected results. That is creolization.

My idea of creolization, as it operates culturally in the world, is based on my conception of the Creole language. Linguists may not agree with this idea. They have their technical reasons, the details of which we won't address here, as I am not particularly interested in any of this. But I do believe that

---

②   In the author's terminology, the distinction between language and speech points to objective and subjective elements, respectively, in the employment of a specific language. [TN]

Ⓒ

my perspective on Creole, as a language rather than a form of speech, affords me a means for approaching what is actually unfolding as a trend of cultures around the world, to which I refer as creolization. Once we consider it as creolization, we should not assume that the elements at stake will necessarily develop into a cultural Creole. The word creolization is only used in reference to the structures of a Creole language. Not a dialect, not a patois, not a deformation, but something new and unexpected.

PC In *La Cohée du Lamentin,*[3] you define creolization as "the most human, dense, and intense form of metamorphosis."

EG Because of the metamorphosis of Being [*l'être, Sein*] into being [*étant, seiend*]. For, given that cultures have thus far existed within the framework of the purity and exclusivity of Being, and given that diversity entails blending, miscegenation, interaction, openness to others, and so on, creolization, once expressed, that is, once it is first practiced and then manifested, is truly the densest form of metamorphosis. But what is metamorphosis? In alchemy, in alchemical practices, metamorphosis is the moment when the ingredients, the elements that have been mixed together, begin to fuse, the useless evaporates, and the residue is what I call a product of metamorphosis. And the residue of the encounter between cultures is to experience the consciousnesses, the sensibilities that feel the world as Being, abandoning any pretense of the world as Being, as something absolute, unique, pure, set apart from everything else. And it seems to me that creolization is a form of alchemy. There are other modes of entanglement. There is dilution, when we become entangled, when we blend with something else and dissolve into it, completely and utterly. We disappear.

With creolization, nothing disappears, everything is transformed. Everything is transformed, but nothing is diluted. Nothing is utterly and completely erased. Another form of entanglement is complete and utter chaos, whose constituent elements are impossible to distinguish, however undiluted they may be. There are forms of chaos that are total chaos, meaning that nothing can be discerned. But I think that, in the Chaos-World, we are able to discern the components. And so, the Chaos-World is not mere disorder, it's not sheer randomness. The Chaos-World is not chaos because it's in disorder, but because it's unpredictable. Chaos is unpredictable. Creolization is, thus, the entanglement that produces unexpected results but preserves the original elements.

[3] Édouard Glissant, *La Cohée du Lamentin. Poétique V.* Paris: Gallimard, 2005. *La Cohée du Lamentin* has not yet been officially translated into English. The title may be interpreted as "The Call of the Lamentin." "Cohée" is an archaic and regionally specific term from Caribbean French, evoking an ancestral call or shouted signal used to mark presence in the dense forest—a gesture of oral memory and collective orientation. "Lamentin" refers both to a municipality and a bay in Martinique, often associated by Glissant with the mangrove and the opaque, relational geographies of the Antilles. [EN]

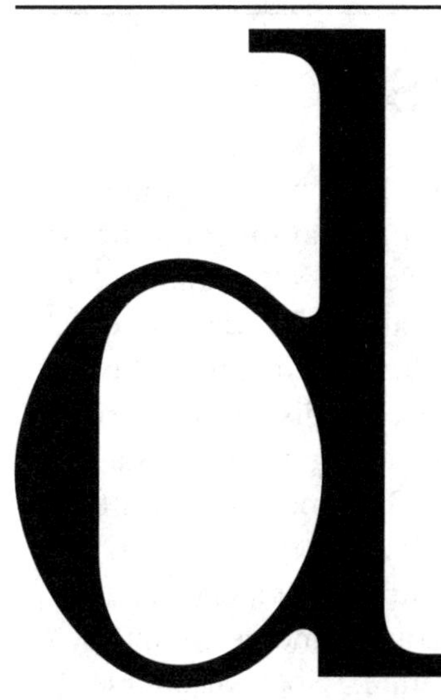

detour

PC　There is already a definition of detour, and it's yours. You say: "This is indeed the detour, which is neither escape nor renunciation, but the new art of 'untangling' the world."[4] In this definition, I see two parts: one that I would call historical, which perhaps refers to the period of slavery, "neither escape nor renunciation." Perhaps it describes the attitude of the slave on the plantation. But the most unexpected part is "the new art of 'untangling' the world." Thus, within the notion of detour, would there be a historical dimension and a contemporary dimension, or maybe one related to the concept of the "Whole-World?"

EG　Yes, "untangling," as in "to untie" or "to unravel." Throughout history, the art of detour has been very important. The trace may constitute a way, a new way of knowing and approaching knowledge; the detour is a new way, devised in the world of plantations, of approaching reality and trying to master it. On the one hand, because cunning is the most effective weapon the slave on the plantation has to oppose the master's actions. The maroon slave, who has rebelled and gone up into the hilly woodland, relies on traces, but not on cunning anymore, as there is no longer any need for it. He has left his cunning down below. But the slave and the farm worker, on the plantation, still need cunning. For example, they need to know, even with their backs turned, when the master's ears are nearby. What they say to their neighbor must not be overheard, and they need a certain skill, a knowledge of all the practices that allow them to maneuver, to tread between the plantation interdictions. The detour is first and foremost avoidance. Avoiding the most significant margin of repression. The detour is also a tactic: when we cannot directly confront something negative, we try to work around it. The detour is also an art of appreciating reality. We do not appreciate reality in a definitive way, once and for all. We appreciate it in all the possible ways the real can be arranged. Therefore, the detour is a very lively practice. It constantly repeats, it constantly restarts. We cannot settle into the practice of the detour once and for all and then… At every turn, we must start again.

---

④　Édouard Glissant, *Introduction à une poétique du divers*. Paris: Gallimard, 1996, p. 70 [*Introduction to a Poetics of Diversity*. Translated by Celia Britton. Liverpool: Liverpool University Press, 2020, p. 44: "This is indeed the detour that is neither fleeing nor giving up, but the new art of freeing up the world"], highlighted here by the interviewer.

The practice of detour cannot be a once-and-for-all given. Because renewing the imperative to exist is perpetual. But so is renewing the impossibility of existing. One could say there is a new appreciation of time. Of time lived in this mode of detour. This is not the architectural and monumental time that European writers, for example, have striven to build. There's a detour that reaches other things: for instance, the search for a time lost, crushed, shattered, and the feeling that nothing is settled once and for all, and nothing is settled within a system. This is what I believe to be significant in the practice of detour: it's an archipelagic practice. It has no concept of a system, neither a system of existence nor a system of reality, just a perpetual scrutiny and a perpetual skirting of the matter at hand. And I am convinced that it was in the Caribbean and in the plantation system that this found its most terrible, most fantastic, most enduring expression—enduring but not systematic. Fragmentation is constant and frequent. There's also a downside to detour. For example, it may be conducive to a tacit acceptance of reality, in the hope that it can be circumvented. One might say: yes, we accept our place as French citizens because the advantages involved may enable us to circumvent the problem of the impossibility of existing, at least the collective impossibility of existing. It may be a mischievous practice of detour, and perhaps a form of alienation. But such form of alienation is not enough to prevent us from considering the practice of detour as a fantastic invention of a new way of being in the world.

The detour has made way for so much inventiveness, so many new ways of approaching others, that I think it truly deserves to be considered as a new approach for the human sciences, or even for human kind, to deal with reality.

discourse

PC There is a word you have used a lot in your work that distinguishes it from Césaire's. For him, a lot of it is about the idea of "cry," while for you, it is more about the idea of "discourse." And I was reading what you said about Cardenas, the sculptor, something like: "Cardenas' sculpture is not a cry, it's a discourse, incessant and deliberate." So, is discourse better than a cry? Do we need discourse more than cries? Is crying still acceptable today, given the complex reality of the world?

EG Let's say the cry is linked to genesis, to the idea of genesis. After all, that cry is the cry of a newborn child. A child is not born 36 times, only once. And the first thing it does in the world is cry. Just like that, to catch its breath. And therefore, from the point of view of literary expression, there are two kinds of cries: the one of communities that are born, that is, that are born to an awareness of themselves. A community can exist for a long time not being aware of itself, and when it does become aware of itself, the poet's cry is the community's first cry. That's how it has always been. There is a second kind of cry: when the community is threatened. Then it is no longer the cry of birth, it is the cry of the community's performance in the world. "I want to be in the world and I want to exist in relation to the world." This second cry may be less organic, but it may be more savage. For example, Allen Ginsberg, one of the great poetic voices of the hippie era in the US, wrote a poem called "Howl."[5] And it's a howl, much like the *Cahier d'un retour au pays*

[5]   Allen Ginsberg. *Howl, and Other Poems*. San Francisco: City Lights Pocket Bookshop, 1956.

natal,[6] but it's the notebook of a hippie road trip across the United States. As we've seen in the movies. There are arthouse films, as they say about those things. Well, it is not a cry of birth. It is a battle cry against something that overwhelms you. And those two cries are two forms of poetic cry. But there is something missing in those cries, and I can only describe it in the following way: the relationship between time and space is missing. The relationship between historical time and geographical space. And the interrelationship of those data for a community. In *Cahier d'un retour au pays natal,* there is a connection to history. There are references to Toussaint Louverture and Schœlcher. And there is a connection to geography, with all the descriptions of Martinican land. All the writing about the land of Martinique: "November purring in the distilleries…" "Where all the mango trees blossom…" And then, I do not precisely recall the text, but there is no mention of the inescapable connection between the inability to master history and the inability to master geography. At least, that's my opinion! Perhaps it is there and I misread it, but I have been teaching *Cahier d'un retour au pays natal* for a long time in my college lectures, and it seems to me that the historical link is immediately provided by one source, an African source, which is not particularly scrutinized. It is genetic in nature, in the sense of an origin story. A genesis. And the geographical link is established in a kind of acknowledgment of our own shortcomings. When Césaire makes those absolutely frightening and fantastic assessment of our flat lives, our flat cities, our shortcomings, our cowardice… The thrilling and trembling link to geography is basically that. And I don't think the two really fit together. In other words, there is no poetic theory! Of the inextricable, of those situations. Yet this poetic theory can only be conveyed by a discourse. Not by a cry, for the cry is genetic, while discourse is digenetic. Because the discourse embraces or captures the impossibilities of history and the impossibilities of geography, namely of the country. And I believe that, for example, the landscape is the autobiographical continuum of a country. There is an autobiographical continuum of a country that can only be found through interpretation. We know how to read the landscape, but not the country! The landscape, because it's what gives a country its autobiographical continuum, that is, what connects yesterday, or yesterday's impossibilities, to tomorrow, or tomorrow's impossibilities. And that autobiographical continuum is not provided by a realistic description. When we give a realistic description of a country, we are not listening, we can't hear the voice of the landscape, a voice that must be deciphered and discovered. All in all, I believe that, just as there are roots reaching out to each other, it's discourse that provides this interpretation, this contact, and this fusion with the voice of the landscape, the autobiographical continuum of the country.

Poetry, the cry contained in ceremonies and in origin myths, for example in Europe, has nevertheless found its way into *The Iliad,* which is no longer a cry but a statement. And the cry of Abraham, for monotheistic societies, has nevertheless been transformed into the Jewish Torah, into the Old Testament, and ultimately into the Koran. All those books had a tendency to replace poetry. Or even to render a certain form of poetry useless. Consequently, the cry does not sum up the whole purpose of poetry; there is a poetry of time and of articulate language, because the cry is inarticulate language. But there is a poetry of time and articulate language, like mine, for example, that appreciates the beauty

[6]   Aimé Césaire, *Cahier d'un retour au pays natal.* Paris: Présence Africaine, 1956; Paris: Gallimard, 1994 [*Notebook of a Return to the Native Land.* Translated by Clayton Eshleman and Annette Smith. Middletown: Wesleyan University Press, 2001].

of the cry but does not consider such beauty as sufficient to establish the very relationship between the individual and the collective.

That's why I don't believe poets are standard-bearers, torchbearers, or beacons. I don't believe it at all! Because standard-bearers and beacons are the ones who cry out. But they are not the ones who weave words together. Those are wordsmiths, not standard-bearers.

PC Yes, it struck me that the discourse can be poetic, just like that. On the heels of Césaire's cry, a poetic triumph, we have Glissant's *Le Discours antillais* [*Caribbean Discourse*],[7] an equally poetic discourse, bearing in mind that it is not merely an analytical exercise, but also a poetic endeavor.

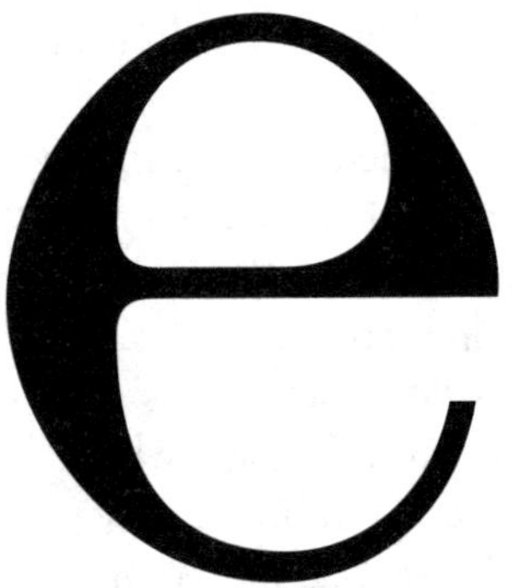

errantry

Errantry is not exploitation, it is not colonialism, nor is it tourism. It is not about visiting countries to enjoy discovering them or their nature. That is the first point. Secondly, one can be errant while immobile, that is, without going anywhere. The peculiarity of it is that someone who is immobile, yet still dwells on the idea of erring, endures an inward struggle.

Errantry is first and foremost imaginary. And then it is relational. There are those two domains. And I was saying that one can practice this errant thought while immobile, that is, in the very place where one is, but in that case, there is a great risk of internal exile. Because the people around you, who are not engaged in this errant thought, isolate you from traditions or rules, or community reflexes, and you can slip into a kind of struggle, an exile within. I have seen many such cases of inner exile. But the fundamental thing about the errant thought, first of all, is that it enables us to imagine geographies, as opposed to consuming them as tourists. When imagining geographies, for instance, there is an imagination of the river, an imagination of the forest, an imagination of the lake, an imagination of the seas, an imagination of cultures, of plains with crops. There is an imagination of the desert and an urban imagination. And then there are many others that we have yet to discover.

There is a sense of poetry within the layout of the land. And errantry allows us to experience it, even without physically moving. When we displace ourselves, errantry brings greater understanding. First, of the relationship between the country we are in and the rest of the world. And it seems to me that this is something we tend to overlook in our country, Martinique. It seems to me that Martinique has a presence in the world that we tend to ignore, precisely because

7 Édouard Glissant, *Le Discours antillais*. Paris: Éditions du Seuil, 1981; Paris: Gallimard, 1997 [*Caribbean Discourse: Selected Essays*. Translated by J. Michael Dash. Charlottesville: University of Virginia Press, 1989].

we lack an imagination of the world. And so, we believe that this world is terrifying for us, or that we don't need it, or that in order to be ourselves and fulfill ourselves, we must separate ourselves from this world that, as we fear, will dilute us, will swallow us up. And I find that errantry, the errant thought, gives us confidence, both collectively and individually. There is no objective in errantry, no interest, no quantitative result.

Apart from being in contact with the world, and establishing the relationship between what we are here and what is there. And that's why most authors from the Antilles, Martinique, Guadeloupe, or the wider Caribbean use the expression *ici-là* [here-there]. *Ici-là* means that "here" only exists by reference to "there." And vice-versa. And that's already the beginning of a new poetics, meaning, a new way of conceiving language, not just as descriptive realism, but as an extension into elsewhere.

expanse

We need to go back to a real historical process, namely the formation of Baroque aesthetics during the Western Reformation and Counter-Reformation. The Reformation, meaning the split within Christianity between the Catholic Church and the emerging Protestant churches, led to a kind of austerity in the Protestant model. In terms of aesthetics, Protestant churches are not as magnificent and extraordinary as Catholic cathedrals. There was a bias towards sobriety and severity. And then there was the Counter-Reformation, and this Catholic drive consciously sought to promote the proliferation and effervescence of the Baroque. It's when the great Baroque cathedrals emerged in Spain, Flanders, and Portugal. So, what is Baroque? It is not

reducible to a kind of classicism, which is splendid and suggests the ancient cathedrals finesse, but it is rather a return to an unstoppable flush of aesthetic sensation. In fact, Baroque churches spread their ornamentation everywhere. Even across the oceans. The churches and cathedrals of Peru, Chile, Mexico, and Argentina, for example, are Baroque temples. As such, they feature an infinite variety of ornamental elements and materials. With their dazzling gold and ivory, those cathedrals are breathtaking and capture the imagination. They are also monuments to colonization. The angels, for instance, are depicted as little Indigenous boys with bows and arrows, and the Virgins are Black Madonnas, like the Virgin of Guadalupe. They have saintly figures, Black saints, performing miracles. Therefore, the very idea of creolization is tied to the concept of an uninterrupted expanse of aesthetic elements and representations of reality. And this also undergoes transformation and is carried over into painting, for example. Latin American painting does not resort to the tricks of perspective, for example. It is flat, layered painting, and that is mirrored in the literature developed in those countries. All the literature those countries have produced is characterized by accumulation, multiplication, repetition, circularity, repetition, assonance, and so on. Like the scrolls and corbels of Baroque aesthetics in the cathedrals and churches of the Americas. What is it, then? It's renouncing the tricks of perspective, renouncing the idea of a depth one must delve into in their quest for the absolute. Paradoxically, the absolute is as much the elevation towards the summit, towards the spire of the bell tower, as it's the search for depth, the catacombs and cellars of churches, and the true source if that pursuit of the absolute. Thus, depth is not only what goes to the bottom, but also what extends toward the ethereal and, by contrast, what tends to expand, hence the notion of expanse. What tends to expand is the motif of cathedrals, but it is also the book that never ends, and the painting that never stops filling the canvas, which even leans over the edge, beyond the canvas, as far as one can imagine. They are all hallmarks of the arts throughout the Americas. And it's all connected to the idea of mixture and creolization.

It's fantastic to see the cherubs as little Indigenous children with their bows and arrows in churches and cathedrals in Chile or Peru. It's absolutely fantastic, and that is creolization in its most direct and complete form.

The expanse has no goal. Depth has one that is unattainable: the ideal, the absolute. Artworks, or intellectual works, also have ideal goals, but they too are unattainable. The expanse has none; as long as it can expand, it expands. So, it has no aim. There is no regulated mode of expanse, whereas there do exist modes of depth. For example, the spire of a church: the more it tapers, the more it soars; the higher it rises, the more it sums up, in its fineness, the search for the absolute. But expanse is not like that. From its vantage point, we could say that "expanse is the inexhaustible manifestation of sensitivity," whereas the absolute would be depth, as "the manifestation aiming at an absolute that can never be attained." Therefore, those are two ways of conceiving one's relationship to the world, to the surrounding environment. And Caribbean storytelling, for example, is a practice based on expanse. It's not a practice rooted in depth. Caribbean narratives are often quantitative in their descriptions, reflections, and analyses. Caribbean storytelling is quantitative, while Western literatures are qualitative. We can say

that, in a Balzac novel, when there is a realistic description of reality, it tends to give meaning to that reality in depth. But you have to guess it, you have to follow it. For example, in *Le Lys dans la vallée* [*The Lily in the Valley*],[8] it is a special case, the landscapes of Touraine are significant of a relationship that is ethereal, infinite, absolute, and therefore ends in failure, lacking any content, as it turns out. But does such literary technique suit us? Absolutely not! Because we don't have to strive for any kind of absolute rooted in the in-depth description of our realities; instead, we must expand them quantitatively before us, on the spot, to try and see how to navigate this inextricable situation. And that is indeed what Caribbean storytelling does, but, unfortunately, many Caribbean writers try to apply Balzac's approach to the Caribbean situation. Yet the Caribbean situation is not a Balzacian situation. It's the kind of situation in which what is hidden, what lies beneath, what is expansive, what frightens, and what reassures, may not be revealed through subtle research, but rather through a multiplication of representations.

The relationship between depth and expanse in the novel can be summarized as follows: the character is a landscape, and the landscape is a character. This is where the connection resides in our literatures. The same cannot be said for European literatures, in which, with the exception of poetry, the landscape is most often a backdrop. It may be a compliant backdrop, or otherwise, but a backdrop nonetheless.

Not only in my books, and here I'm being bold, but also in Faulkner's books, for example, I have noticed the absence of character descriptions. The characters are described through their reactions or through their actions, but there is no description as

---

[8] Honoré de Balzac, *Le Lys dans la vallée*. Paris: Gallimard, 1977 [1836] [*The Lily in the Valley*. Translated by Peter Bush. New York: New York Review of Books, 2024].

such. "He had small, sly eyes, and a thick mustache" is not something you would find in Faulkner.

In other words, the description is seen from the perspective of history, of Yoknapatawpha County, that is, the original curse of having introduced slavery. The series of characters that stem from this original curse are all incredibly well defined, but Faulkner never says, "he had blue eyes," or "he had gray eyes," or "he had eyes like so and so." Instead, he manages to make us picture the characters in front of us with no actual description. In such an astonishing book as *As I Lay Dying,*[9] for example, there are a dozen characters who take turns having their own inner monologues, but they never take the form of confidences or dialogues. It's an incredible interweaving of elements from the landscape. And each person seems to be a character in their own right, and there are girls, there are boys, there are adults, there are shepherds. None of them describe themselves by saying, "my beard…" But there is an incredible precision in how each of those characters is portrayed and outlined. Because the character is a landscape, and because the landscape is a character. In novels from the Americas and the Caribbean, the tree is a character, the river is a character, the mountain is a character, the forest is a character, and the city is a character.

Baroque has no metaphysics. So, expanse has no metaphysics, but depth does. Moreover, depth goes both ways, from top to bottom and from bottom to top. It does have metaphysics. Baroque, in contrast, has only aesthetics. Malraux said that the 21st century will be either spiritual or it will not be at all; I say that the 21st century will be either aesthetic or it will not be at all.

landscape

I believe that, in our times—and it's both commonplace and worth repeating— landscapes are the most threatened things. That much is fairly certain, all over the world.

For me, landscape is the country… The country clad in an autobiographical continuum. Meaning the country, successively over time, and even when time is disrupted, is clad in guises that make up its biographical continuum, cycling from degeneration to degeneration, or from regeneration to regeneration, or from catastrophe to catastrophe, and so on. Just as a forest regrows after a cyclone. And the landscape is the country, the structure of the country overlaid with this, clad in this autobiographical continuum and the changes that the flow of historical, prehistoric, or non-historical time has extended across the country.

And I can increasingly see that humanity has a conception that links its fate to that of the biographical continuum of landscapes. In other words, environmental thought arises from this awareness of the

---

[9]   William Faulkner, *As I Lay Dying.* New York: Vintage, 1990 [1930].

relationship… once again, between humans and the landscape; and once again, we return to pre-Socratic terms.

So, is a river a landscape? But it's also alive! What is a forest in a landscape? It's also alive. What is the sea? It's a landscape, but it too is alive. That is for sure, but such relationship calls for the fusion of humans and landscape, that gives rise to the environmental thought we see today!

Landscape is a character, because it's an acting part of the historical continuum with all its leaps and variations. And if landscape is a character, it interacts with other characters, human characters, in human society. I think Maroonage was an alliance between the hills and woods with a fellow in search of freedom.

PC Is there a connection between major resistance movements in the contemporary world and the landscape?

EG The most important aspects in the relationship between landscape and humans are threat and suffering. To me, it seems to be the most critical factor. Today, it's not so much about resources and assistance as it was in the days of the Maroons: the forest was both a resource and a lifeline for the Maroons, but I don't believe that is the case today. Precisely because all landscapes around the world are under threat. Absolutely all of them. Any thought is a thought about the relationship between landscape and humans.

language

PC There is another very famous phrase that introduces another term, that of language. You express it as follows: "The poetics no longer requires the adequacy of language, but the precise fire of language. In other words: I speak to you in your language, and it is in my language that I understand you." ⑩ What do you mean by that?

EG It means there is a truth that has always been around but was never really acknowledged, namely that, when we use language, we use it differently depending on our imagination and our mental imagery. We can use it, for example, by believing that the language's words are constitutive of our being. That's what Mallarmé did, to name one example. A poetics that links the extraction and intricacy of the language's words to the aspirations of Being. In other words, the language's words are constitutive and representative of Being. We can experience it by treating the language's words with distrust. Because we tell ourselves that the language's words have some kind of power, that their use can deceive me, make me believe things. I distrust the language's words. I adopt an attitude of reserve, severity, and even avarice towards the language's words. I use them prudently and sparingly in the construction of my literary work.

We can use them, the language's words, with great confidence and generosity. We think that the more we use the language's words, the

---

⑩   Édouard Glissant, *L'intention poétique. Poétique II*. Paris: Gallimard, 1997 [1969], p. 52 [*Poetic Intention*. Translated by Nathanaël with Anne Mallena. New York: Nightboat Books, 2010, p. 46].

more meaning is conveyed. So, we accumulate them, we repeat them. And anything that, for instance, might count as a mistake in the traditional economy of the French language, well, we use that too. And what does that mean? It has to do with the difference between the language we use and the speech we employ. Speech is the manner, the attitude we have toward the words of the language. But something that is very clear and that we were not aware of, is that it comes into play in all languages. For example, we Caribbean writers place our trust and generosity in the language. A Caribbean writer who was to create minimalist literature, as what's trending now in France, would only be doing so to follow a French fashion.

In other words, though he writes in Spanish and I write in French and thus we may have different languages, we still employ the same speech, the same confidence in words and terms, the same generosity in their use. We do not shy from repetition, we do not shy from redundancy, we do not shy from our way of inhabiting the language. It is one of the unavoidable facts of today's inextricable world that I can write in much the same way as a Chinese author.

"I write in the presence of all the world's languages," [11] meaning I am no longer monolingual in my use of the language I speak. What typically occurred in Western literature in general was that each writer was monolingual in their use of their language. They could not imagine that there could be other languages as valid for writing as their own. The French thought Shakespeare was a savage. The English thought Racine was effeminate literature. They could not imagine

otherwise. So, everyone was monolingual in their own language.

Today, that is impossible. You cannot use one of the world's languages today without being in the presence of all the world's languages, even if you do not know them. And, of course, you do not know them.

That translates into openness and availability in terms of speech. By that I mean the attitude we have towards languages, which is, to give an example, what Classicism achieved in the 17th century: making obvious the organic unity of language, or in other words, tightly binding language around its organic principles. But now the French language can be stretched. We can send it to the other side of the world. We can catch it, we can make it jump. Whereas, according to the principles of Classicism, what I call a measure of measure, that tightening meant we could not imagine the world through it. We imagined the depth and generality of the human race through language. But we could not possibly imagine the diversity of the world.

"We will not save one language by letting the others perish," [12] for if languages perish and one language prevails, that particular language reverts from being a language to become a code. Given the diverse realities of the world, if they all rely on the same idiom, the same language, that very language can only serve as a code. It cannot be a language meaningful to all. For what is a language? It is a medium of communication that becomes a medium of creation, which becomes a medium of knowledge. And the language has its advances and retreats. Depending on whether the community that speaks it advances or retreats. It has moments

---

[11]   Édouard Glissant, *Traité du Tout-Monde. Poétique IV*. Paris: Gallimard, 1997, pp. 26, 85 [*Treatise on the Whole-World*. Translated by Celia Britton. Liverpool: Liverpool University Press, 2020, pp. 15, 52].

[12]   Glissant, *Traité du Tout-Monde*, p. 85 [*Treatise on the Whole-World*, p. 52].

of stagnation. It has moments when it's in danger. It has moments when it becomes obscure, when it becomes excessive, when it becomes baroque. It has moments of perfect clarity. It has moments of retreat, when its use becomes stilted and shabby. And then it has moments of outburst. A language is a variance. But if all the realities of the world use the same language, then that language is no longer a variance, it is merely a code.

Saving one's language and holding on to it means withdrawing from relationships. No actual human society is capable of doing that, of simply withdrawing.

I do not believe in the *Francophonie* because I do not believe in any uniformity with regard to the use of the French language. There are dozens of different forms of French, depending on whether you are in Quebec, Martinique, Mali, or in a small village in Tonkin where, miraculously, people have kept the language alive. In each case, the speech will be different, in terms of how the language is put into practice and in relation with other languages across the world.

m

matta

Matta is one of the greatest contemporary painters. He takes painting into another space, an interstellar space. Matta's spaces are truly interstellar spaces. And, as a result, they are utterly beyond the bounds of the world. Beyond the boundlessness of the world.

It's an exceeding of the excess, which I believe would result, for example, in a town or city with no bounds, a city with no horizon. Even megalopolises have their limits. And when the Chinese build megalopolises, they stash them away in swamps. So, the swamp is the city border, but it's a city whose limits we could not possibly find. We would not know whether they are above, to the right, to the left, or below. It would be a city of excess. Movies often illustrate this concept. Notable examples are films envisioning New York City in 200 years, depicting multiple New Yorkers stacked on top of each other with no communication between them. That's what excess looks like.

n

notebook

For me, a title is a Whole. And I cannot conceive of a Whole scattered across disparate, separate sheets of paper. For me, that is not a work. When I write a poem, I don't usually write just one poem, I write books of poetry, and when I write a book of poetry, it's a Whole, and it must occupy its own space. And the space I make for it in a notebook is practically the same as in the eventual printed version. It doesn't exist at first. So, a title is not a collection of passages. A book of poems is not a collection of poems, it's a single long poem. That's why the idea of a notebook, which is already nearly a book, a book-bound journal, is very important. The notebook size and volume often determine the nature of the work, but that's not an artifice. It's a technical way of overcoming and mastering the technique. There is probably also the fact that notebooks were very rare during my childhood, during the war. Diaries were very rare. My fondest memory is of one day when I was given a plantation logbook. It was a big notebook like this, with two huge black covers made of very thick cardboard, black with lines like this, and those were the plantation logbooks in which the managers and accountants kept all the accounts and the workers' payments. It was an unimaginable gift for me, on which I wrote my poems, my essay drafts, etc. And there was that idea of the rarity and symbolic value of the bound notebook. And probably also the cultural influence of Césaire's *Cahier du retour au pays natal* [*Notebook of a Return to the Native Land*].

That was the first time I had seen the word "notebook" in a book title. It was not "Return to the Native Land" or "Memories of Returning to the Native Land." It was "Notebook" of a return to the native land. And there was a kind of mythical dimension to the notion of a notebook that surely influenced me.

I do not use tricks. I write the first sentence, I write the last sentence, and then I carry on from the first sentence until I have inevitably reached the last sentence. In other words, I don't find my way to the last sentence through tricks, I wait patiently until I reach the last sentence. And when I reach it, then the novel is finished. I have done this several times. I did it for *La Lézarde* [*The Ripening*], I did it for *Le Quatrième siècle* [*The Fourth Century*]. Not for *Malemort* because it was a much more fragmented and unstructured novel. But I did it for *Mahagony*, I did it for *La Case du commandeur* [*The Overseer's Cabin*].[13] The fact is that the substance of the work embodies its own need for space, which effectively imposes itself on you. It's not up to you to decide; you set the bounds, but you don't decide when to move away from them and when to move back toward them. The work itself decides it. It's the neat economy of telling stories the French way. It's a narrative economy. When you get there, it means it's good, it works.

[13]   Édouard Glissant, *La Lézarde*. Paris: Seuil, 1958; Paris: Gallimard, 1997 [*The Ripening*. Translated by Frances Frenaye. New York: George Braziller, 1959; Translated by Michael Dash. London: Heinemann, 1985]. *Le Quatrième siècle*. Paris: Seuil, 1964 [*The Fourth Century*. Translated by Betsy Wing. Ann Arbor: University of Michigan Press, 2001]. *Malemort*. Paris: Seuil, 1975; Paris: Gallimard, 1997. *Mahagony*. Paris: Seuil, 1987; Paris: Gallimard, 1997 [*Mahagony*. Translated by Betsy Wing. Lincoln: University of Nebraska Press, 2021]. *La Case du commandeur*. Paris: Seuil, 1981; Paris: Gallimard, 1997 [*The Overseer's Cabin*. Translated by Betsy Wing. Lincoln: University of Nebraska Press, 2011].

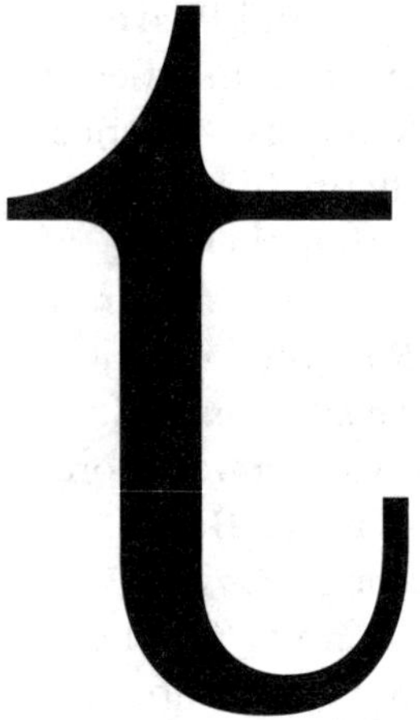

tremors in your thought

We have previously discussed the poetics of measure and the poetics of immeasurability. And, obviously, the cyclone and the earthquake fall within the poetics of immeasurability. As a rhetorical figure of both speech and thought.

We cannot really contemplate beyond the potential inconsistency of the earthquake. While in European countries, even though there are occasional disasters, even though there are particularly harsh winters that wreak havoc, we can still contemplate a kind of measured economy of time progression. Consequently, a kind of measured possibility of calculating the impulses of collective or individual thought. This is the first point.

Above all, though, I believe the world is entering a period when it's impossible for the whole world to measure thought, to have a measured relationship with the passage of time. That's practically impossible today. I think the inconsistency inherent to seismic tremors is no longer unique… It may be more prevalent in specific regions such as Martinique or California because we are located atop fault lines, where tectonic plates meet, or perhaps because we are both atop fault lines and on the shores of oceans where cyclones relentlessly form, we may be uniquely threatened.

But my idea is that the whole world is under threat today. And that there are nearly no places left in the world where we can contemplate in the tranquility of boundless, calm, or peaceful stretches of time, a sort of measure of the flow of thought, of sensitivity, and their expression.

The expression of the world, of the Whole-World, no longer follows any measure, and certainly no measure of measure. Because the world has become immeasurable, for reasons that still elude us, yet not entirely. We can think of all sorts of potential causes—such as global warming, or pollution—that can explain why the world has become immeasurable.

But we can no longer calculate, in any measured way, the flow of the world's matter through time.

I believe we feel this poetically. For example, the people of Martinique are not fatalistic, and that's wonderful, they are not fatalistic, they are not resigned, but they take things into account, they take detours, they calculate possible risks. And I appreciate the subtlety in how they take ownership of the world. That is valid for the Whole-World. Consequently, the whole of humanity is coming to think on the basis of instincts, practices, intuitions, and even types of tremors. In other words, getting a feel for the world's tremors.

The tremor is by no means doubt, dread, or fear. It's the fundamental intuition that systematic thought, flying high above the world, would overshoot it, fail to reach it, and have no bearing on it. It's the realization that systematic thought no longer serves the world, it can no longer operate within it, and it can no longer accomplish anything for it.

Systematic thought was once the source of greatness and splendor in western cultures, and it enabled them to colonize the world. However, it is no longer effective. With systematic thought, you cannot simultaneously grasp the forest fires in California, the impact of acid rain on another forest in Australia, the carbon emissions from a megalopolis in Brazil, a unique biological survival experiment carried out in a small country, and so on. You simply cannot grasp all of this with systematic thought.

Your thinking, and therefore your politics, must be tremorous, that is to say, it must sink here, rise there, branch off here, run along there, have a kind of operational hatch that allows it to engulf the constitutive hatch of the current world.

The trace thought is a way of thinking, a category of tremor thoughts. But the trace thought is the tremor applied to something from the memory realm, to something from before the flood—the flood being, in this case, the crossing of the Atlantic aboard slave ships. But the trace thought goes beyond any original catastrophe to retrieve something. The tremor thought. The trace thought is therefore an instance of the tremor thought.

But the tremor thought is also the examination of a series of current catastrophes, not a single, primordial, original catastrophe, but a series of ongoing catastrophes that enable us to assess not one, but a series of possibilities for restorative change amid the global catastrophes. A series of possibilities for restorative change. And such is, I believe, the politics of our time.

true / alive

PC In *La Terre magnétique* [The Magnetic Earth], your latest work with Sylvie Séma Glissant, you have this magnificent sentence: "Nothing is true, everything is alive."[14]

EG I contrast the system of truth with the unexpected, unpredictable, inextricable nature of life. That's a view I ascribe to part of the people of Easter Island. Because it's a people that, based on an undeniable truth—of having lived for thousands of years isolated from the rest of humanity, but never forgetting its origins—was capable of conceiving a total absolute, which is to say, a total truth.

That struck me as fascinating! And it seemed that one of the resources of that remnant of a people was systematic creolization, meaning systematic miscegenation! There was systematic crossbreeding with their background, their Oceanian sources. They found their origins in Polynesia. They went back; there was always a desire to return, but they no longer had boats.

And they reconstituted themselves both in the sense of maintaining their background… their absolute origins, and in the sense of practicing relations with the invaders—a term we need to to stress, as there is no other word for it. In the meantime, they reached a state of absolute nakedness. That is to say, they had become once again a naked people, adorned only with the tattoos they applied to themselves, replicating the patterns of the ancient absolute.

Alternatively, there is an incredible amalgamation and a condensation. After remaining isolated for hundreds of years, this

(14)   Édouard Glissant and Sylvie Séma Glissant, *La Terre magnétique: Les Errances de Rapa Nui, l'Île de Pâques*. Paris: Seuil, 2007.

people suddenly experienced, in two or three hundred years, a condensed version of all the colonization, all the massacres, all the self-denials, all the debasements, and it was reborn under a new principle of composite truth, which is almost true! And a truth that draws on a previous absolute, which is almost true! But one that is based on an exchange of life!

So, I don't know if it's indeed a people. I don't think it's a denatured people, but rather a very lively people with a lot of energy… That's why the statues they erected, the Moai, are so impressive, because we have lost their meaning, they have lost their eyes, but they are still standing there, like a fantastic presence of the world!

I guess that sums up the formula I used: "Nothing is true, everything is alive."

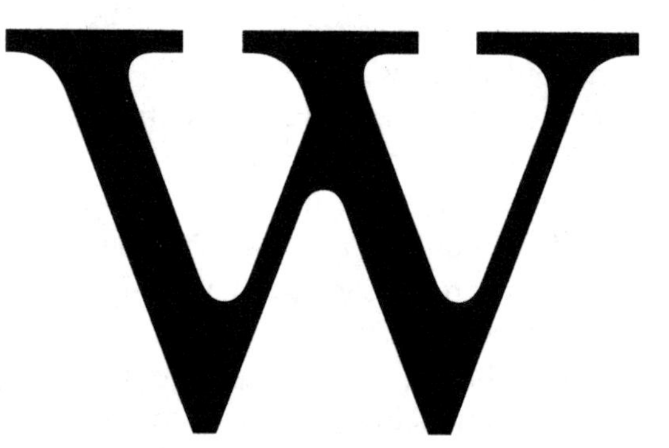

wifredo lam

As we conclude this alphabetical guide, I would prefer to avoid ending on the letters X, Y, or Z. Needless to say, I would be delighted to discuss Wifredo and *La jungla* [*The Jungle*] (1943) as an absolute object.

When I say the jungle is an absolute object, it's because of the reception of that painting, which is a seminal work in the aesthetics of the New World, of the Americas.

You may recall my analysis, as I have stated that the aesthetics of representation in the Americas are entirely different from the aesthetics of representation found in European cultures.

Because European cultures are primarily based on this remarkable discovery of sensitivity and formidable technical device known as perspective, whereas in the aesthetics of the Americas, to this day, perspective is not used as a technical means suited to the sensitivity of American countries and communities.

What prevails in those aesthetics, as we have already said, is contemporaneity and simultaneity, not perspective, which is a projective technique, a refined form of projection that connects the distant with the near, the outside with the inside.

The aesthetics of the Americas are all about simultaneity. Yesterday and today, inside and outside, are all in the same place, and a layering of elements makes it quite simply evident. That's amusing because the structures of Giotto, an Italian painter who could be described as a precursor of perspective, are surprisingly reminiscent of Inca sculptures, with a stacking in which the present is at the bottom, yesterday is in the middle, and the past is at the top.

And this idea of the simultaneity of time, of accumulation, is at the heart of Latin American art. And *La jungla* is the very symbol of this. If I say that "*La jungla* is an absolute object," it's because when it first made its way to the United States, the prevailing aesthetic sensibilities in the country were strongly Europeanized. Thus, it was perceived as a rather relative object, as the representation of a colonial subject, a semi-savage, so to speak. They were at the same time fascinated and a little appalled or a little dismissive. They considered it a relative object, as the product of a culture that had not yet achieved self-mastery.

And when I say that *La jungla* is an absolute object, it's because the jungle represents in absolute terms—not in a rigid, definitive way, but rather vividly and prolifically—the meaning and direction of all aesthetics in the Americas.

That's why it is an absolute object, at least in the sense I understand it. But not absolute in the sense of an absolute truth. When I say absolute, thinking about what we just said about Easter Island, I mean absolute in the sense of an absolute worldview and way of life, like a totality that is made real.

"We write in the presence of all the world's languages.

We share them without knowing them, we invite them to join the language that we use. Language is no longer the mirror of any Being. The languages are our landscapes, which the thrust of the day changes in us. ¶ Opposed to standardization, to banalization, to linguistic oppression, to the reduction to universal pidgins. But knowing already that we will not save one language by letting the others perish. For with every language that disappears a part of the human imagination is lost forever: a part of the forest, of the savannah or the crazy sidewalk. ¶ The taste of tin plates, the flavour of food. The price of hunger. ¶ The imagination radiates and reforms itself in the mingling of the Whole-World. The mingling of languages in turn is made comprehensible to us by the language that we use: our use of the language can no longer be monolingual."

Édouard Glissant, *Treatise on the Whole-World.* Translated by Celia Britton. Liverpool: Liverpool University Press, 2020, p. 52.

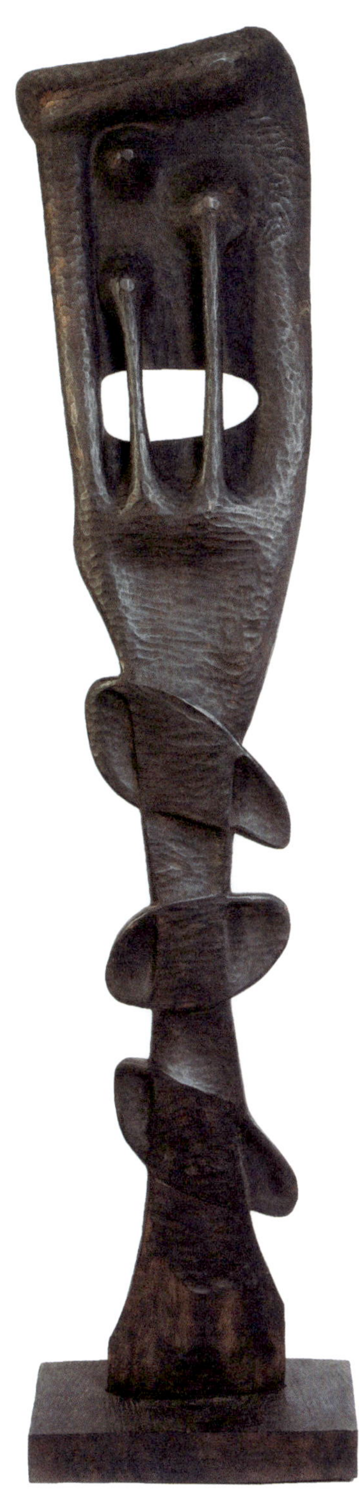

AGUSTÍN CÁRDENAS

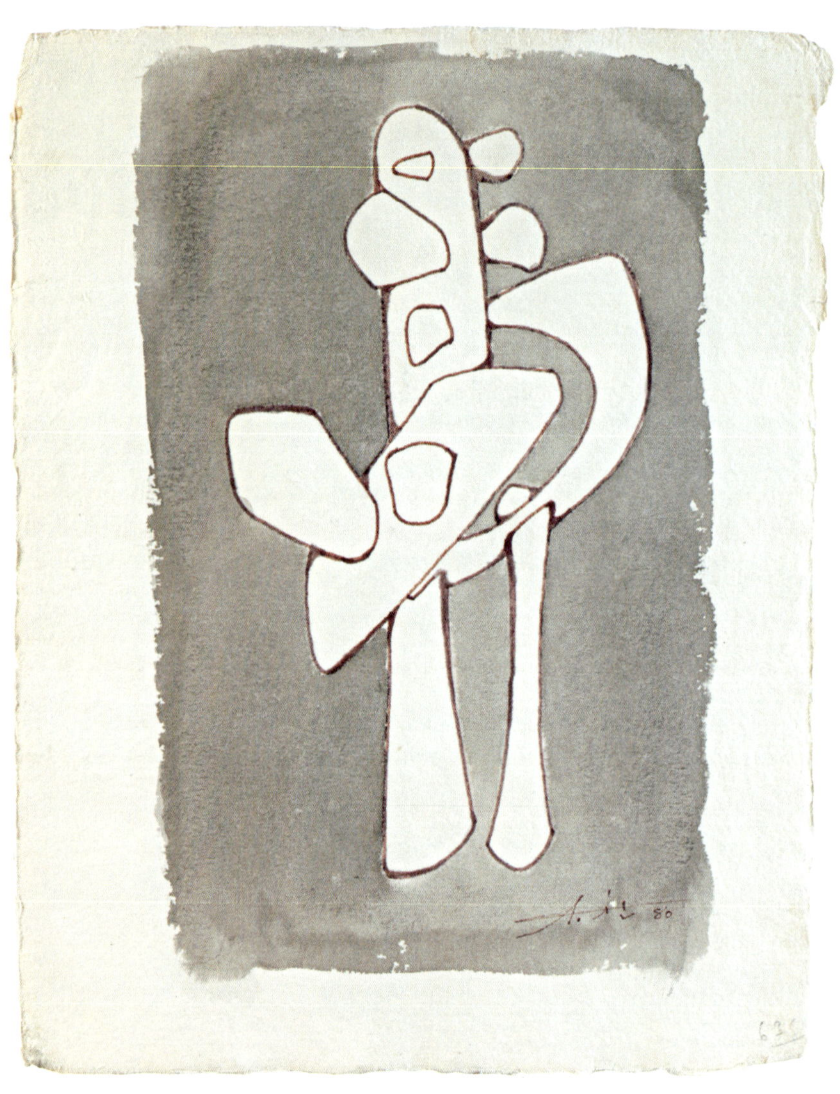

Sem título [Ilustração do *Discurso antilhano* de Édouard Glissant] / Untitled [Illustration of Édouard Glissant's *Caribbean Discourse*], 1980

AGUSTÍN CÁRDENAS

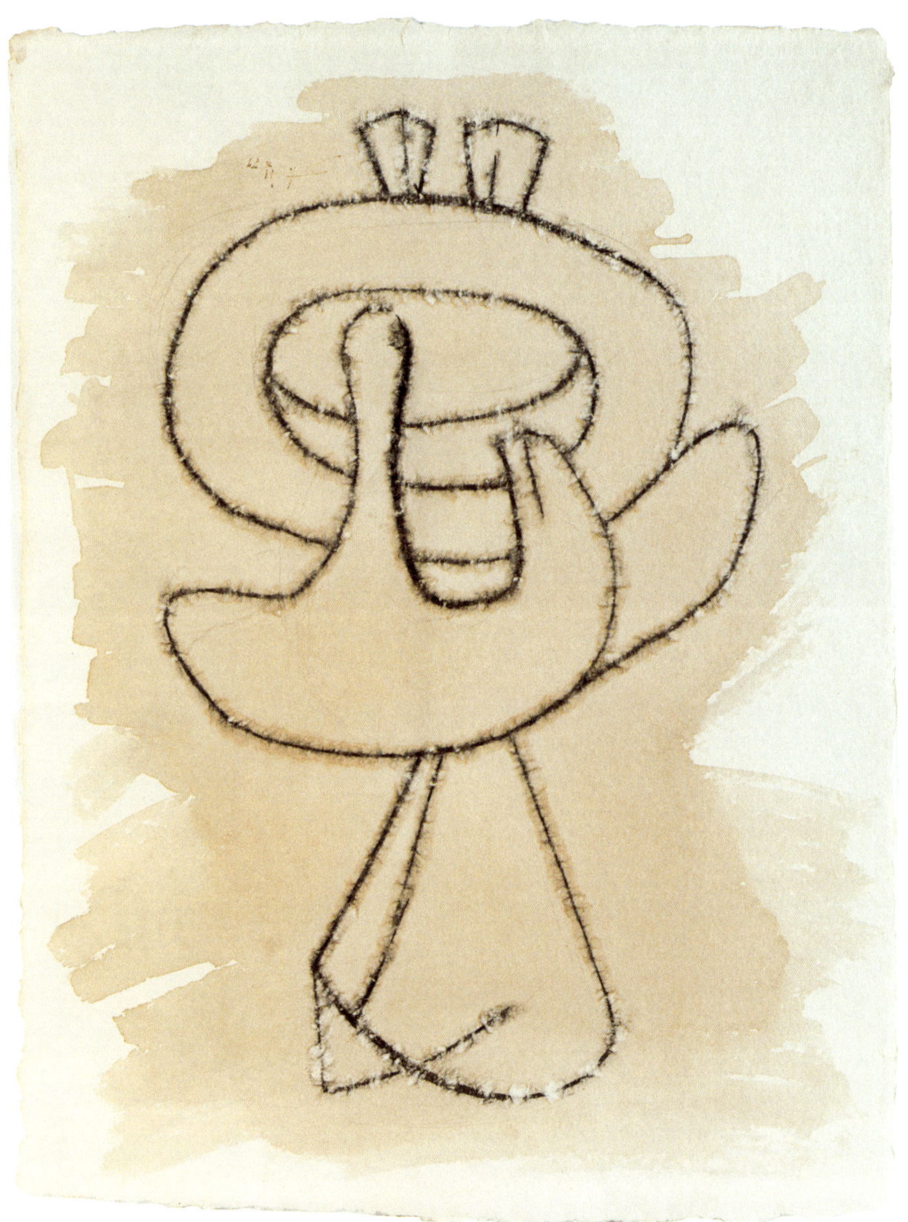

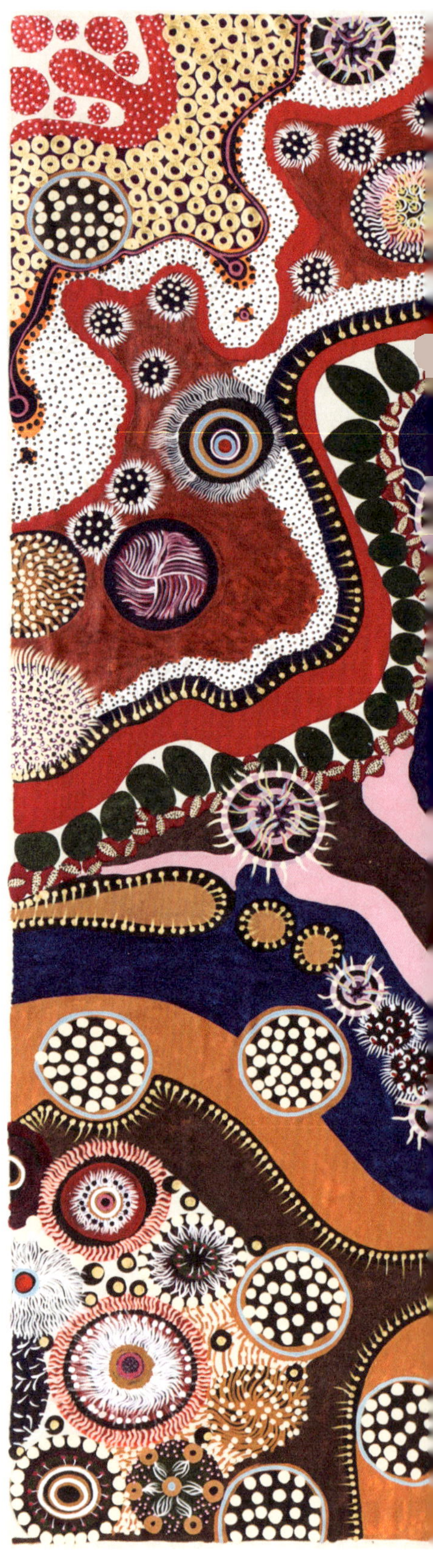

AISLAN PANKARARU

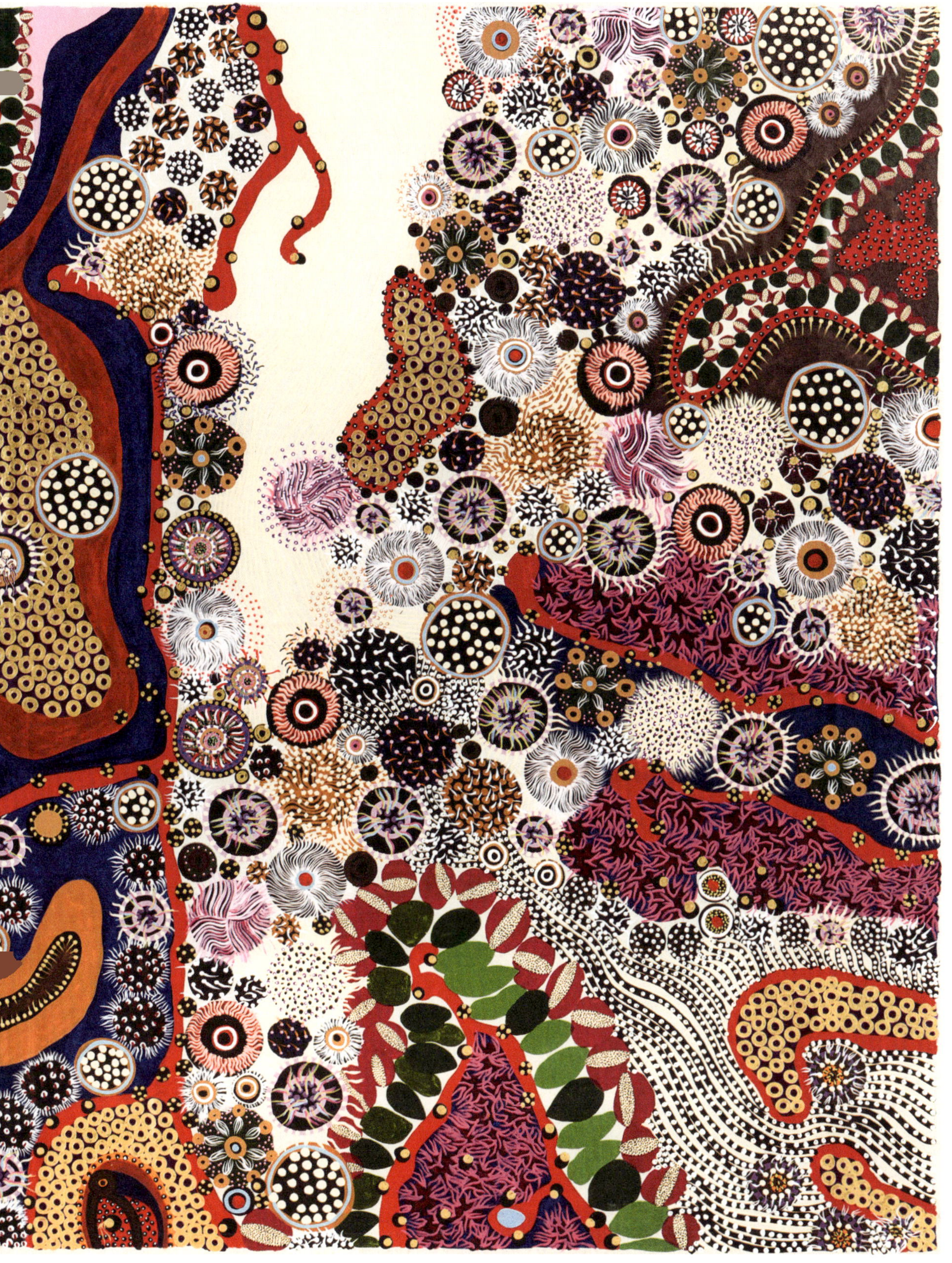

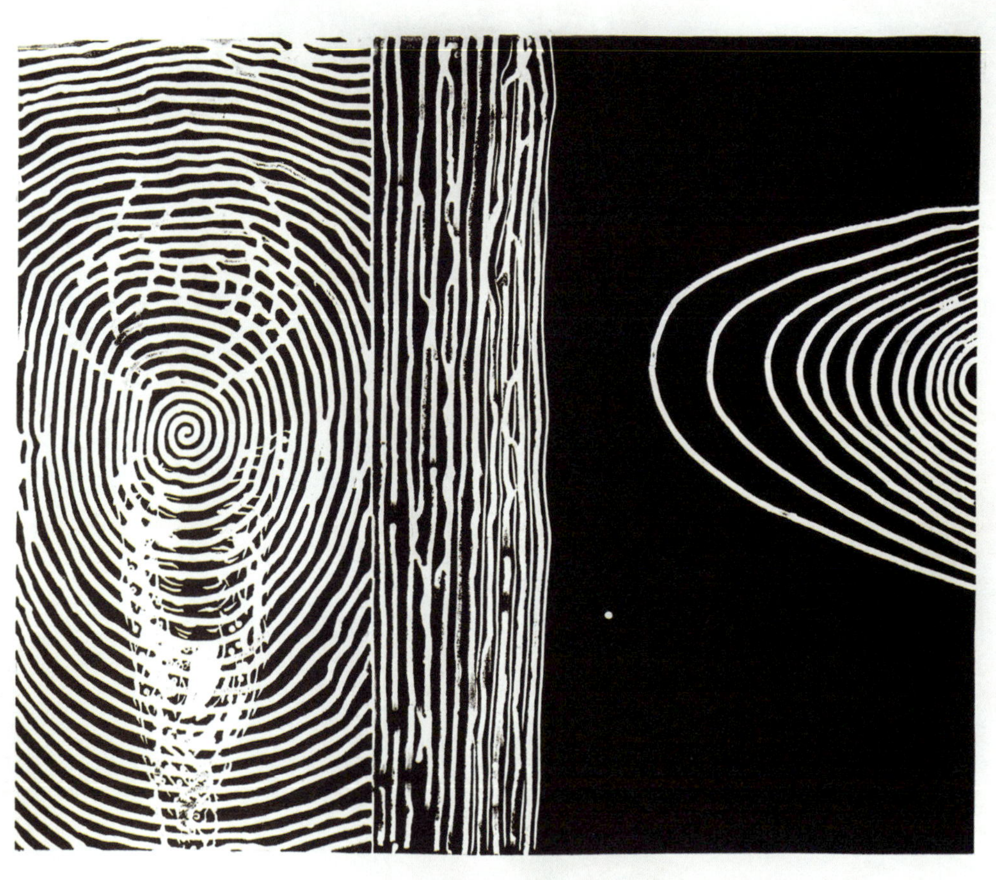

AMOEDAS WANI & PATRICE ALEXANDRE

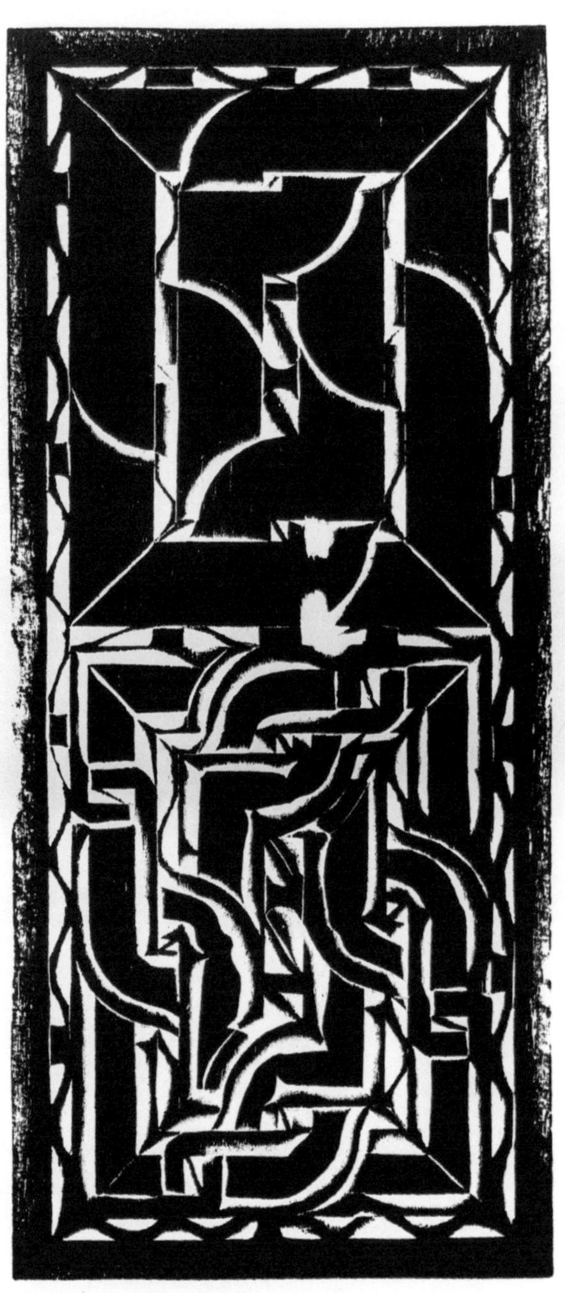

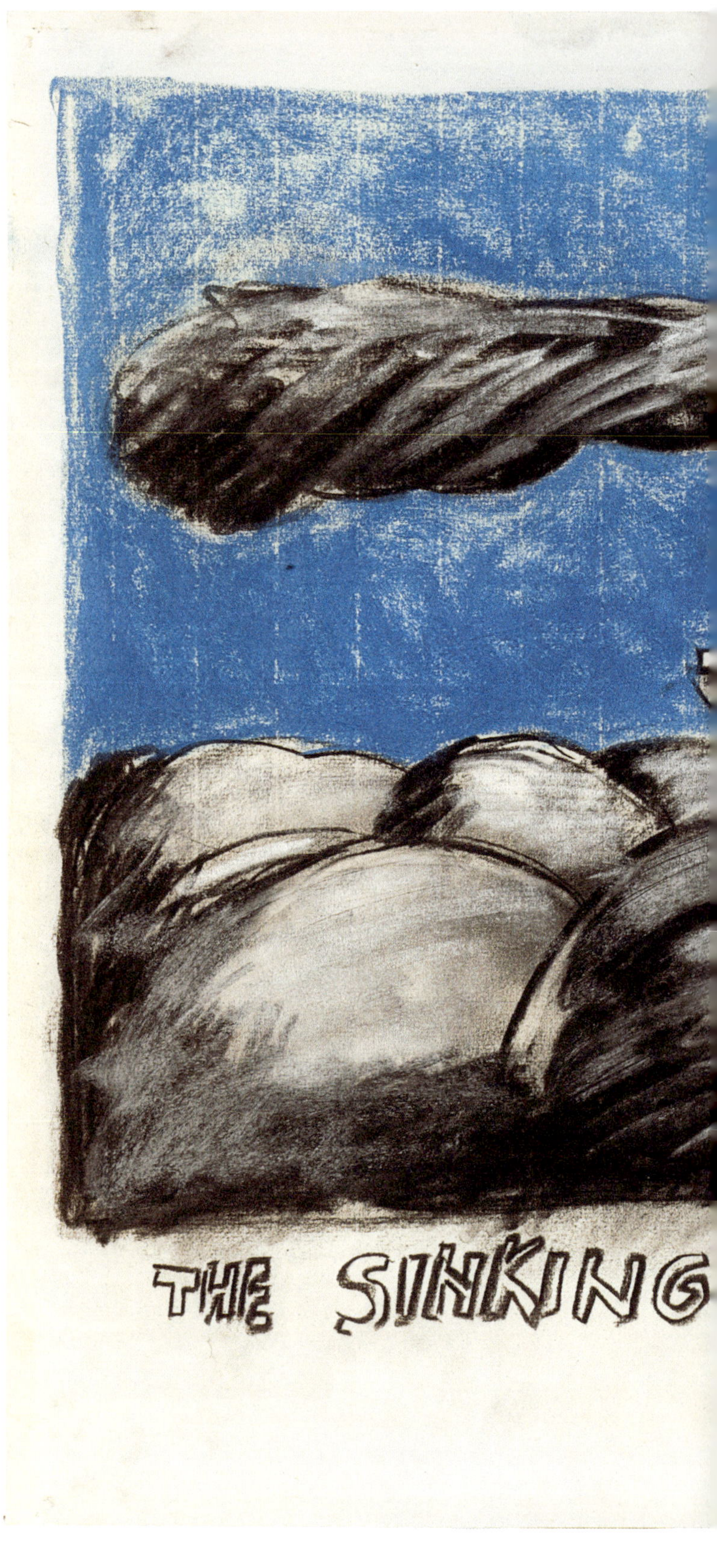

ANTONIO SEGUÍ

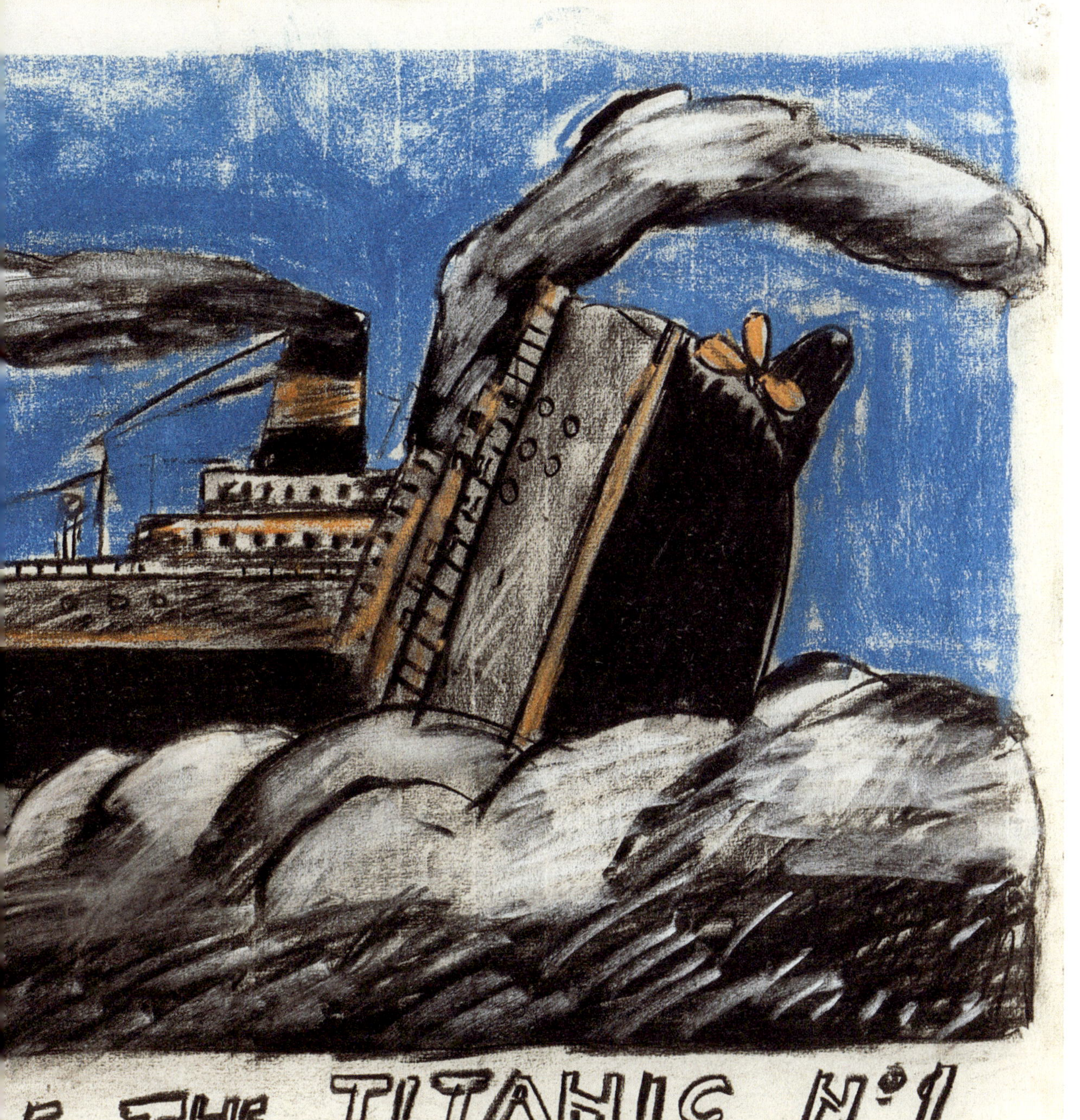

F THE TITANIC Nº1

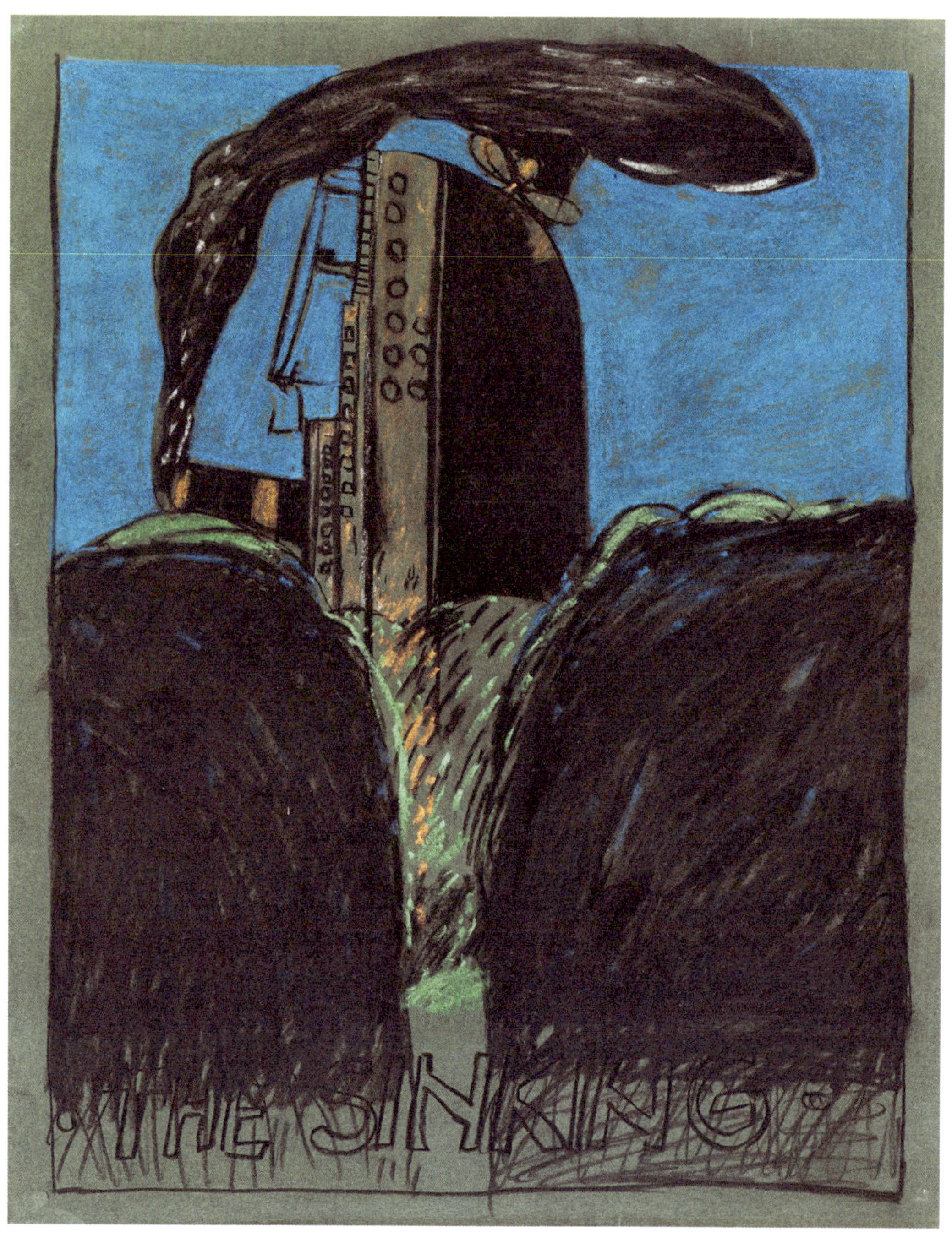

ANTONIO SEGUÍ

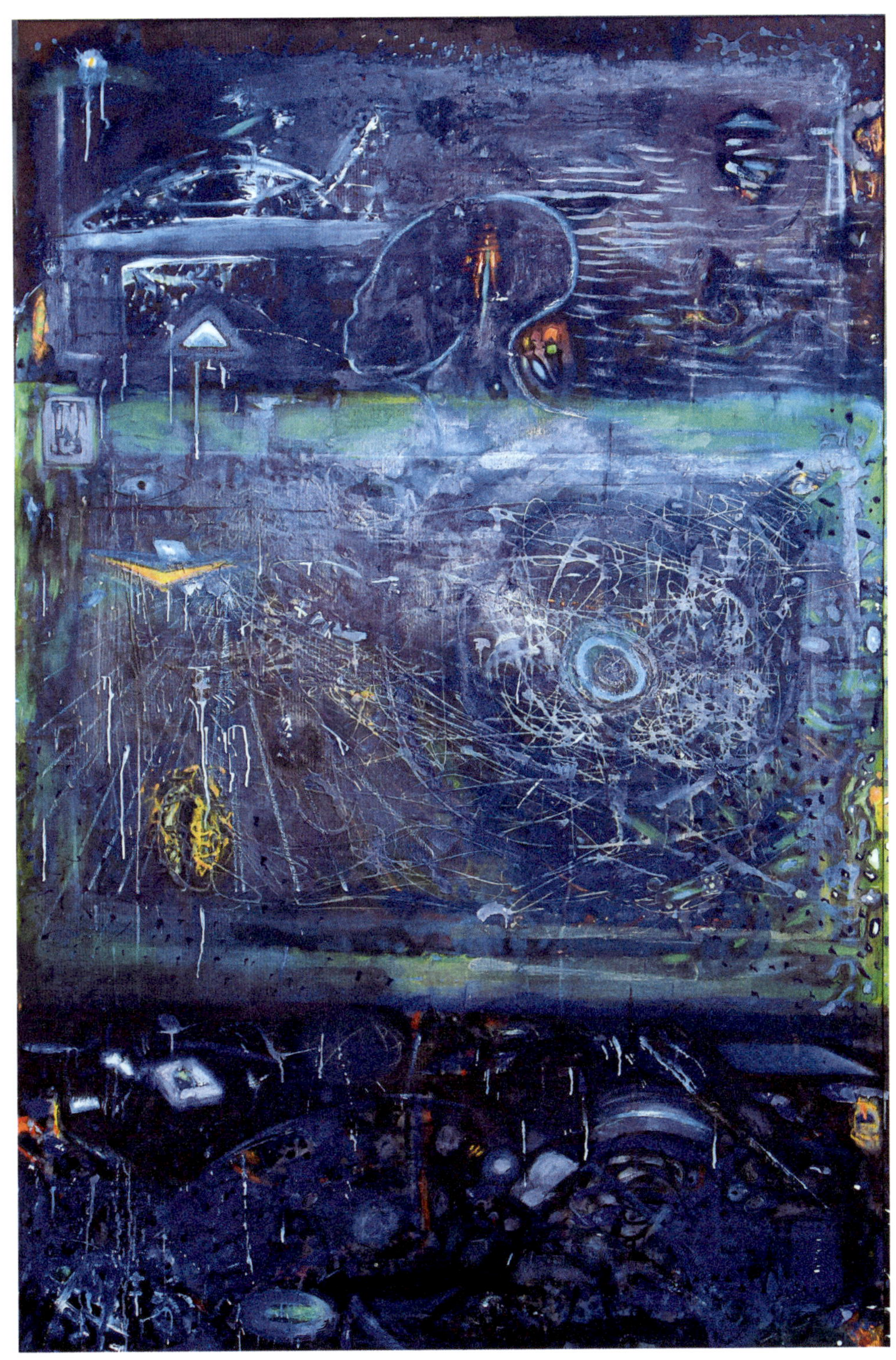

ARÉBÉNOR BASSÉNE

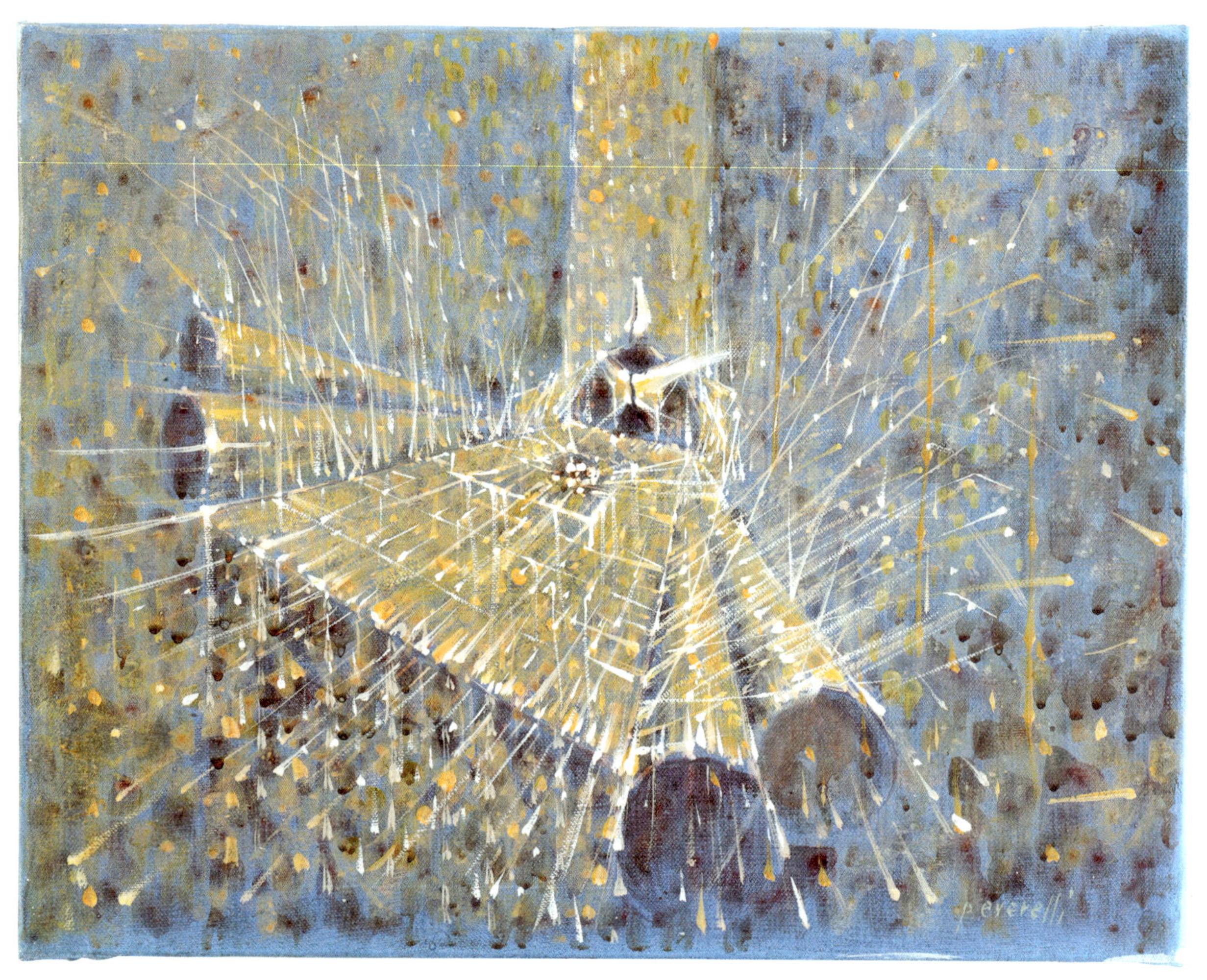

CESARE PEVERELLI

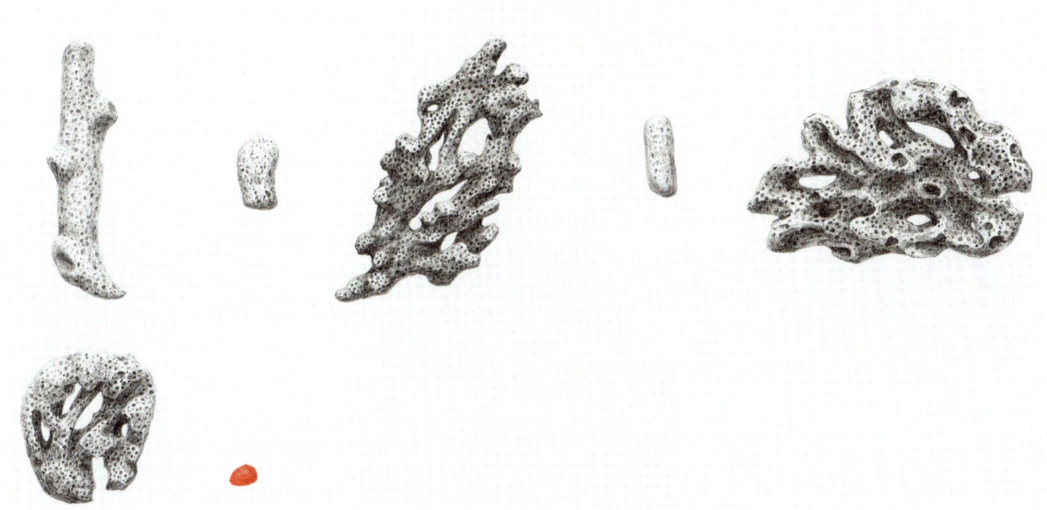

Penulis itu menjalin sebuah cerita khayalan.

That writer is composing a fantasy story.

那作家撰写一部奇幻故事。

	penulis (pena)	writer (pen)	作家 (笔)		menjalin (jalin)	to plait / to braid / to compose (plait)	编织, 组织 / 编, 梳理编 / 撰写, 编辑, 编者 (编)
	itu	the / that	那个 / 那		cerita	story / tale	故事 / 传说
	sebuah	a / an	一个		khayalan (khayal)	fancy / imagination	假想, 虚构 / 幻想

CHANG YUCHEN

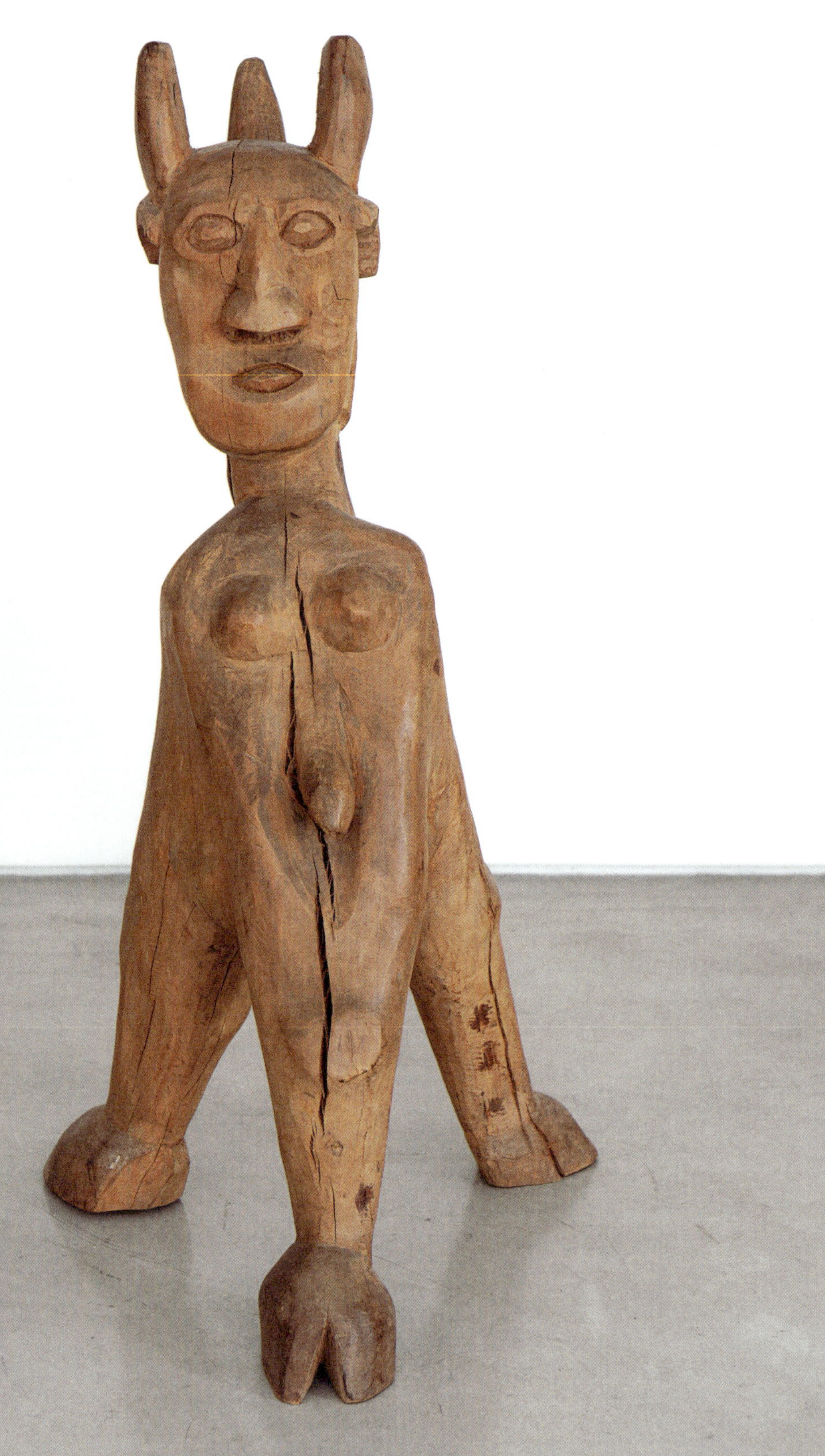

CHICO TABIBUIA

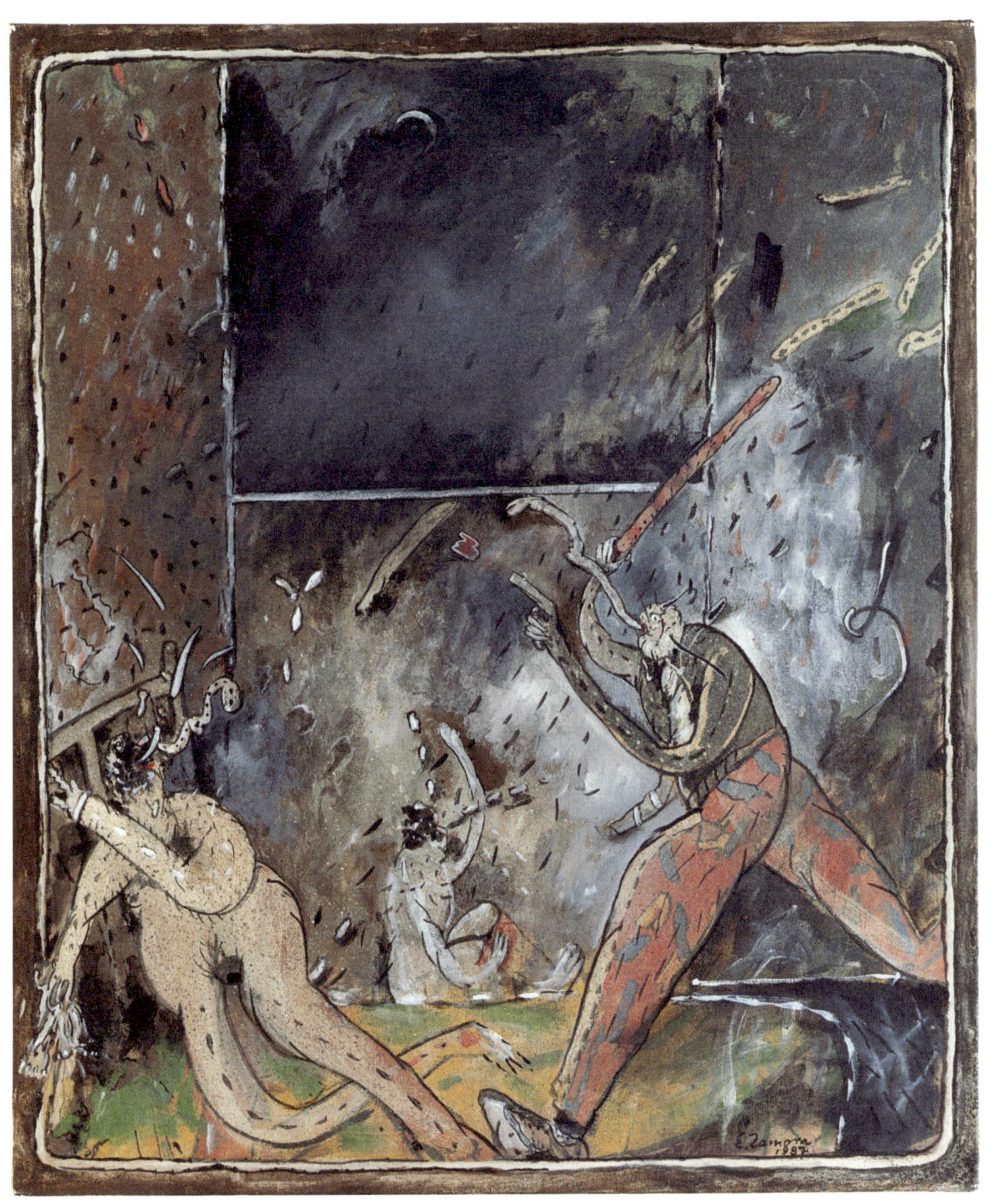

EDUARDO ZAMORA

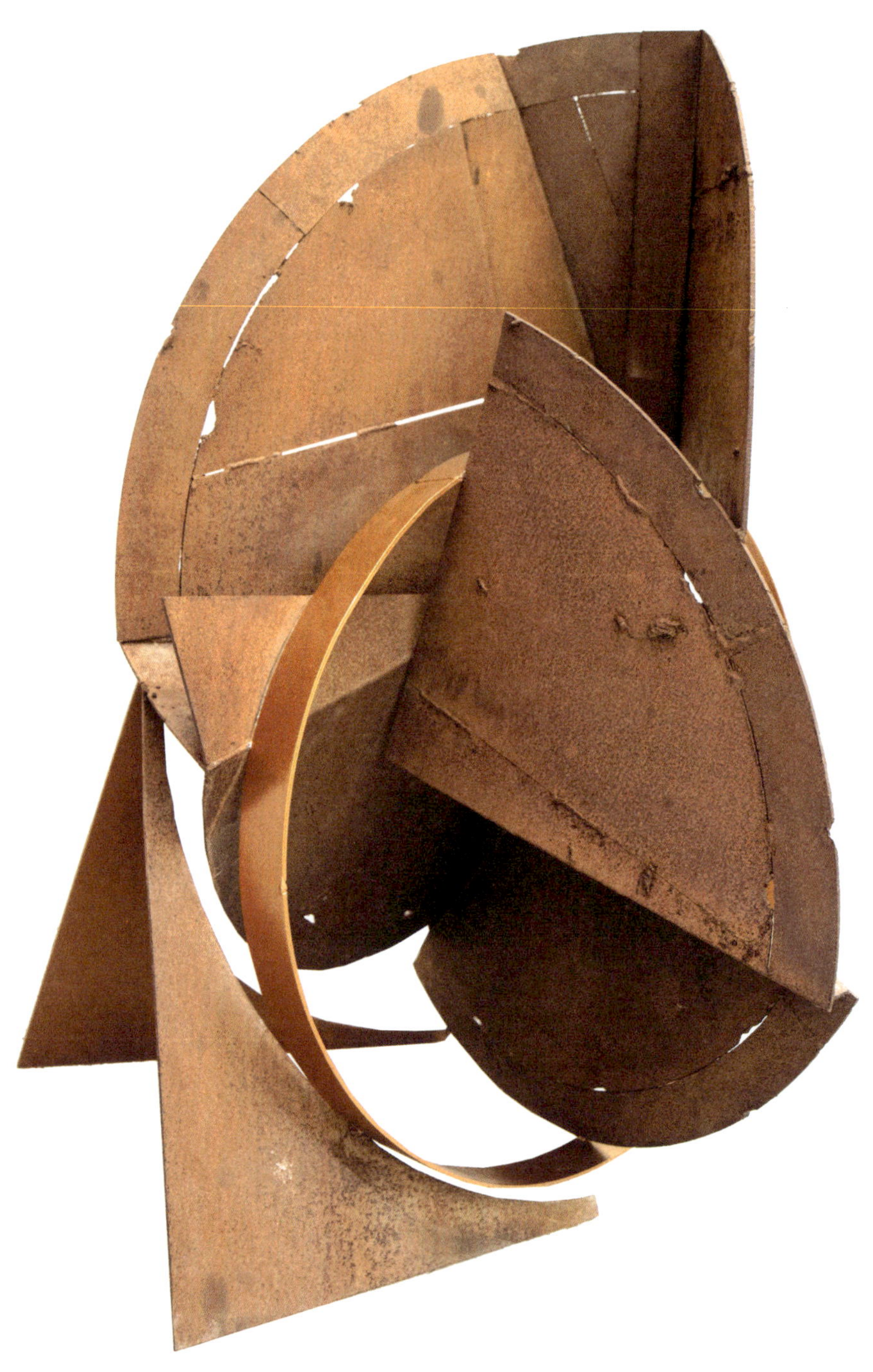

EMANOEL ARAÚJO

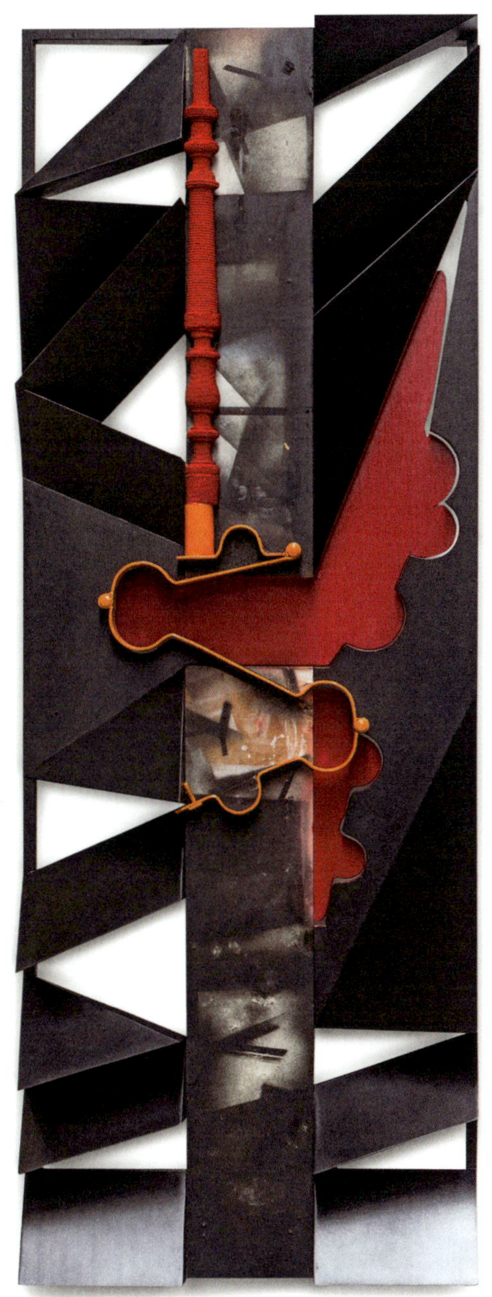

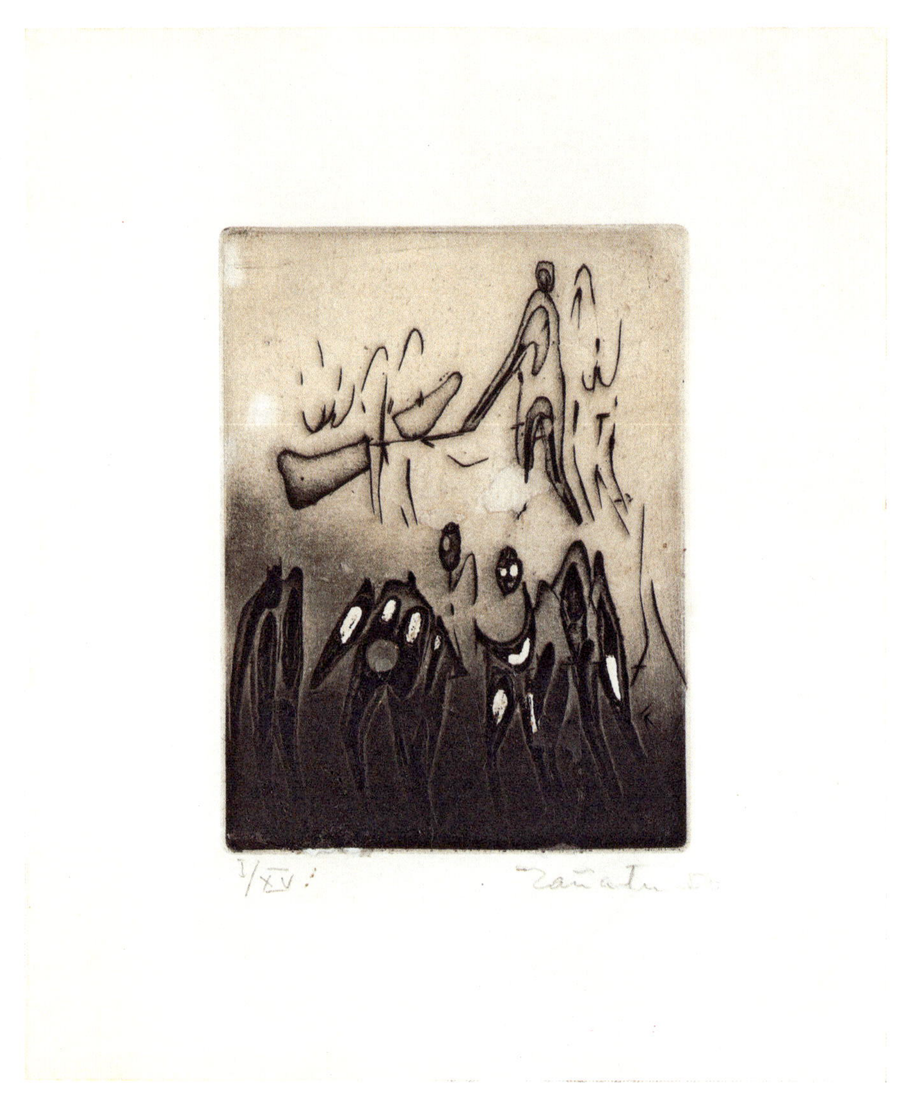

ENRIQUE ZAÑARTU

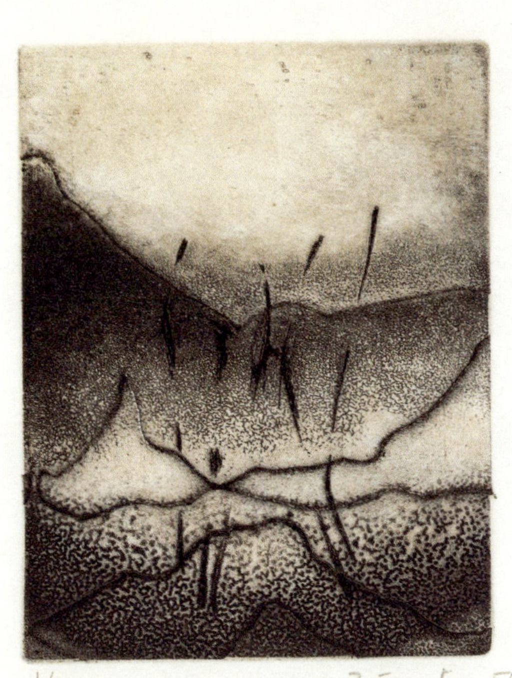

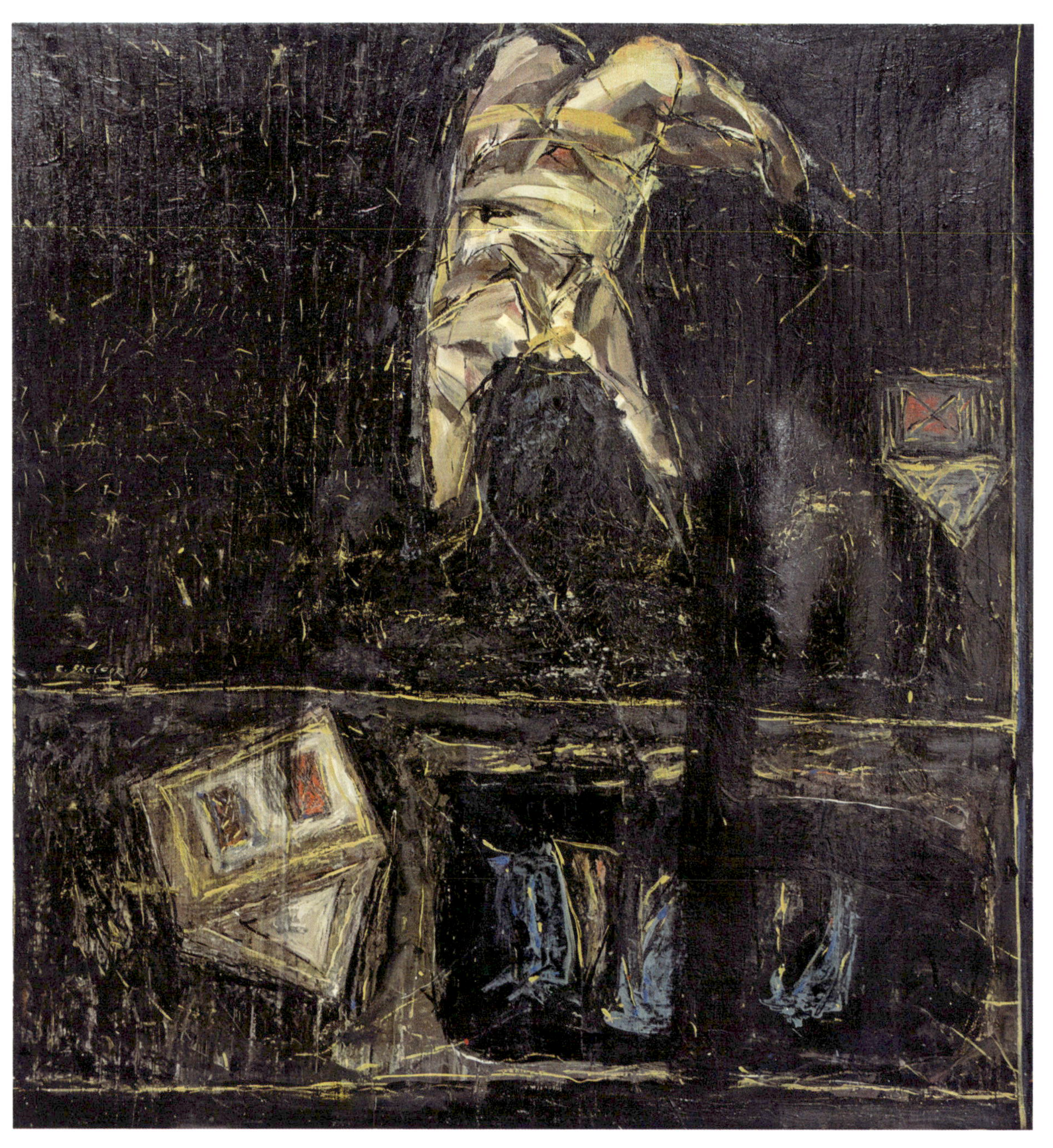

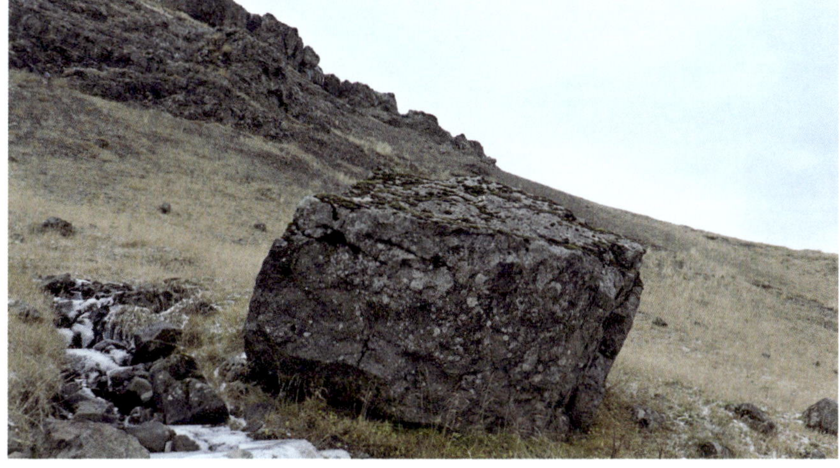

O dizer das pedras / The Telling of the Stones, 2025

ETIENNE DE FRANCE

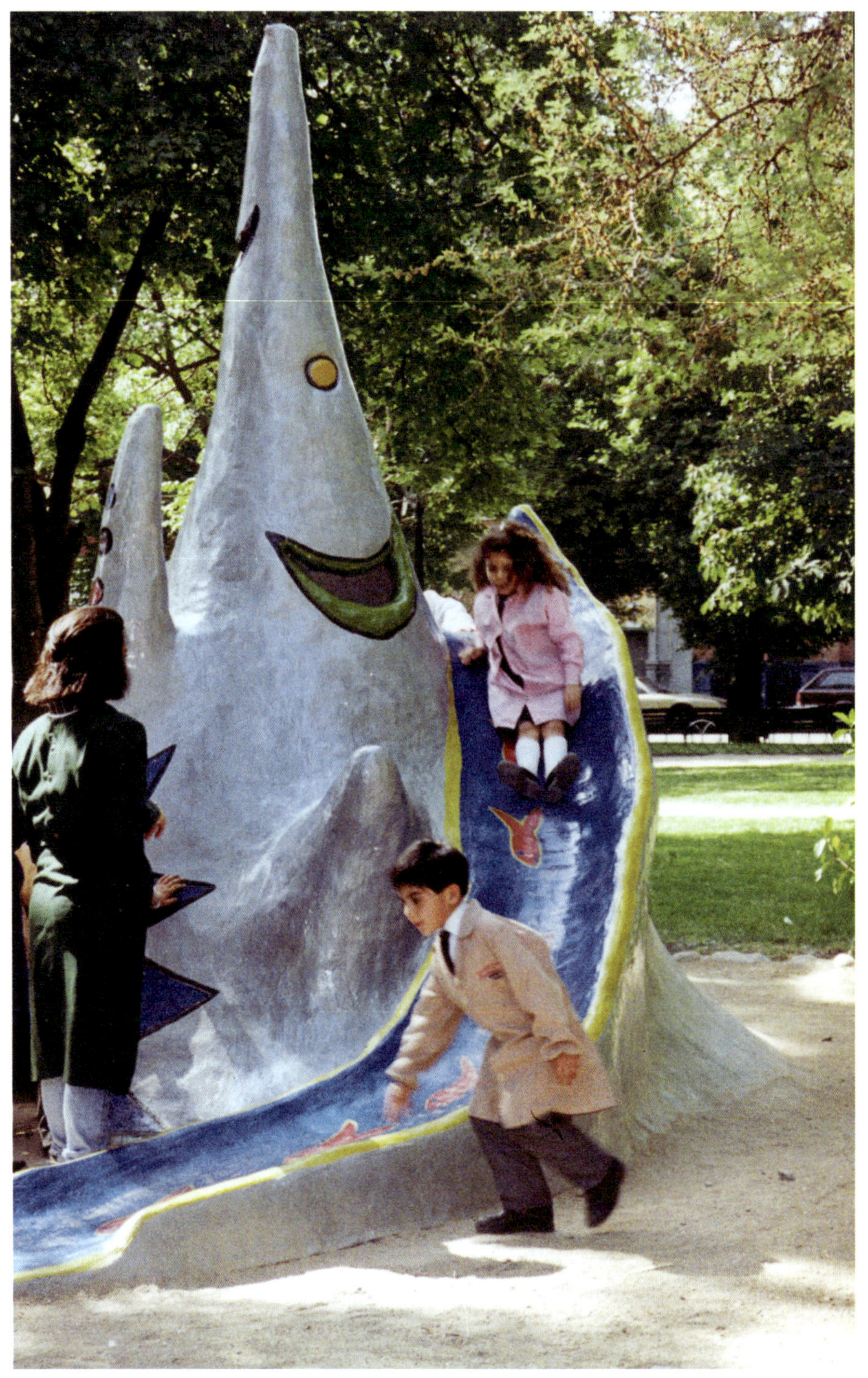

FEDERICA MATTA

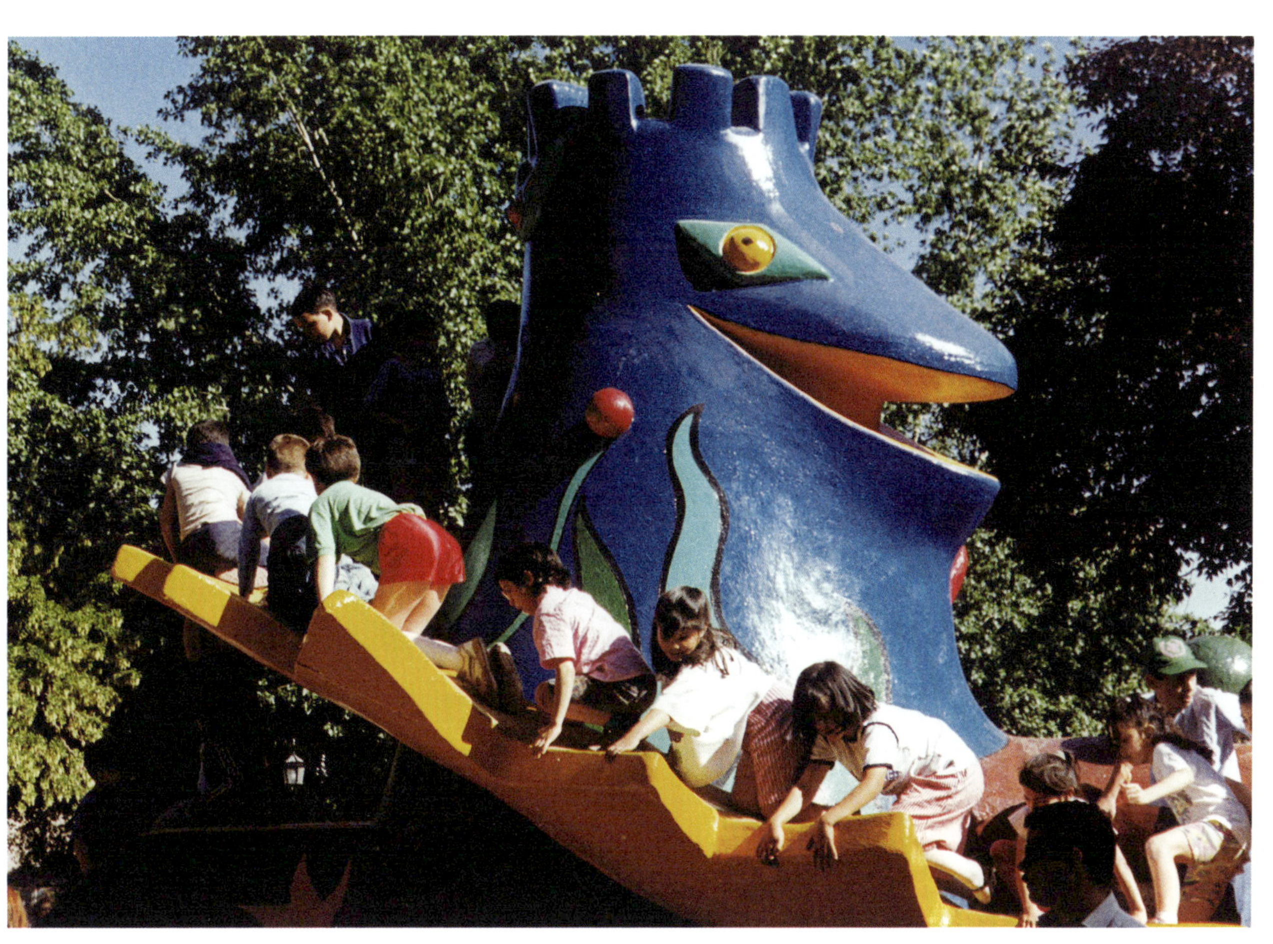

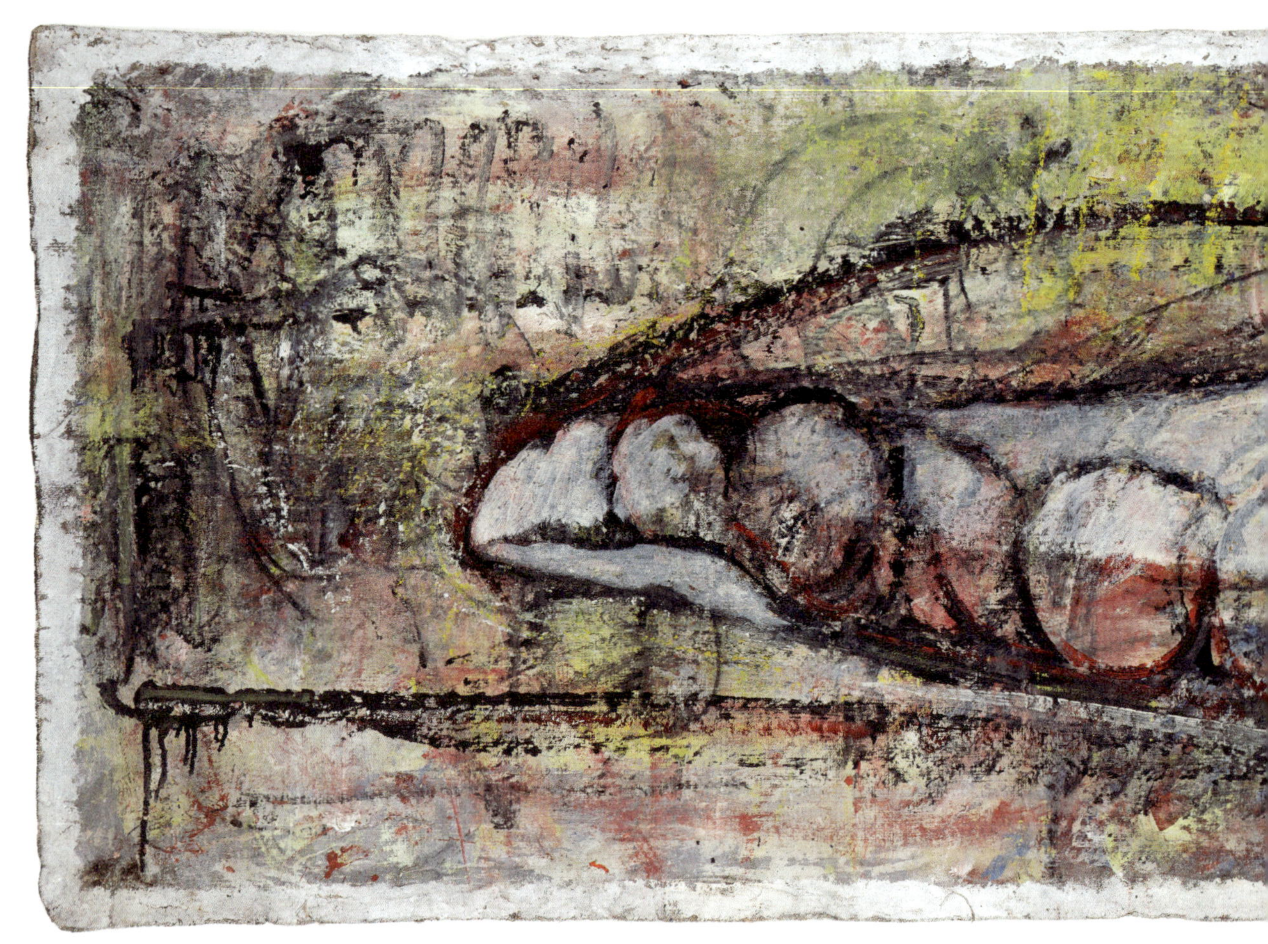

FLAVIO-SHIRÓ

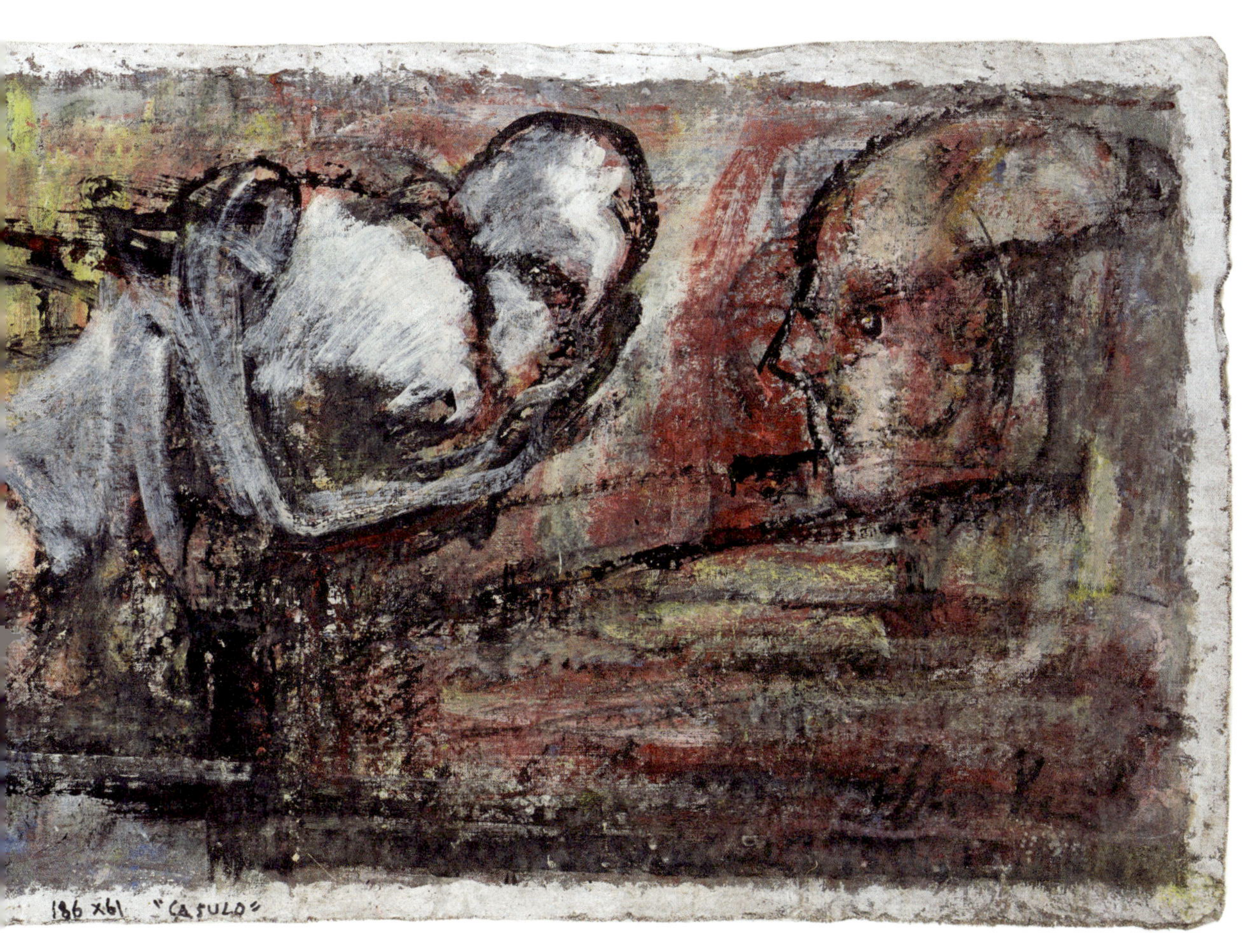

186 x61 "CASULO"

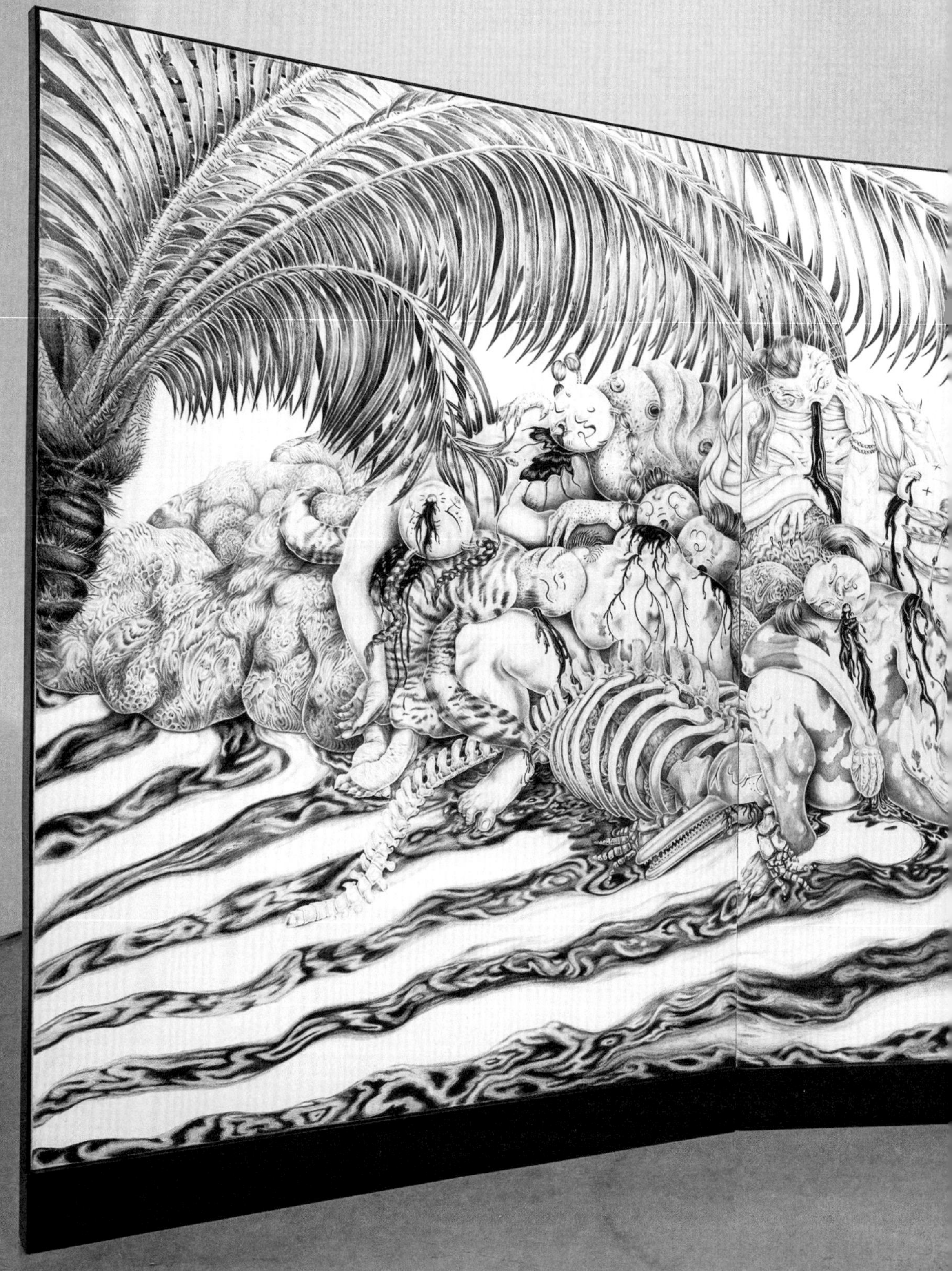

FLORENCIA RODRÍGUEZ GILES

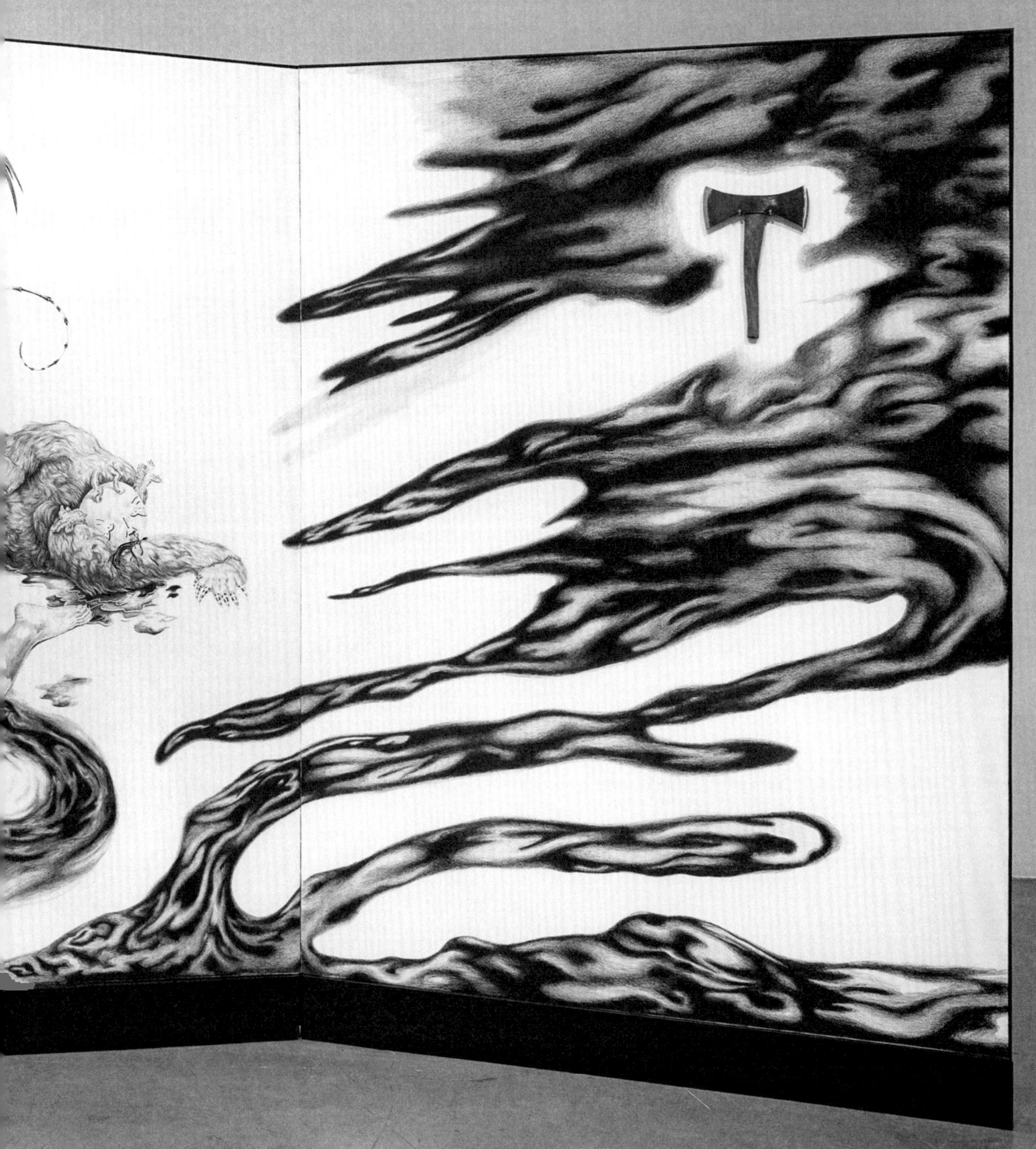

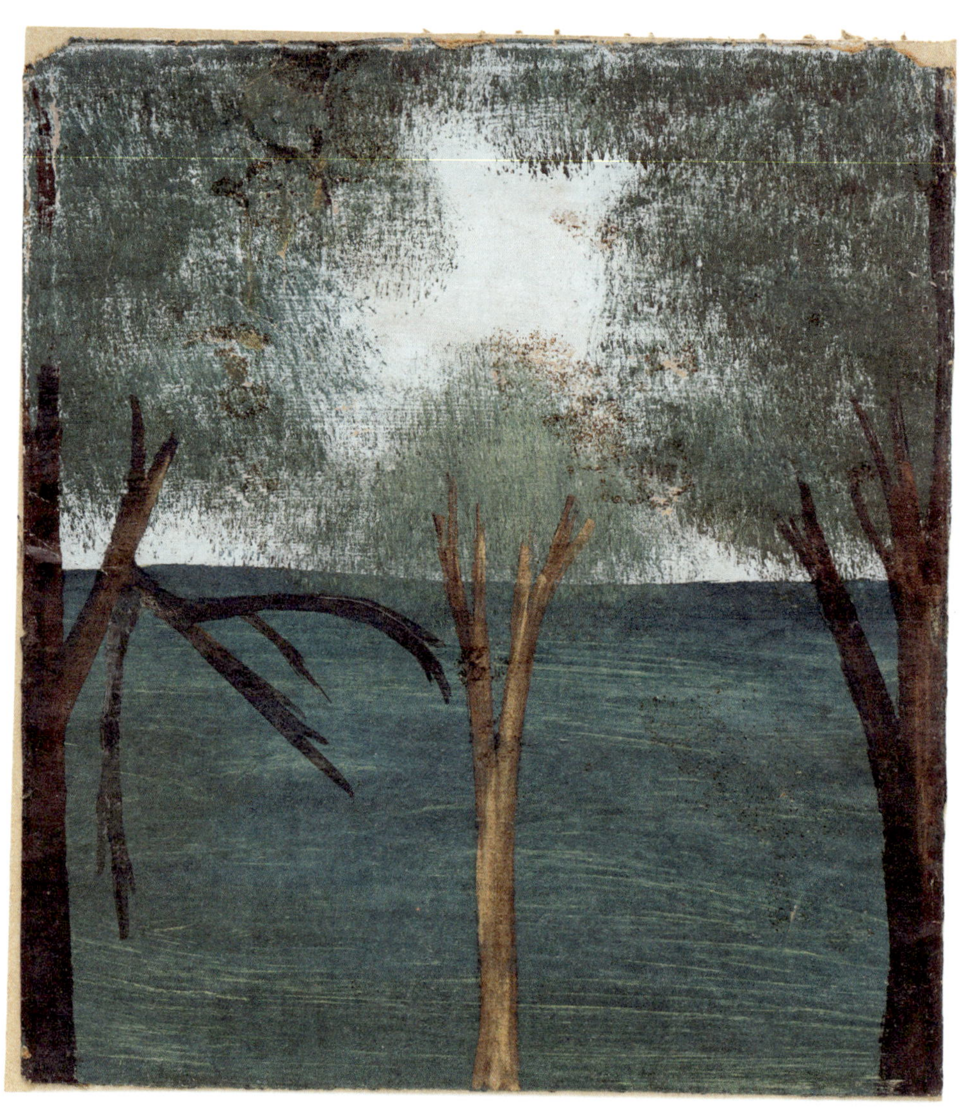

FRANK WALTER

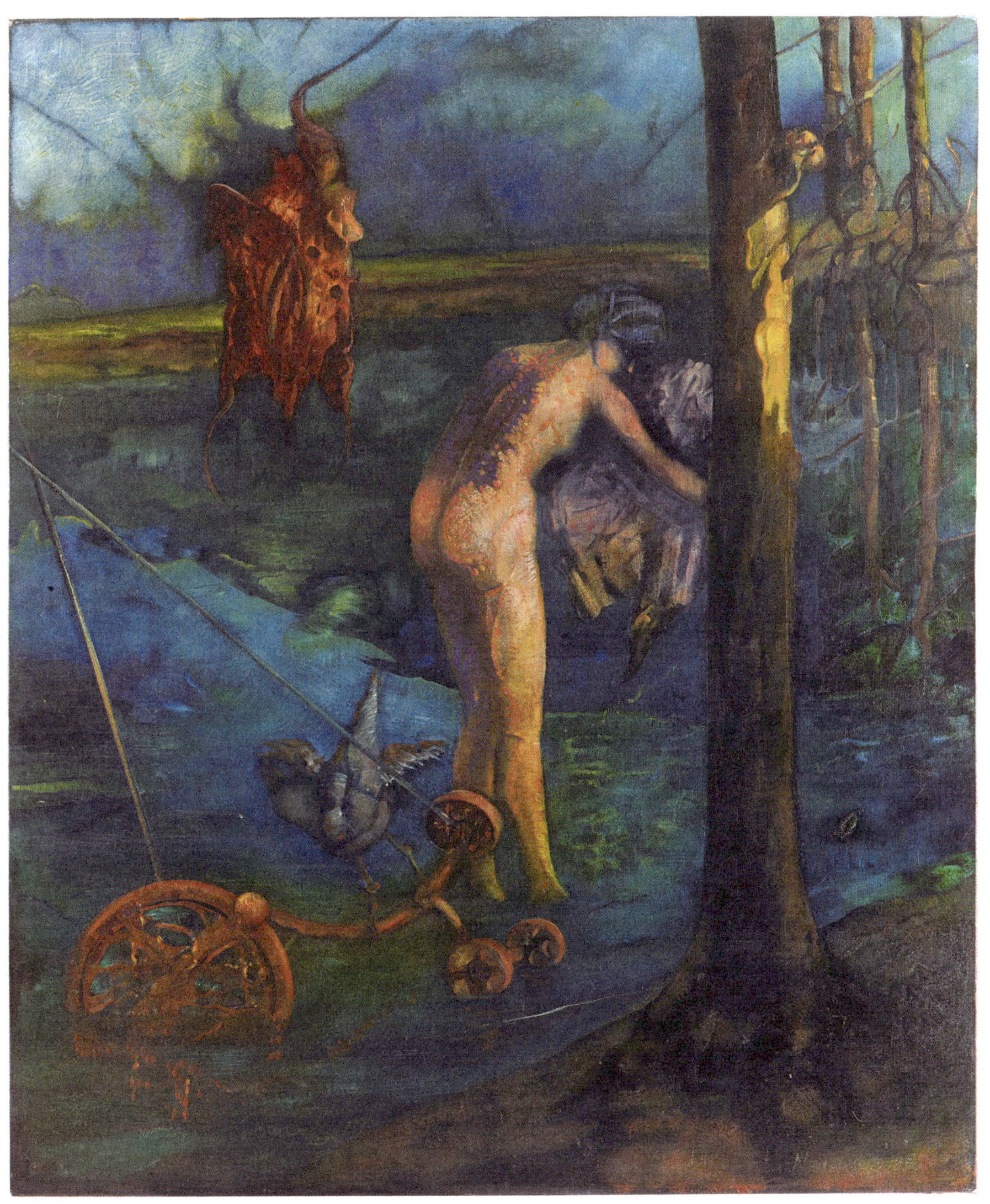

GABRIELA MORAWETZ

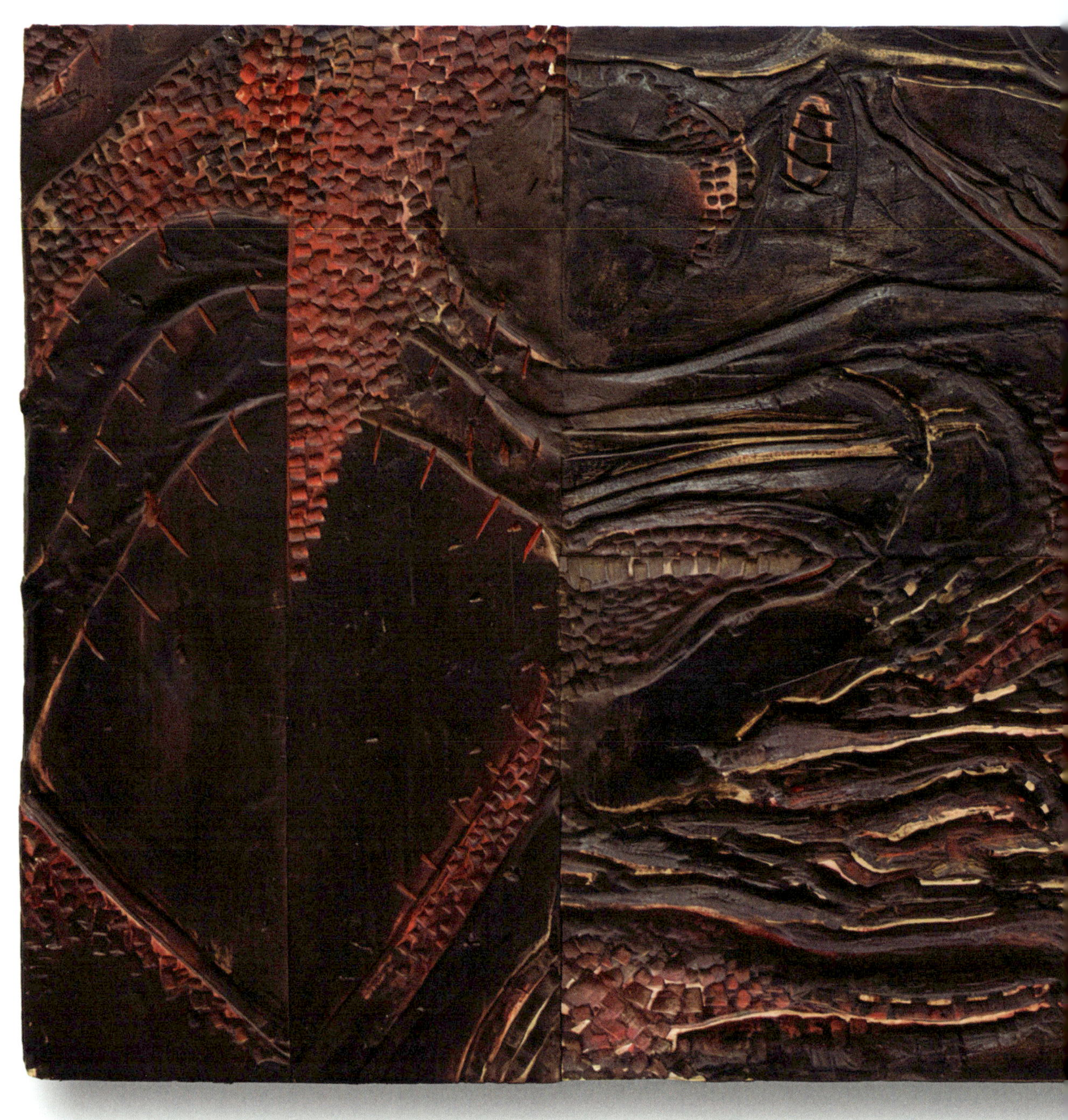

GENEVIÈVE GALLEGO

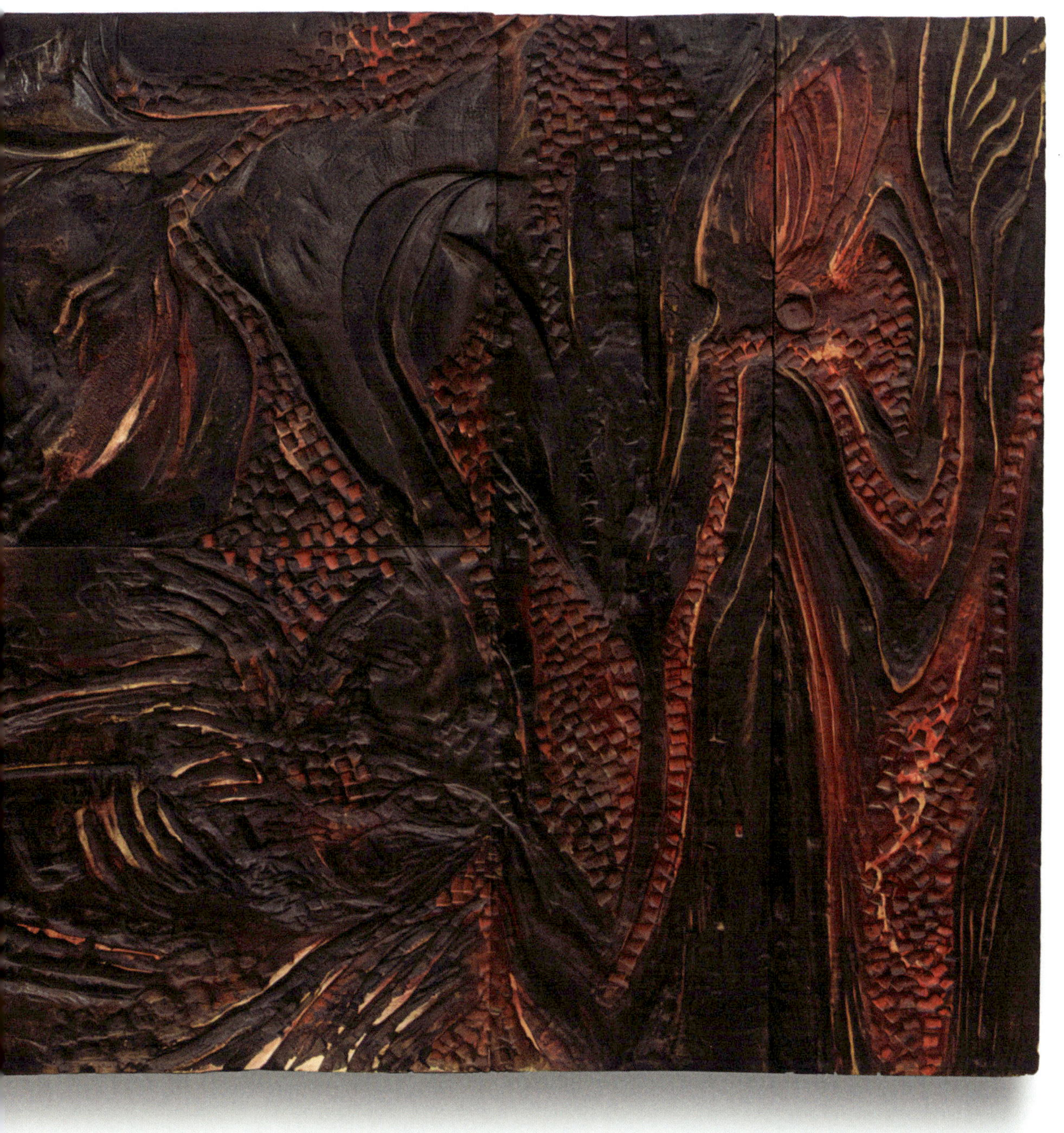

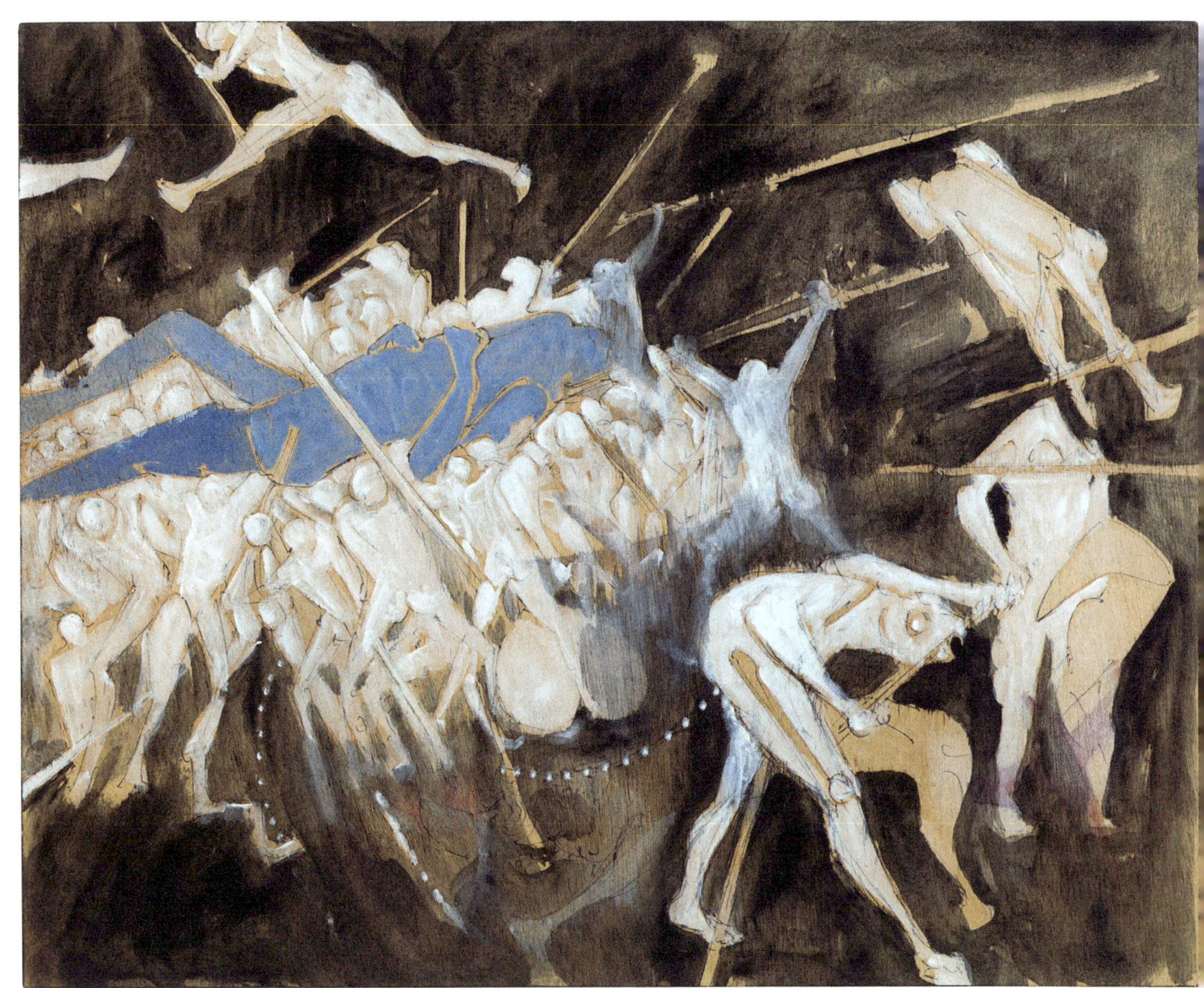

GERARDO CHÁVEZ

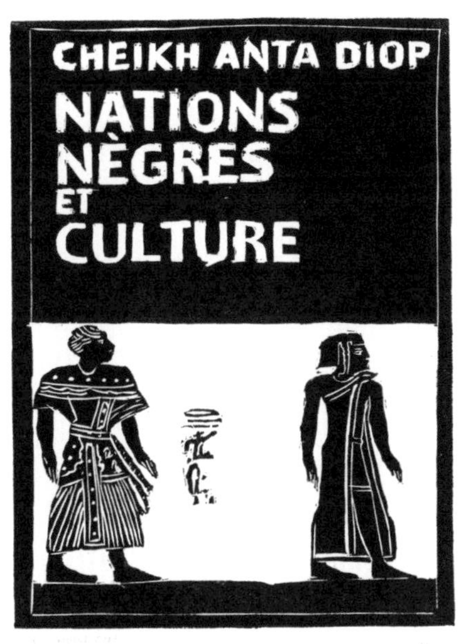

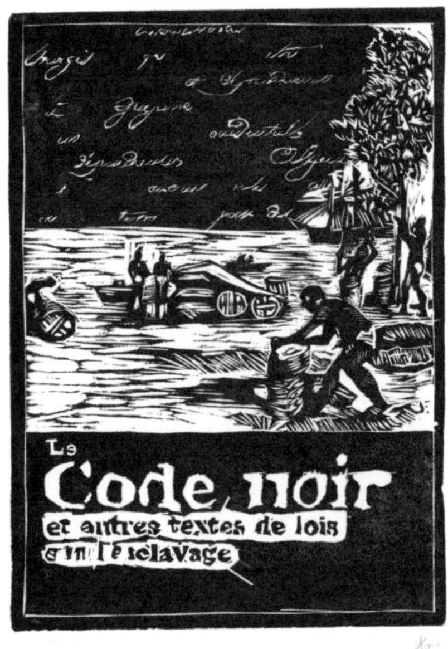

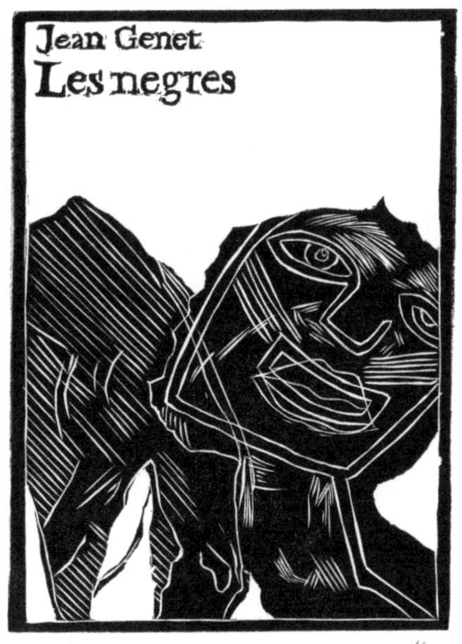

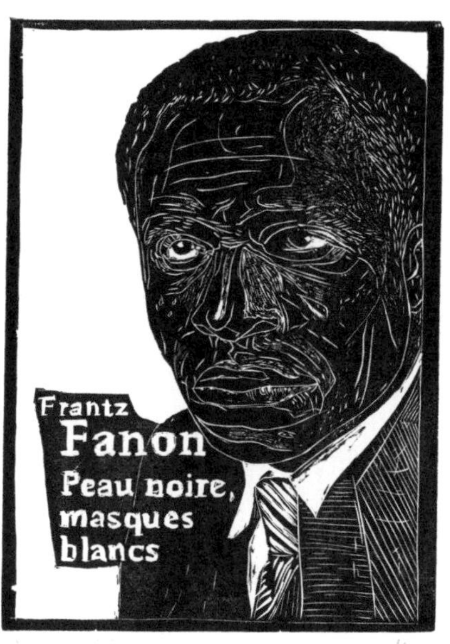

HAMEDINE KANE

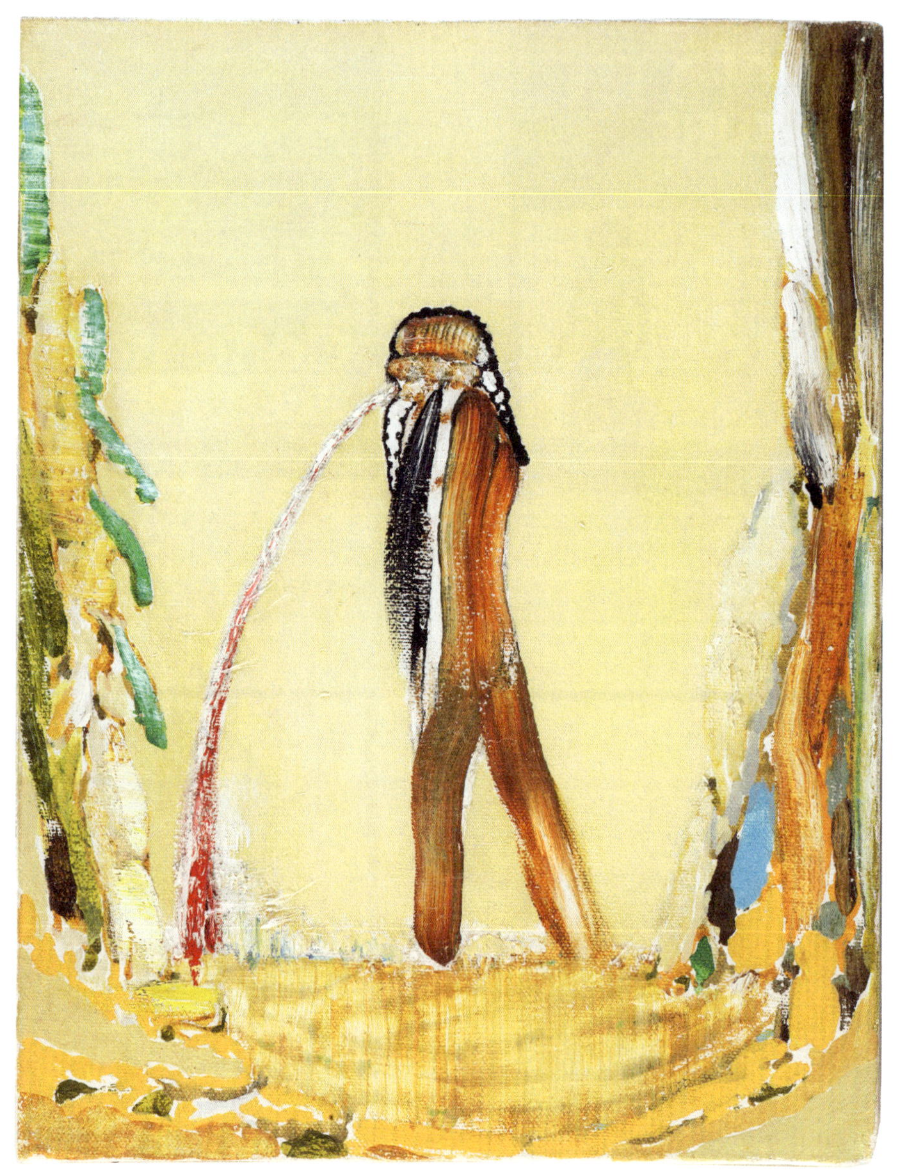

IRVING PETLIN

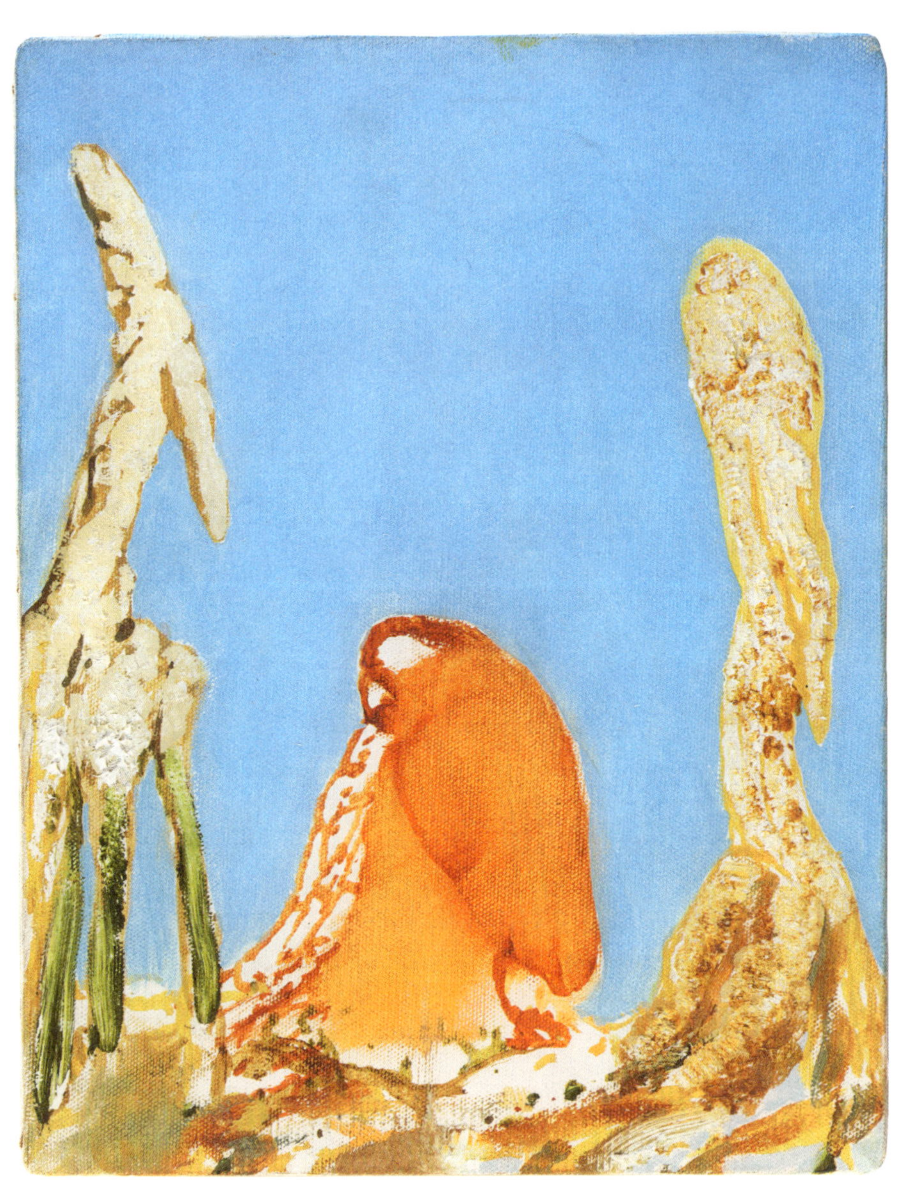

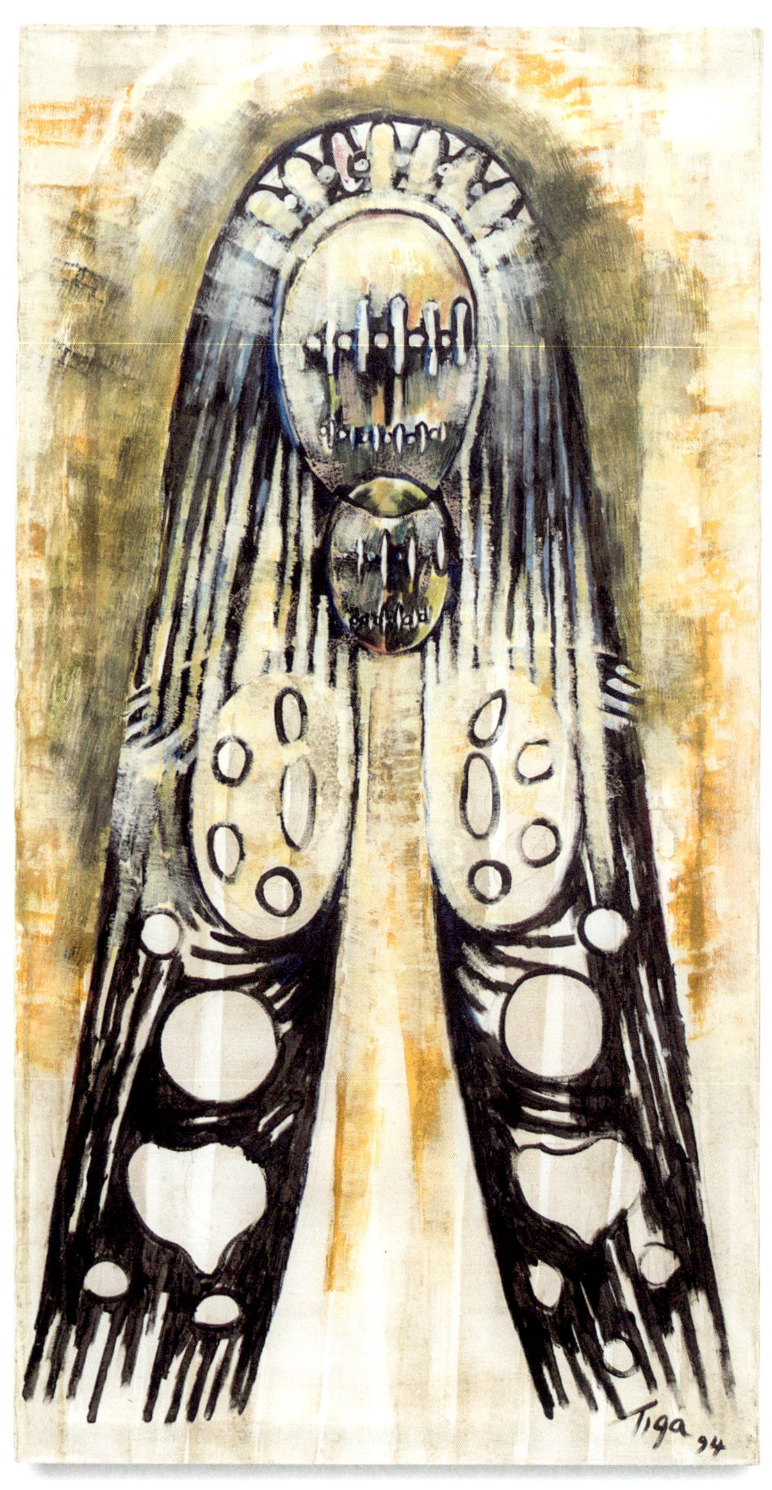

JEAN-CLAUDE GAROUTE (TIGA)

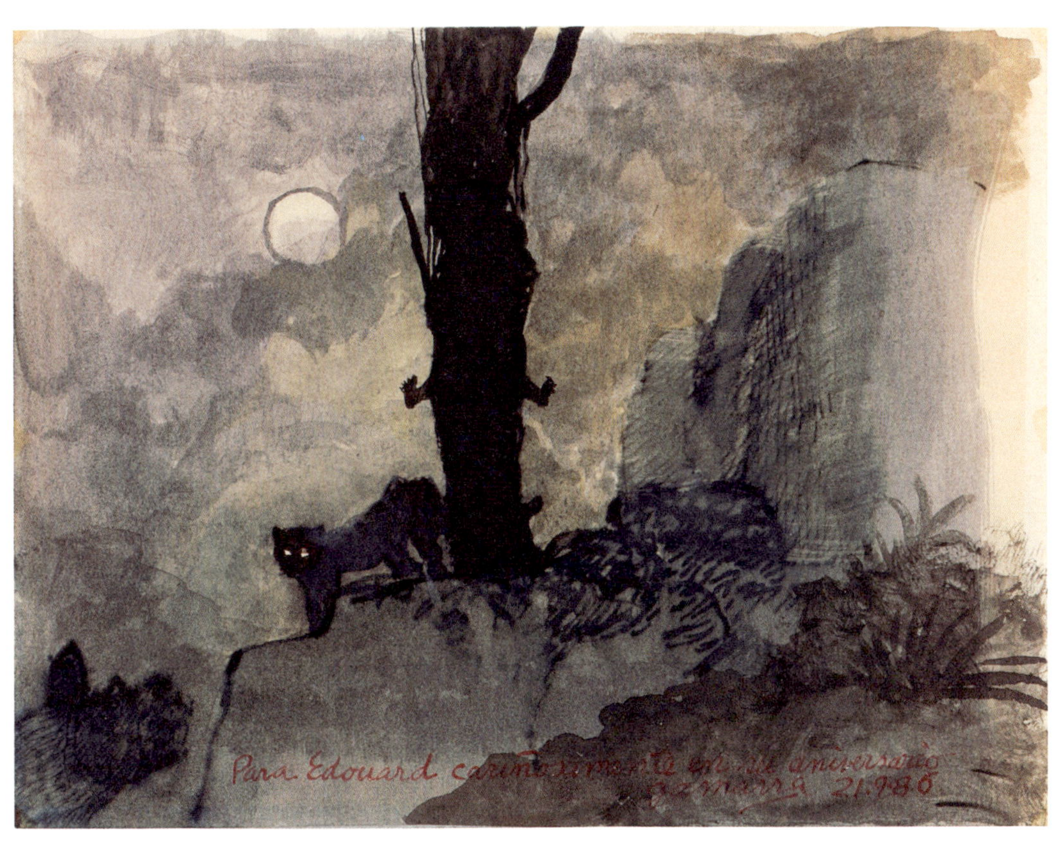

JOSÉ GAMARRA

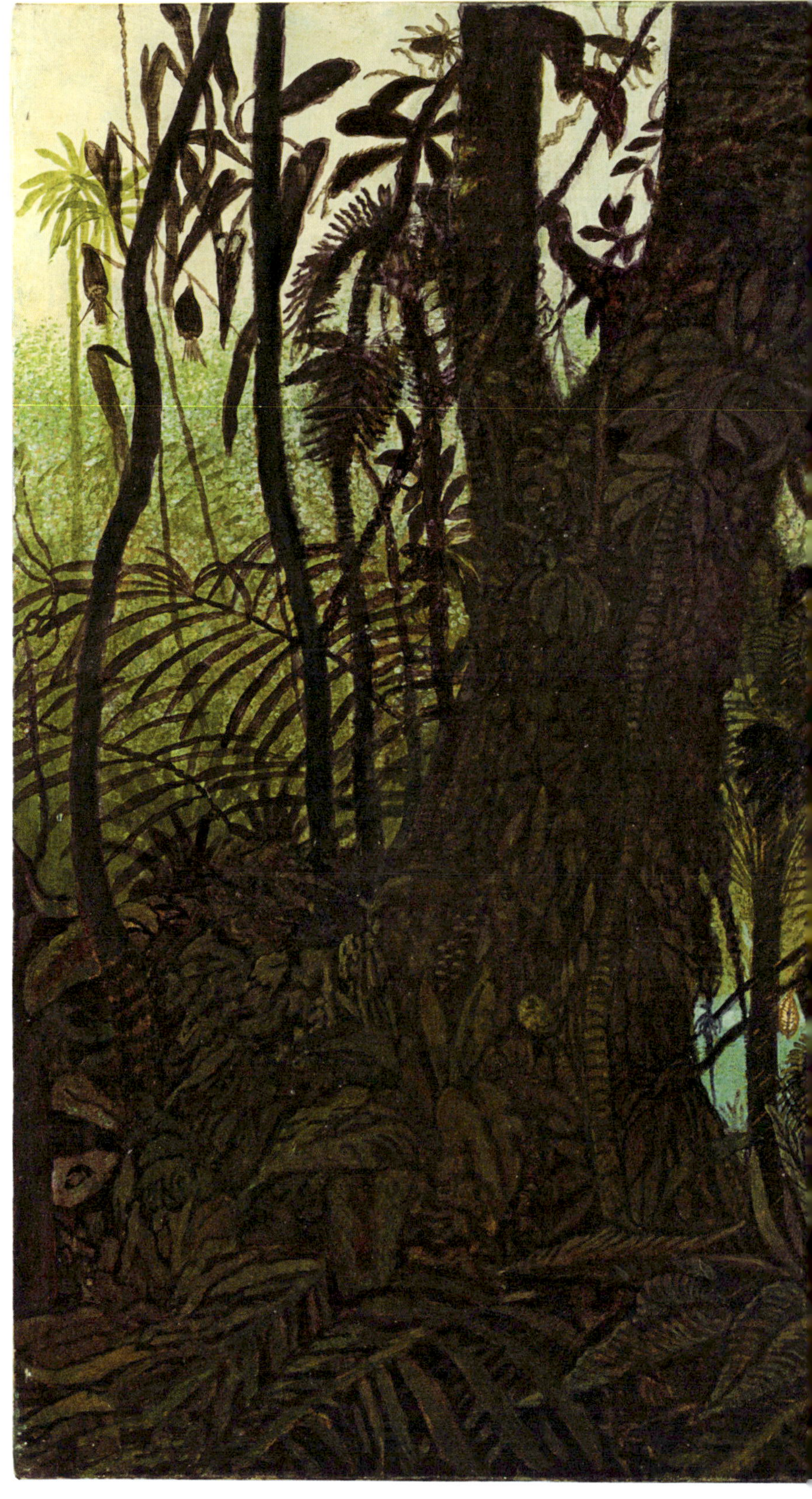

JOSÉ GAMARRA

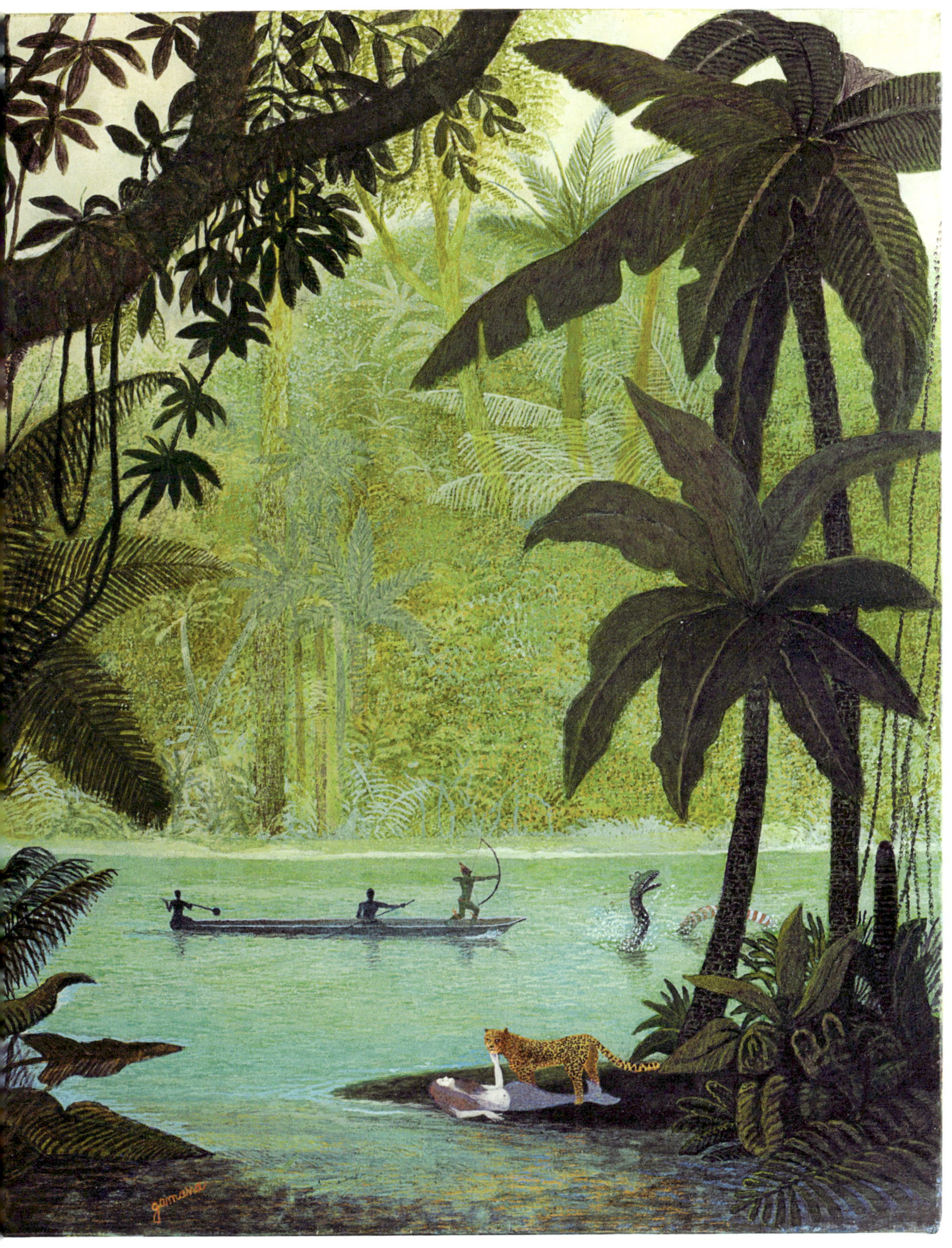

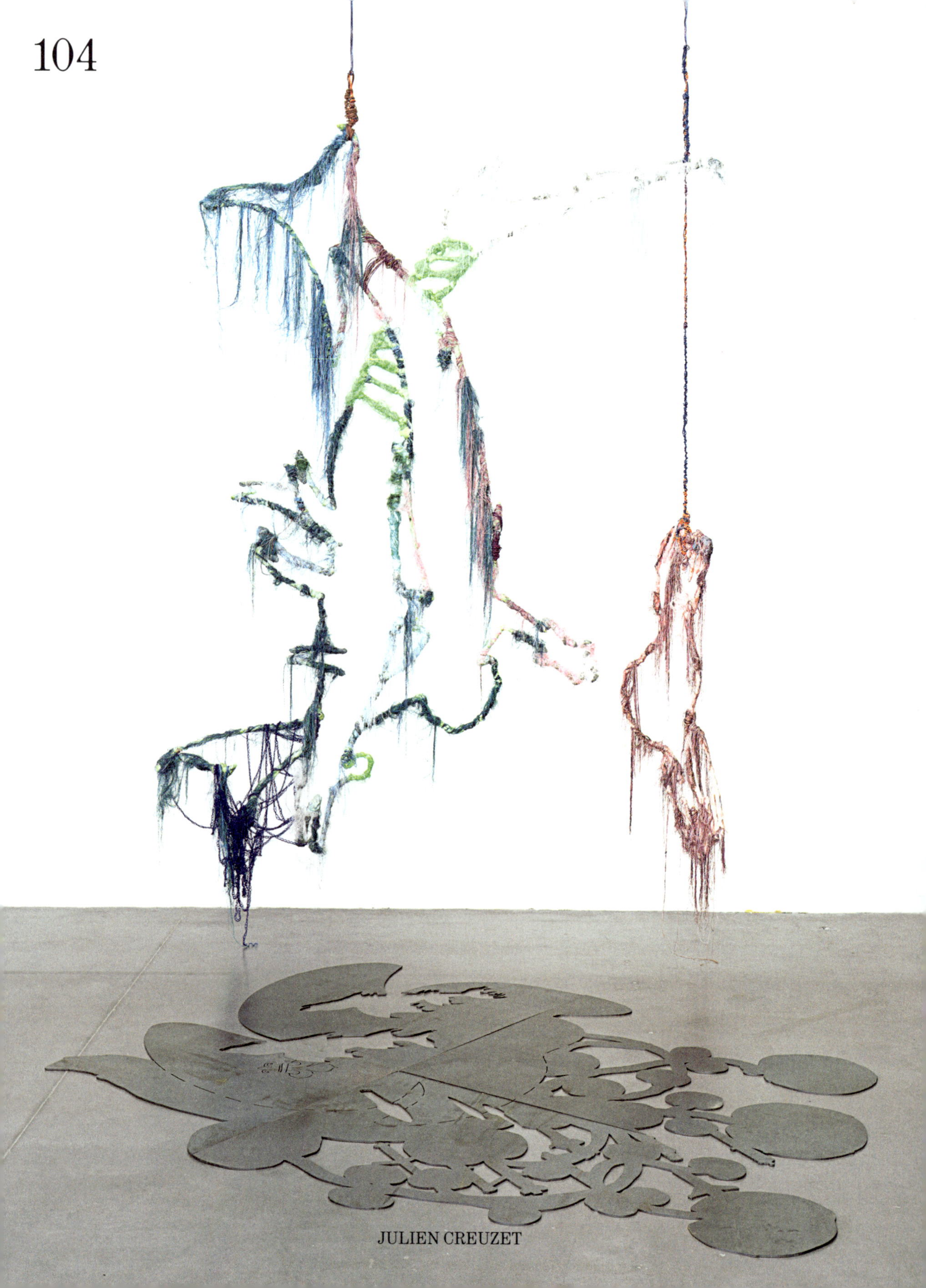

JULIEN CREUZET

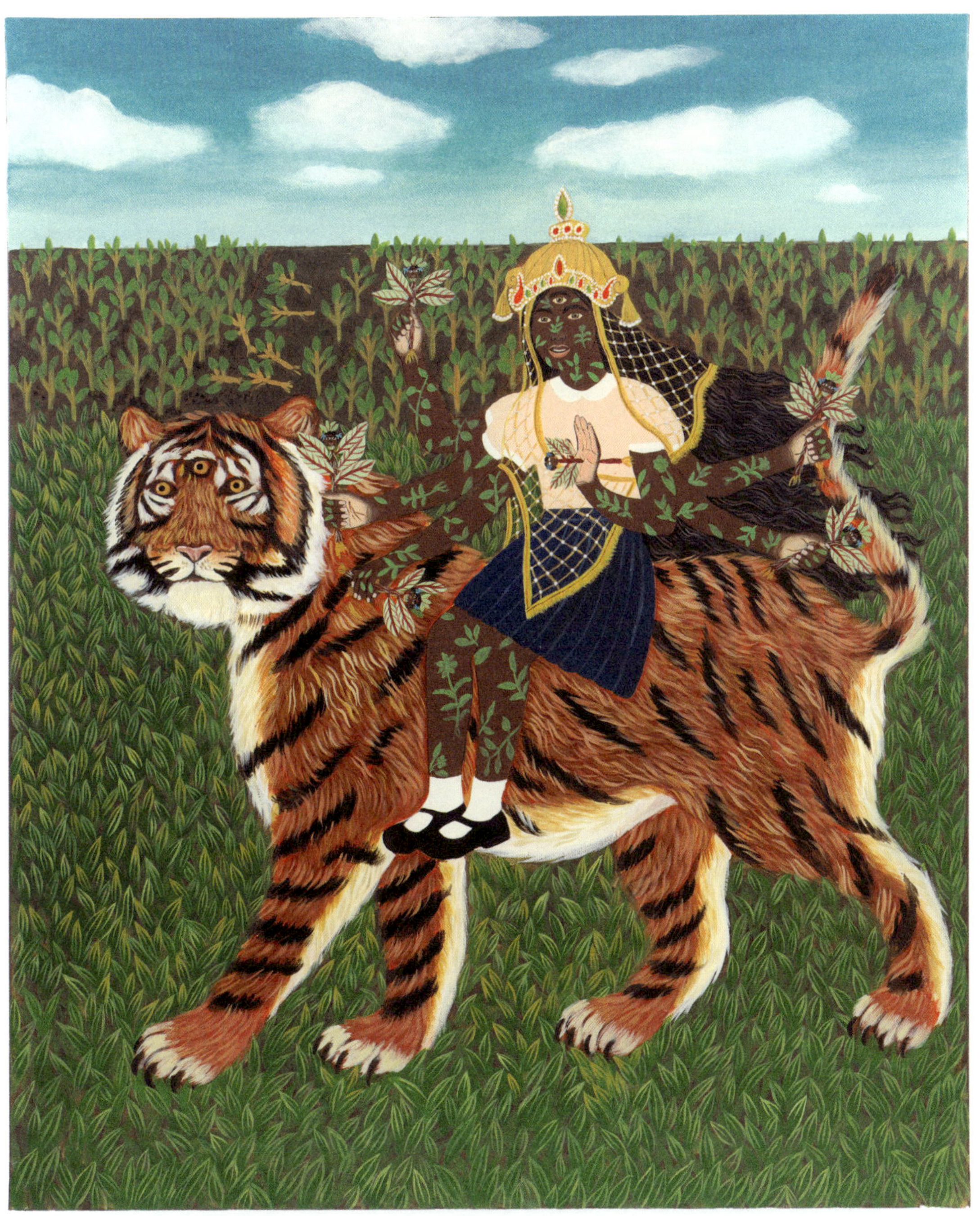

KELLY SINNAPAH MARY

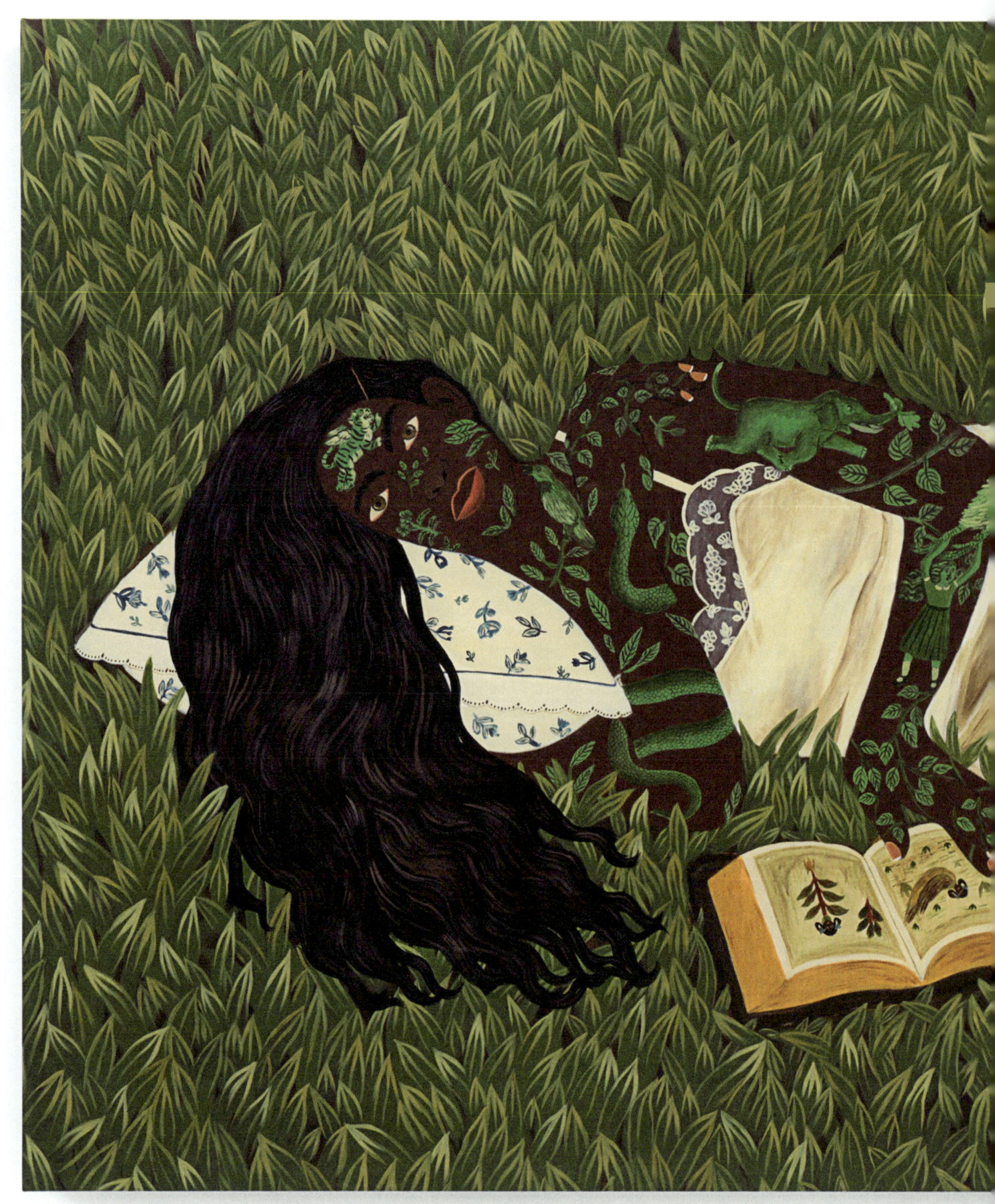

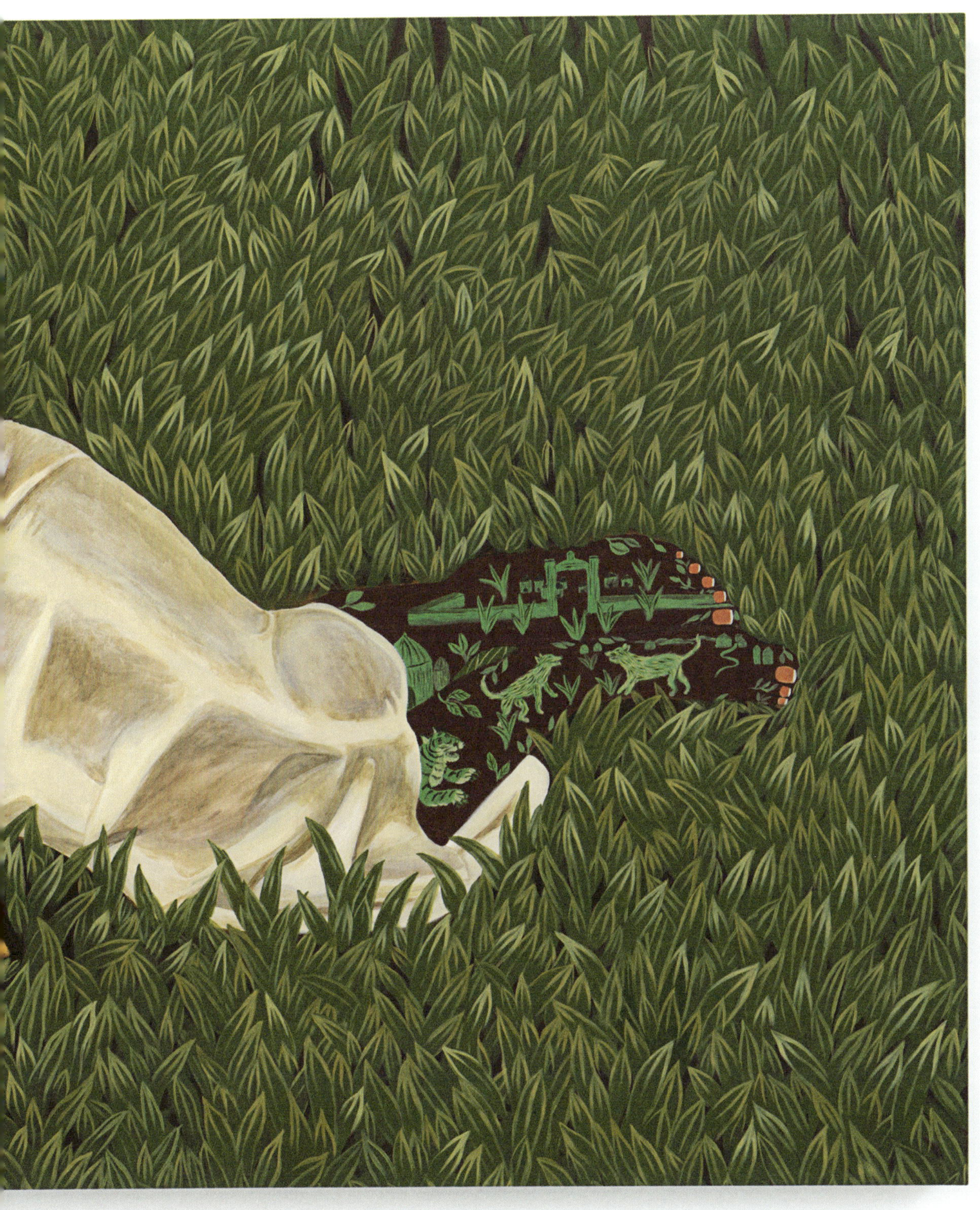

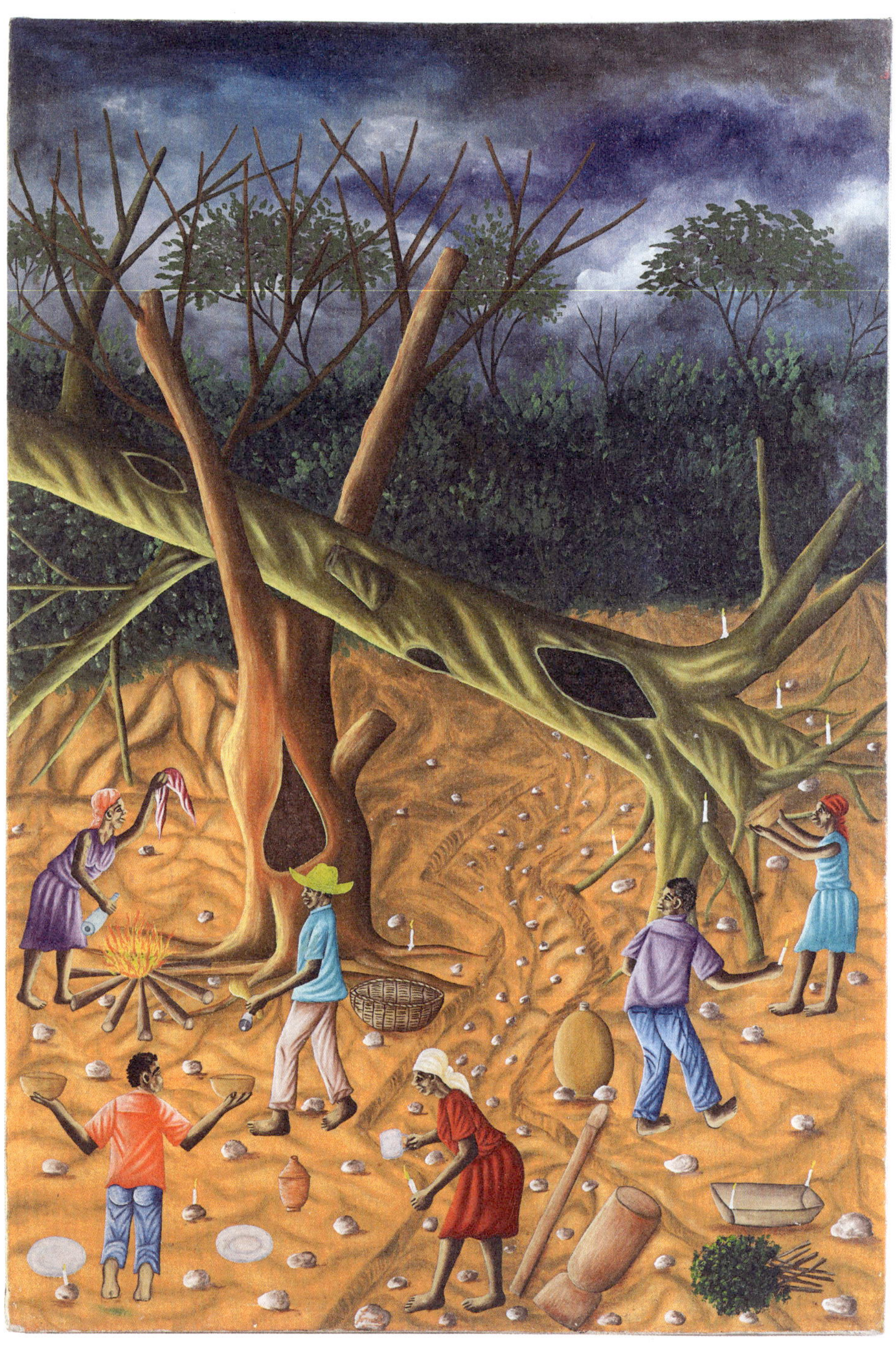

M. EMILE

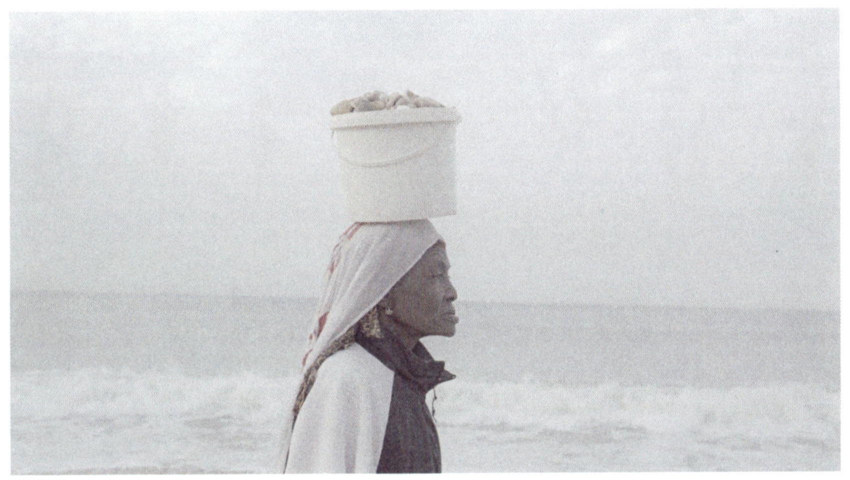

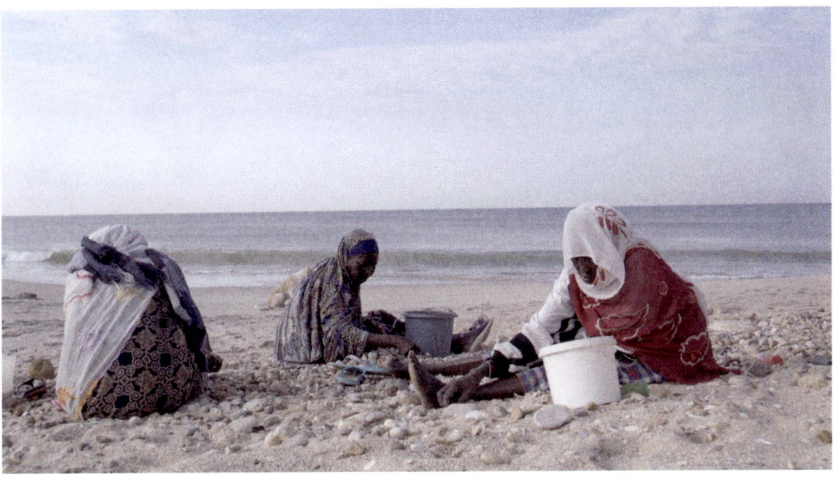

MANTHIA DIAWARA

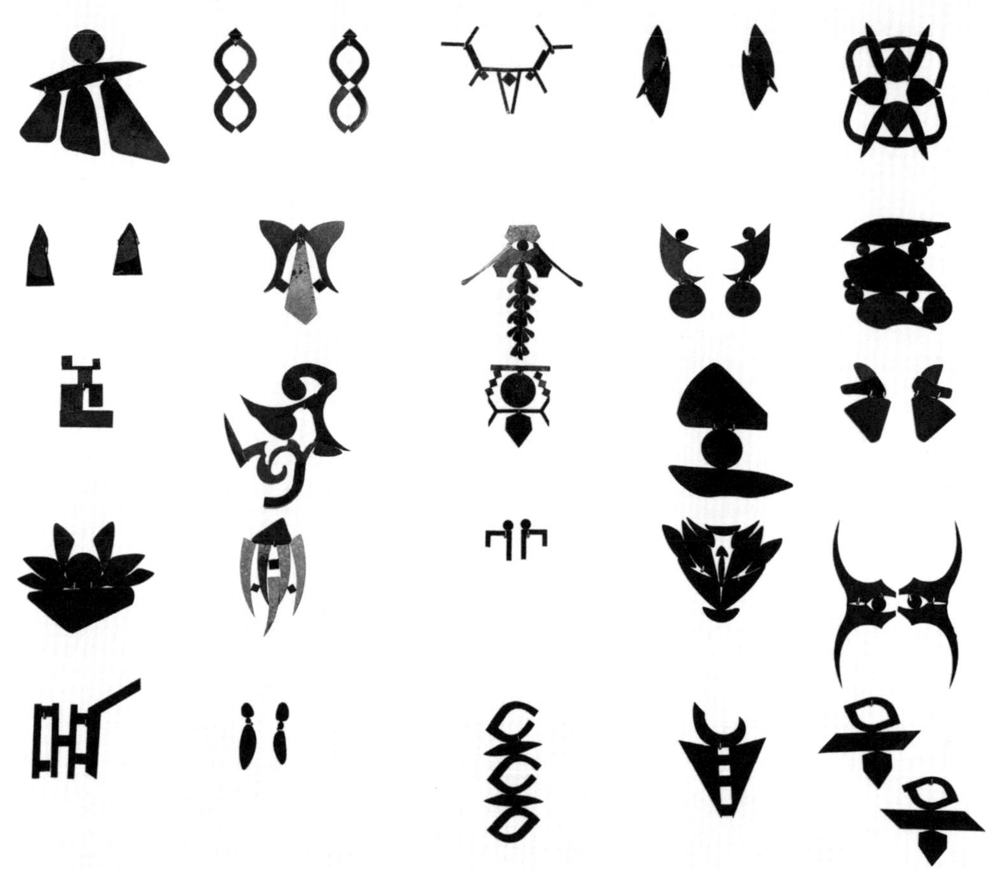

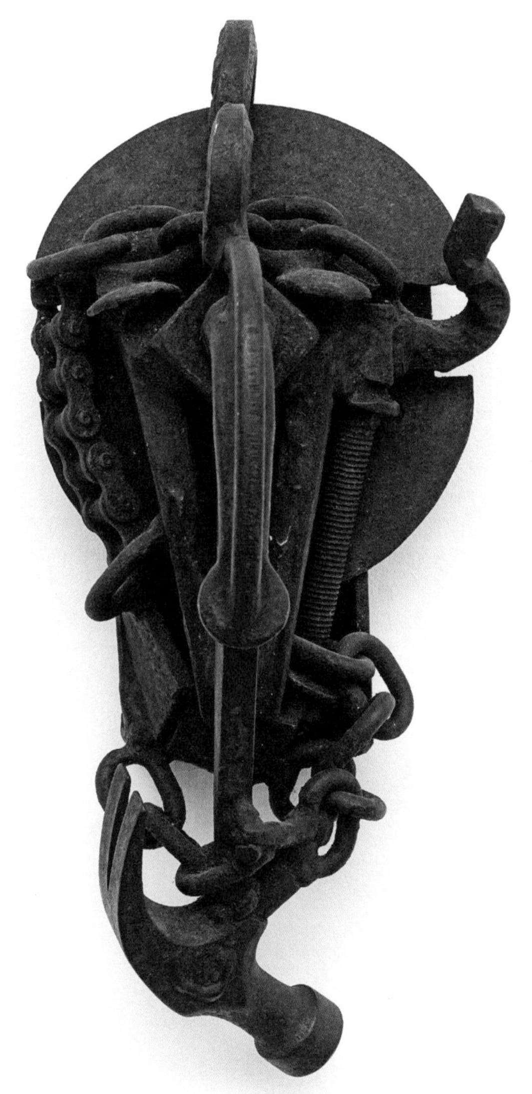

MELVIN EDWARDS

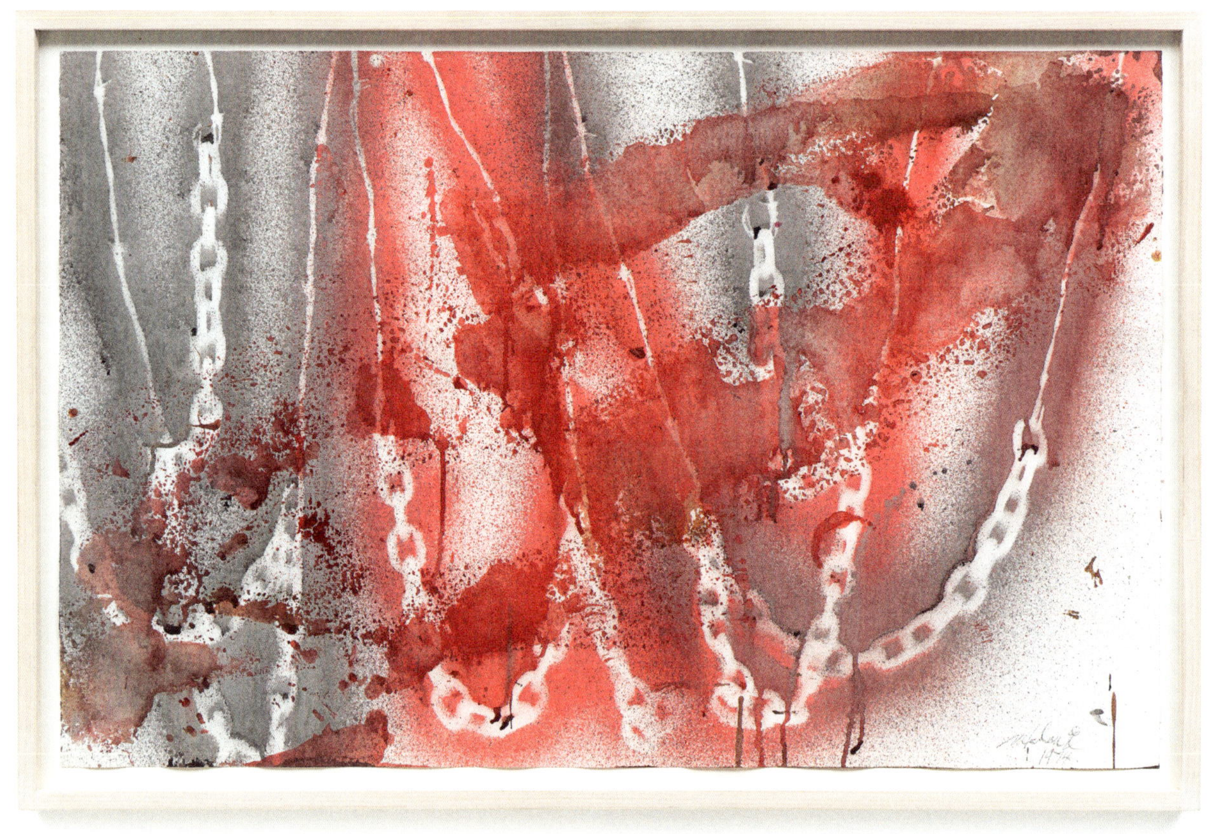

MELVIN EDWARDS

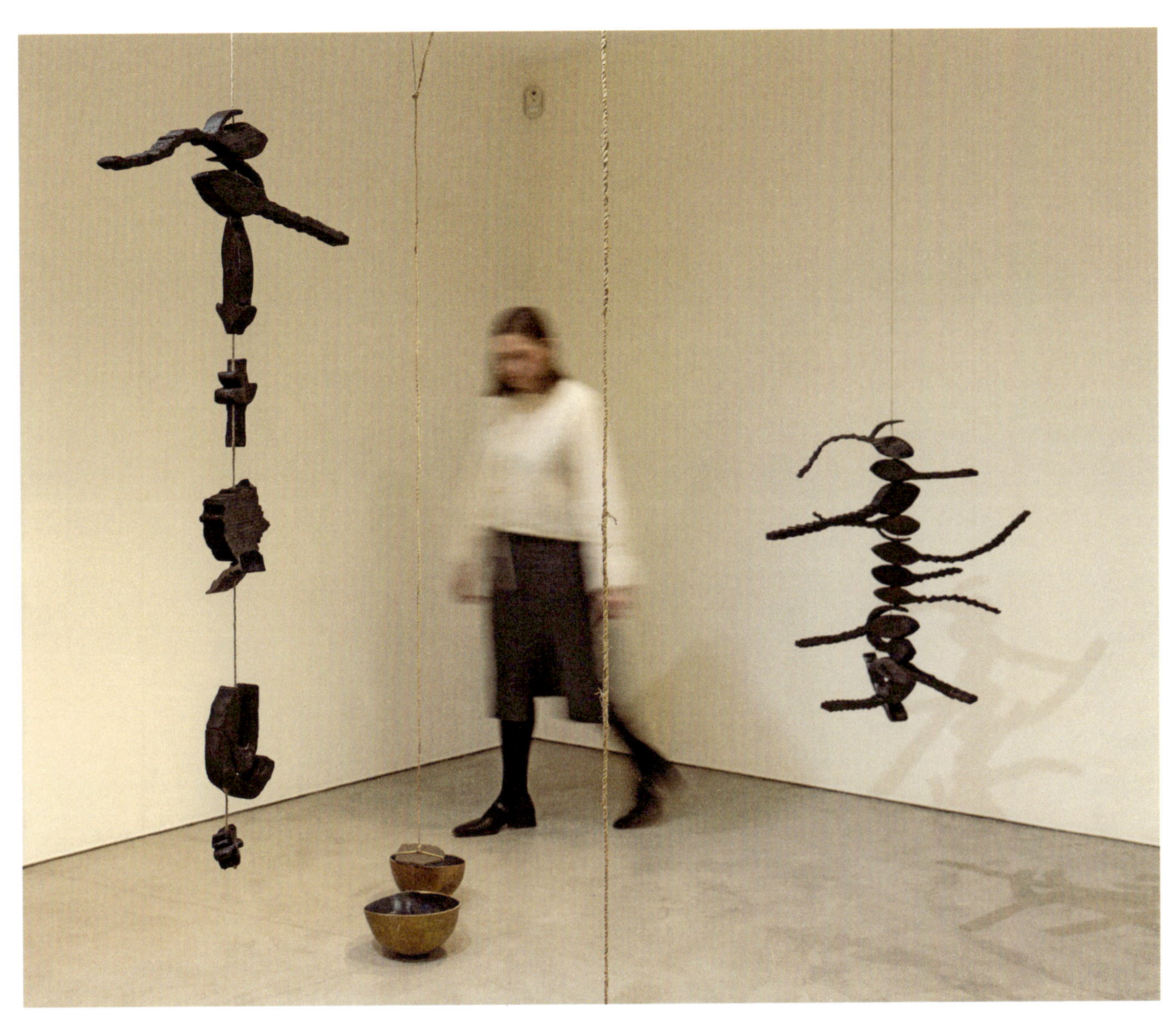

MINIA BIABIANY

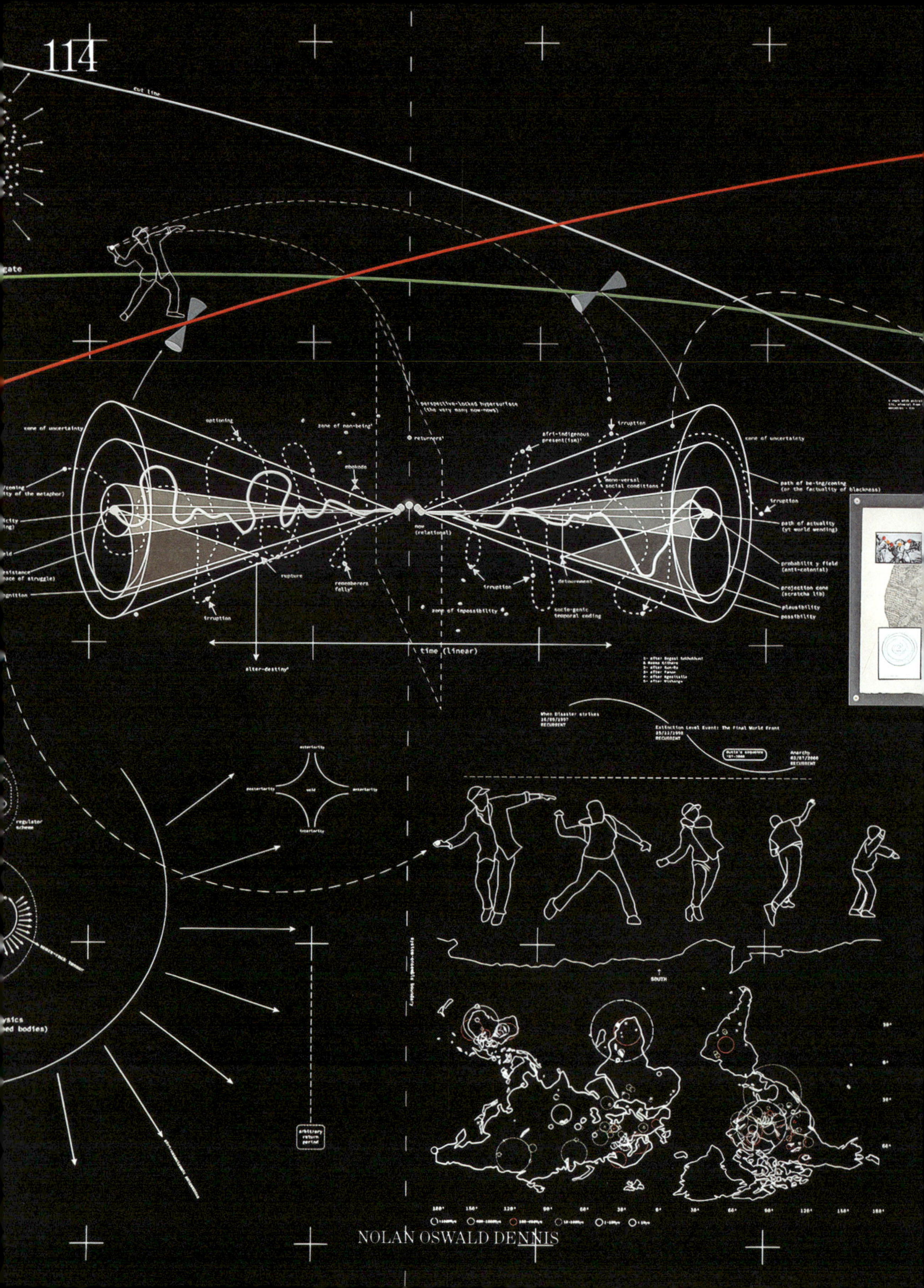

cut line
gate
perspective-locked hypersurface
(the very many now-nows)
irruption
cone of uncertainty
cone of uncertainty
returners'
afri-indigenous present(ism)'
non-versal social conditions
path of be-ing/coming
(or the factuality of blackness)
irruption
path of actuality
(yt world wending)
probability field
(anti-colonial)
projection cone
(scratcha lib)
plausibility
possibility
optioning
zone of non-being'
embokode
/coming
(ty of the metaphor)
resistance
(ace of struggle)
gnition
rupture
rememberers folly'
irruption
alter-destiny'
now
(relational)
detournement
socio-genic temporal coding
zone of impossibility
time (linear)
1- after Bogosi Sekhukhuni
& Manna Githens
2- after Gumbs
3- after Fanon
4- after Agostinis
5- after Wichengo
When Disaster strikes
16/09/1997
RECURRENT
Extinction Level Event: The Final World Event
15/11/2000
RECURRENT
Anarchy
02/07/2000
RECURRENT
exteriarty
exteriarty
void
exteriarty
interiarty
regular scheme
SOUTH
arbitrary return period
NOLAN OSWALD DENNIS

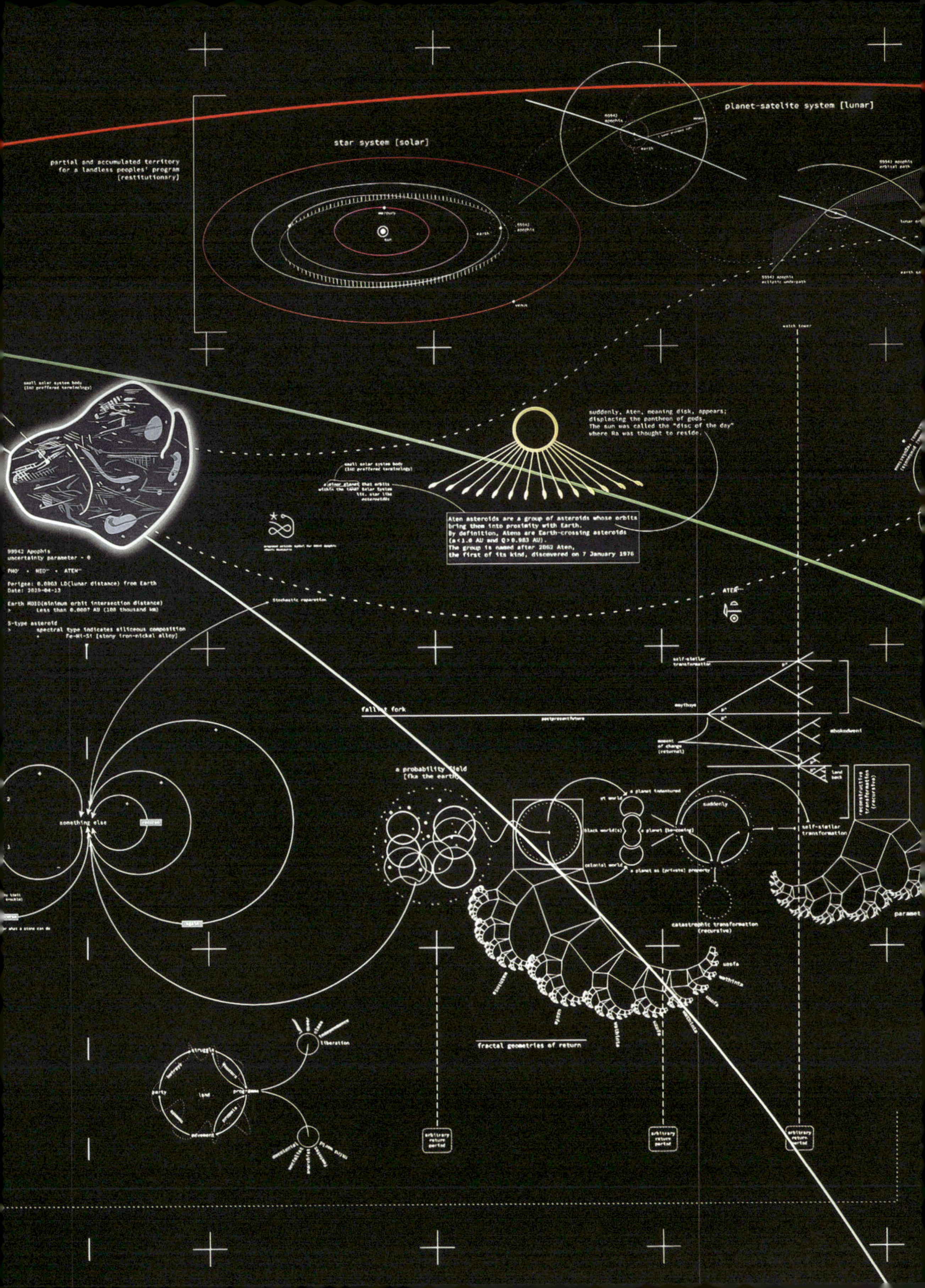

planet-satelite system [lunar]
star system [solar]
partial and accumulated territory
for a landless peoples' program
[restitutionary]
small solar system body
[IAU preferred terminology]
suddenly, Aten, meaning disk, appears;
displacing the pantheon of gods.
The sun was called the "disc of the day"
where Ra was thought to reside.
a minor planet that orbits
within the inner solar system
its star like
asteroids
Aten asteroids are a group of asteroids whose orbits
bring them into proximity with Earth.
By definition, Atens are Earth-crossing asteroids
(a<1.0 AU and Q>0.983 AU).
The group is named after 2062 Aten,
the first of its kind, discovered on 7 January 1976
99942 Apophis
uncertainty parameter = 0
PHO* · NEO** · ATEN**
Perigee: 0.0963 LD(lunar distance) from Earth
Date: 2029-04-13
Earth MOID(minimum orbit intersection distance)
Less than 0.0007 AU (100 thousand km)
S-type asteroid
spectral type indicates siliceous composition
Fe-Ni-Si [stony iron-nickel alloy]
ATEN
stochastic reparation
self-stellar transformation
anything
past/present/future
moment of change (returnal)
abandonment
loop back
reconstructive transformation (recursive)
self-stellar transformation
a probability field [fka the earth]
yt world
a planet textestured
black world(s)
a planet [be-coming]
colonial world
a planet as [private] property
suddenly
catastrophic transformation (recursive)
uoofa
paramet
fall out fork
something else
fractal geometries of return
liberation
arbitrary return period

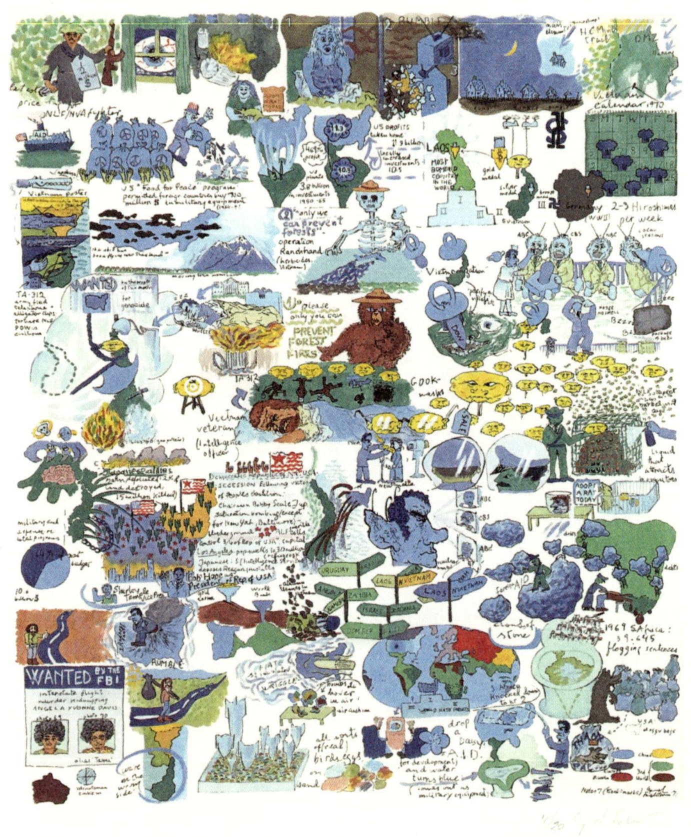

ÖYVIND FAHLSTRÖM

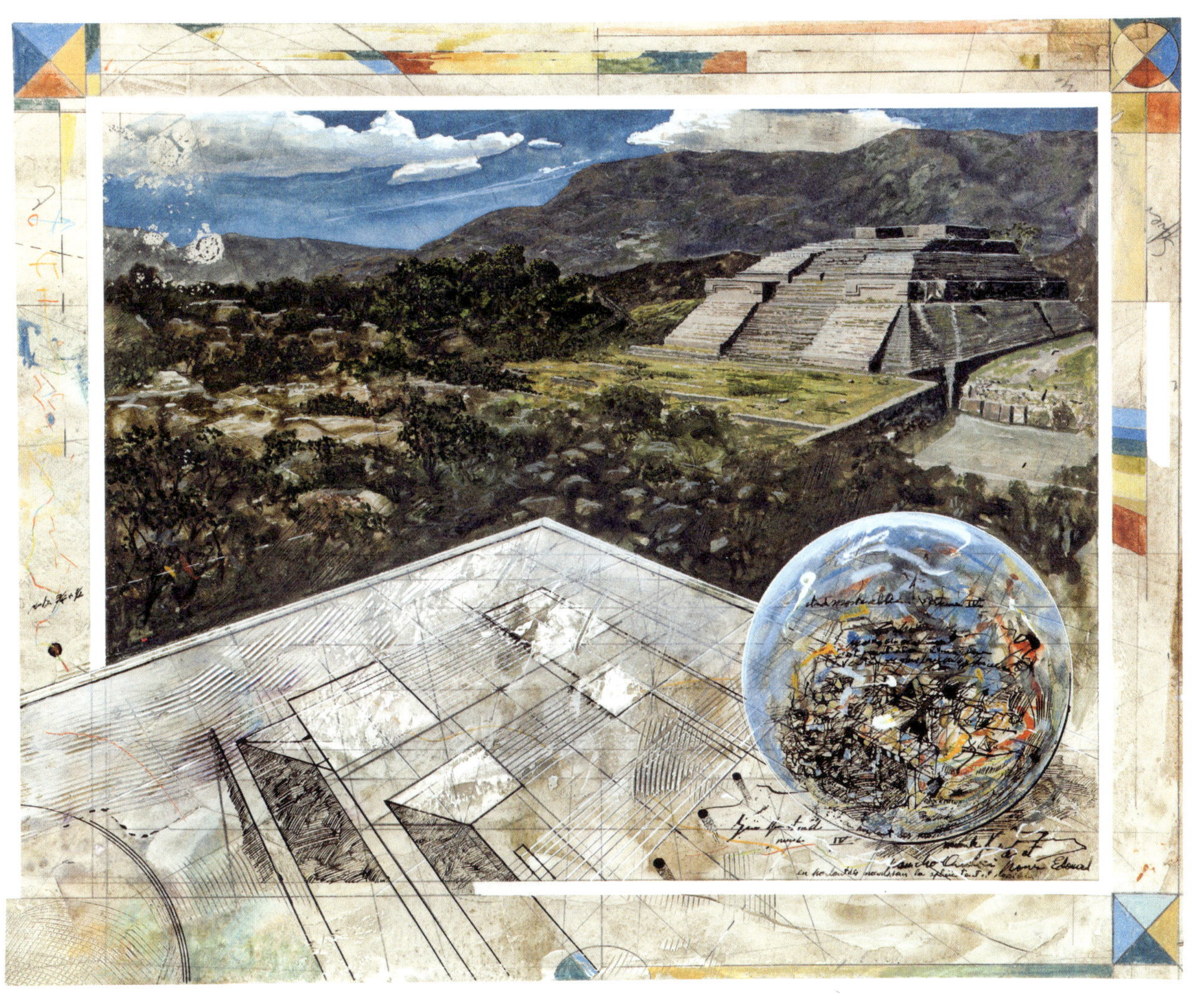

PANCHO QUILICI

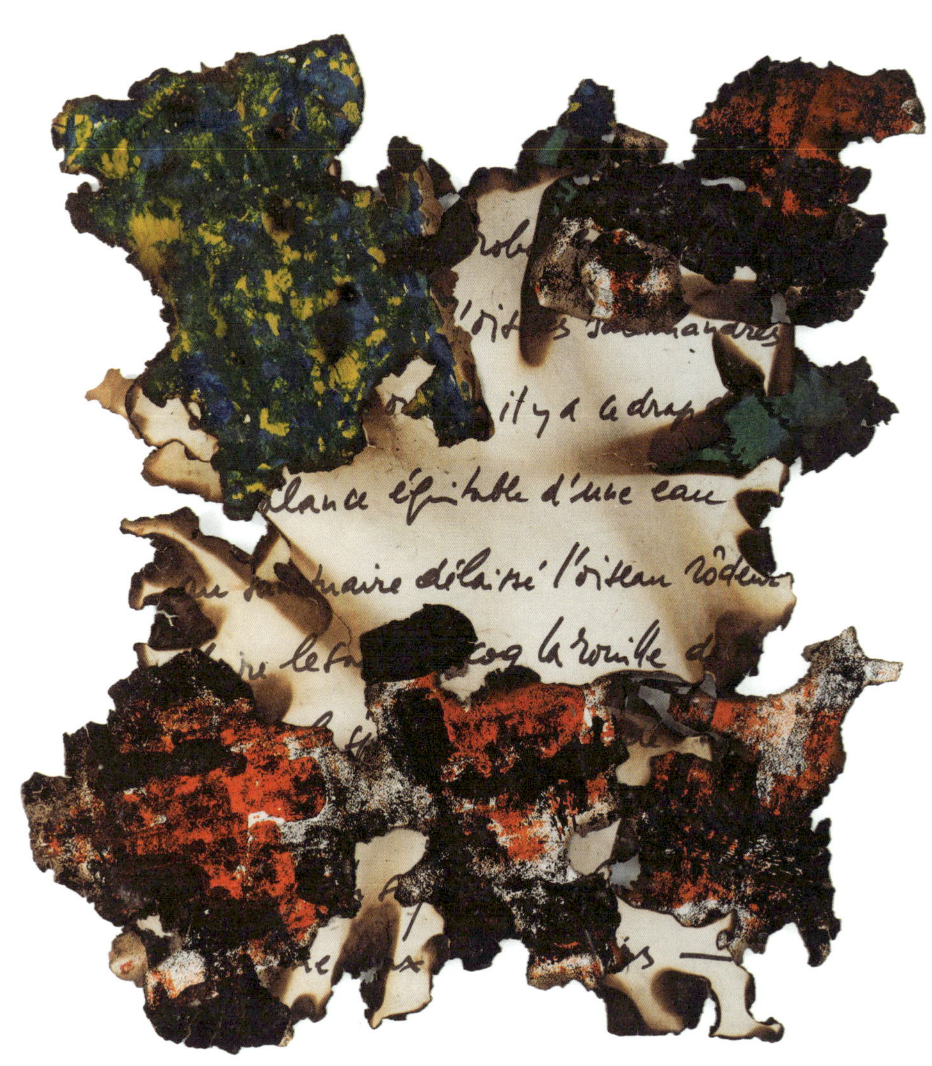

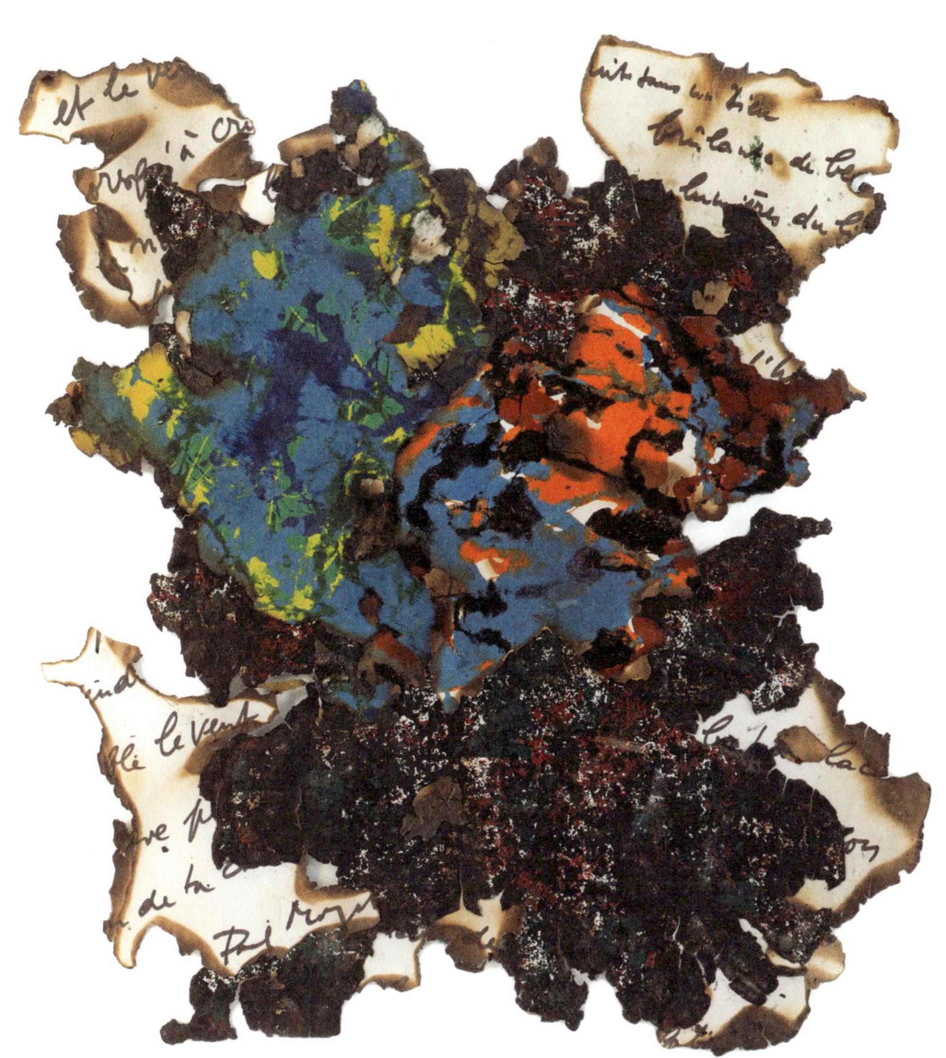

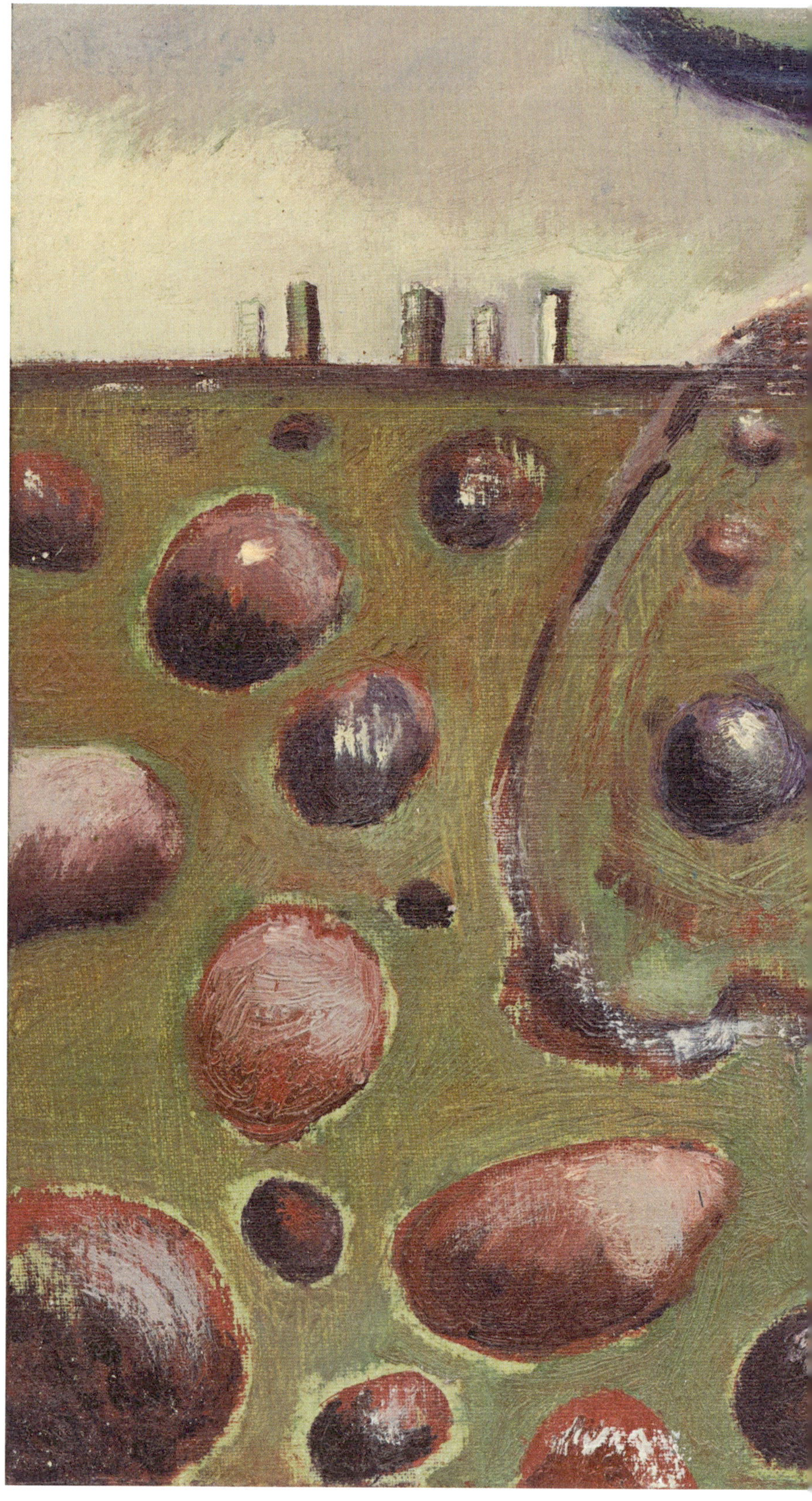

PEDRO FRANÇA

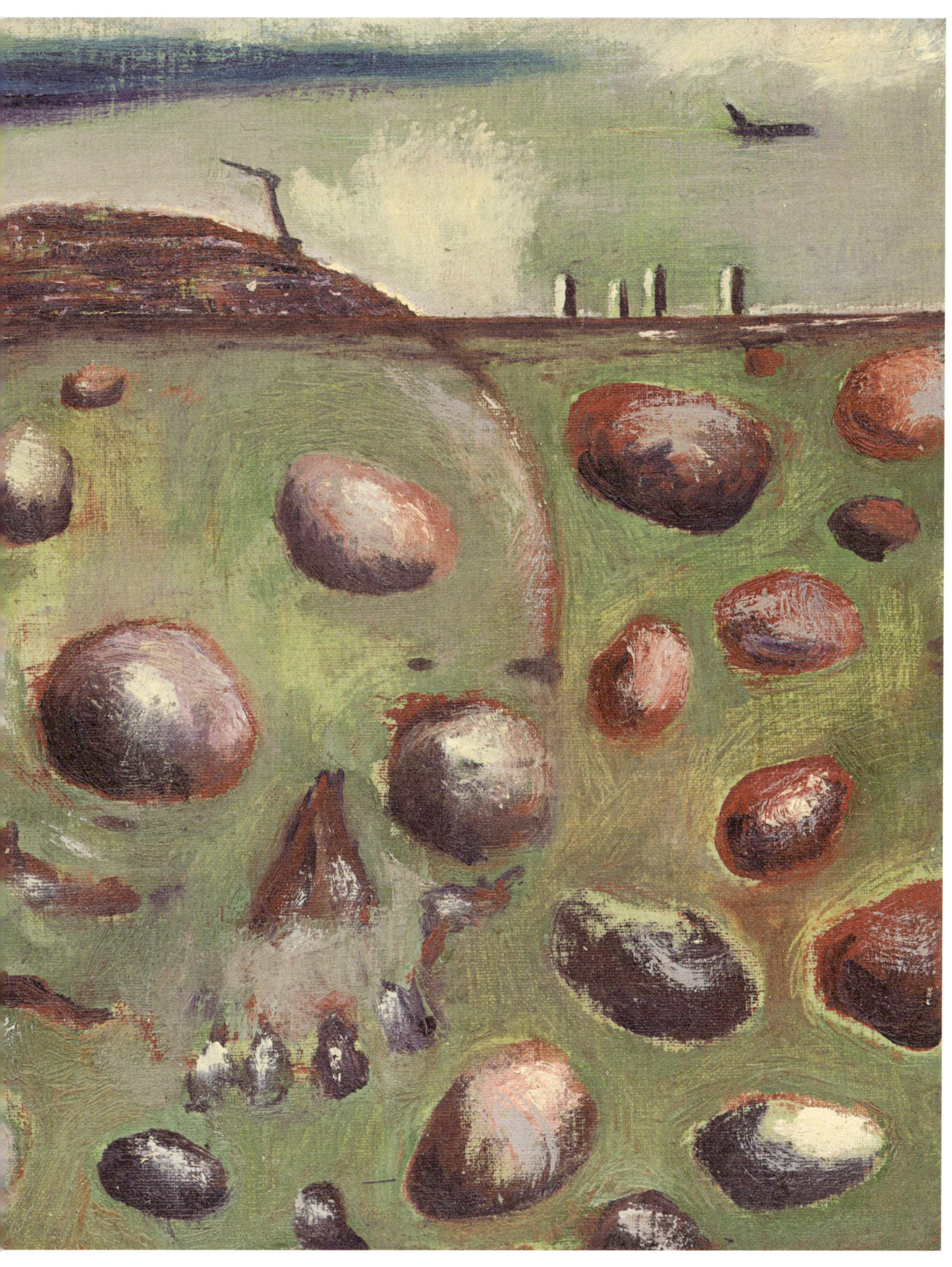

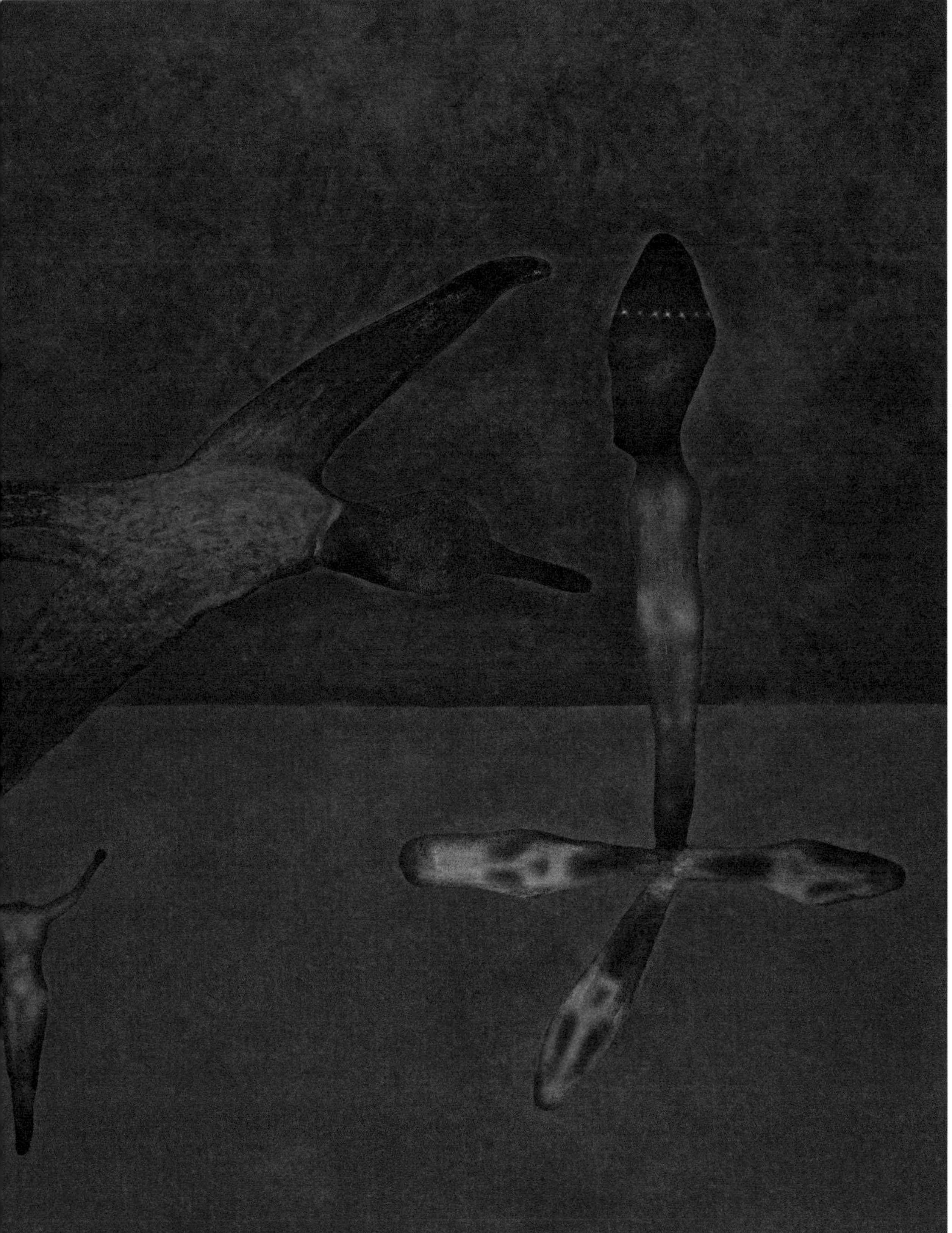

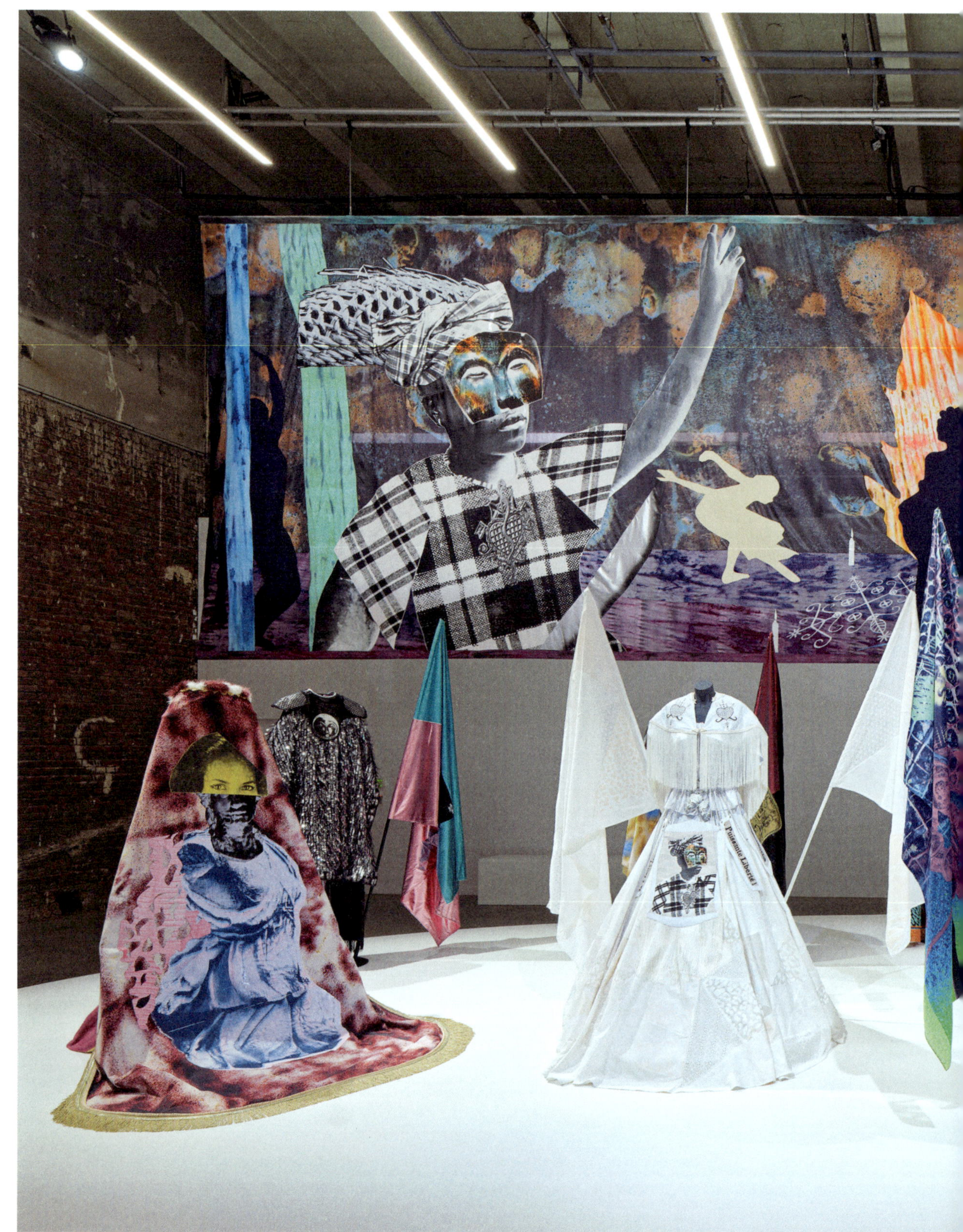

RAPHAËL BARONTINI

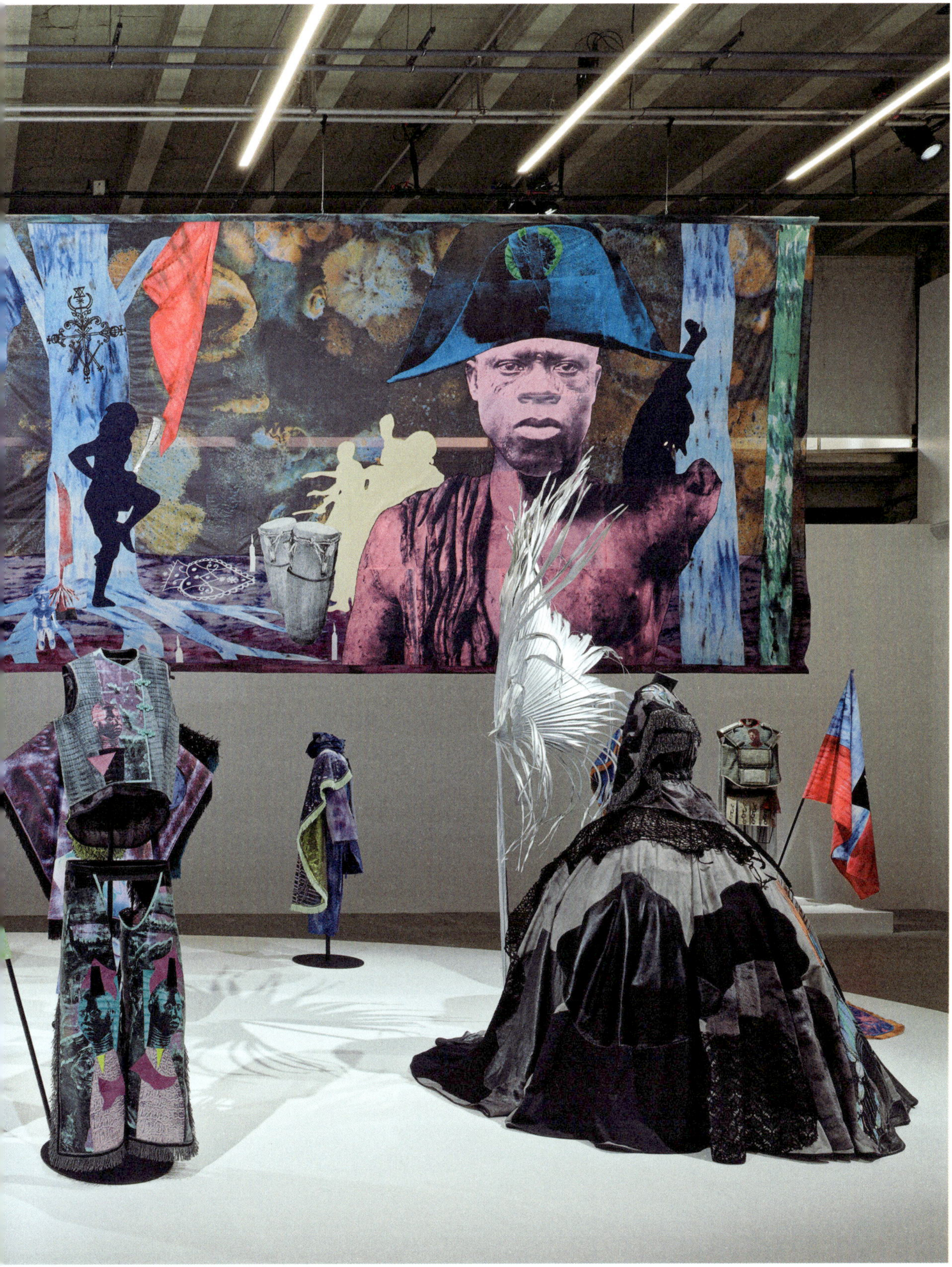

Raphaël Barontini, vista da exposição / exhibition view, *Somewhere in the Night, the People Dance*, Palais de Tokyo, Paris, França / France, 2025

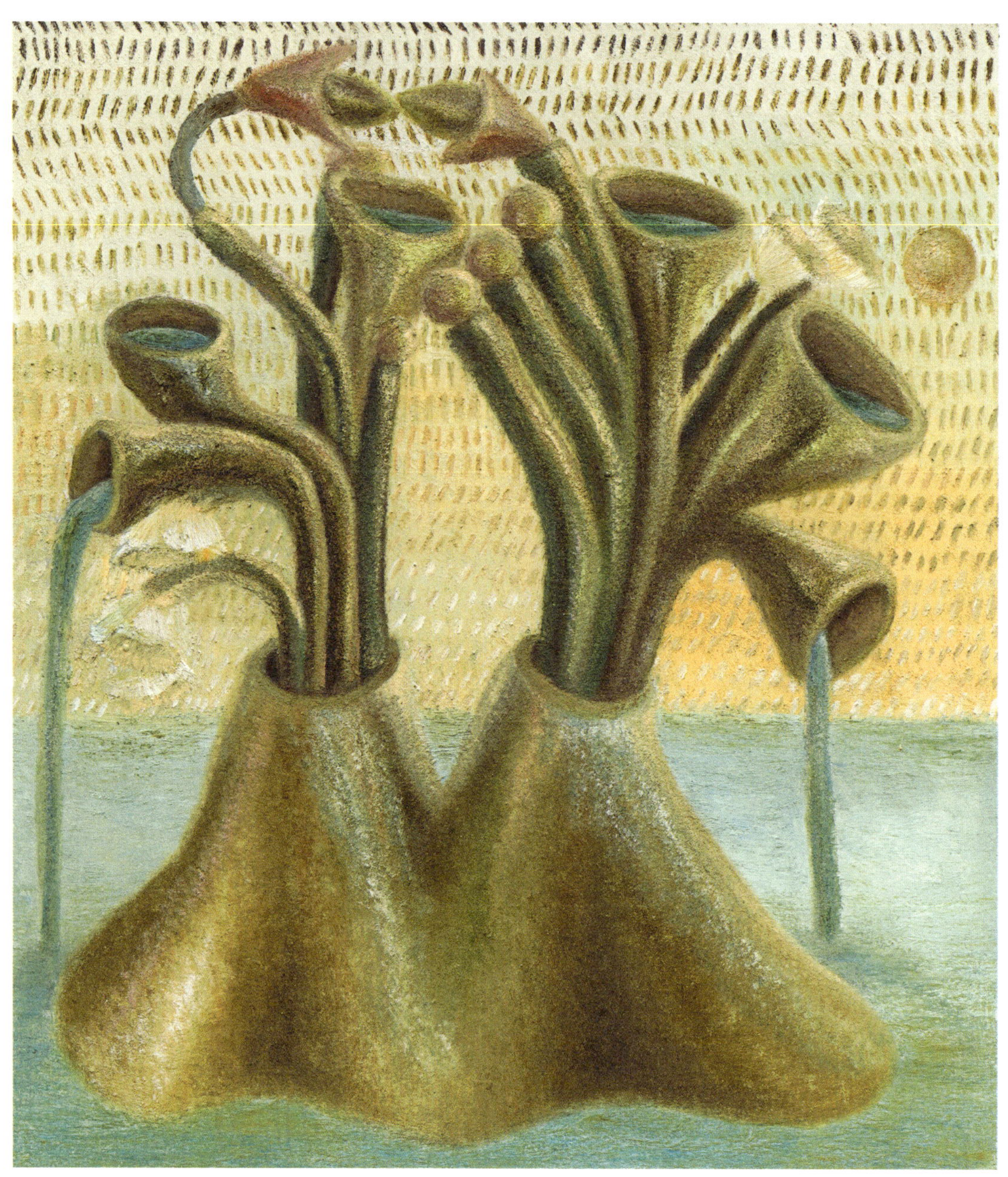

RAYANA RAYO

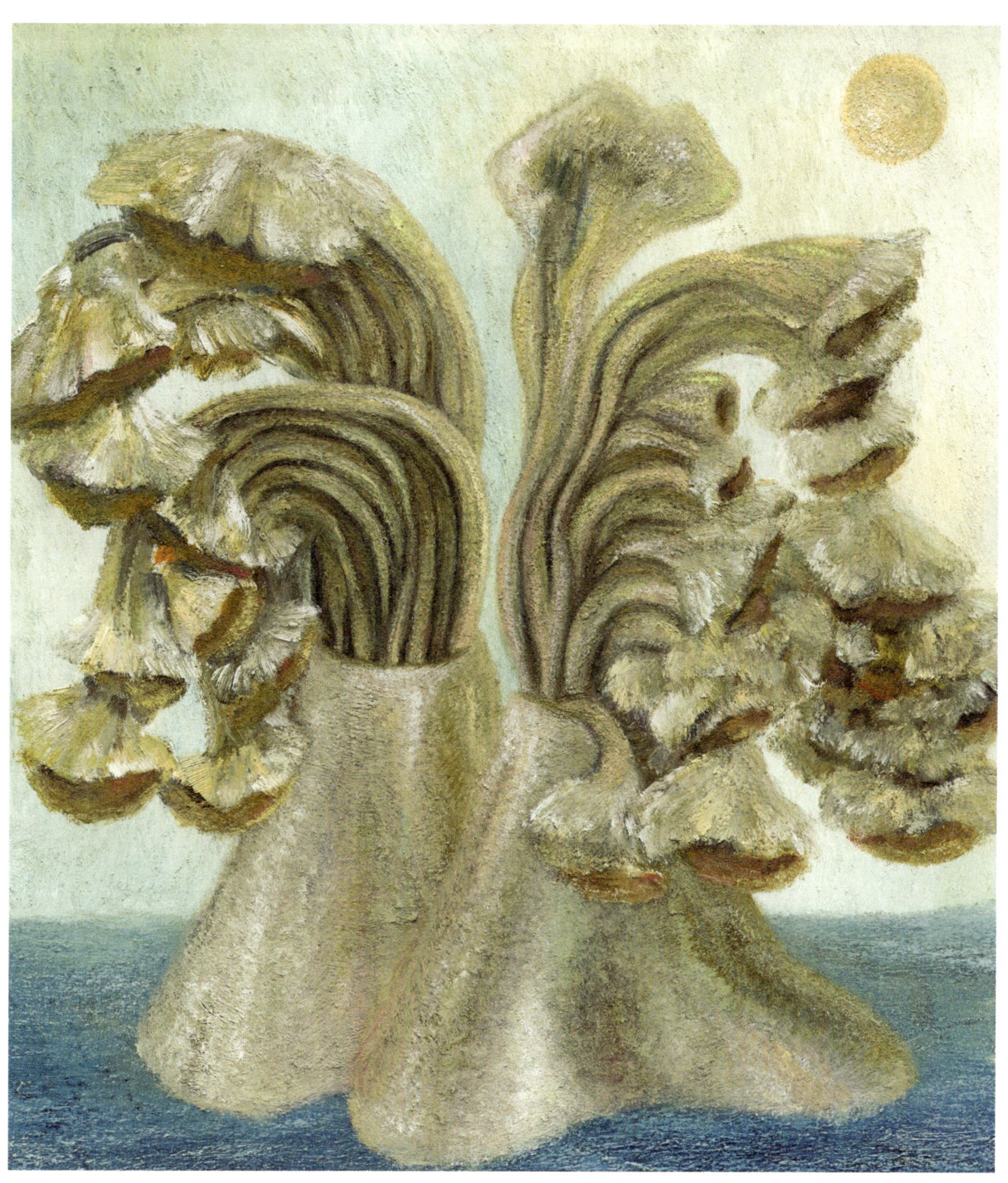

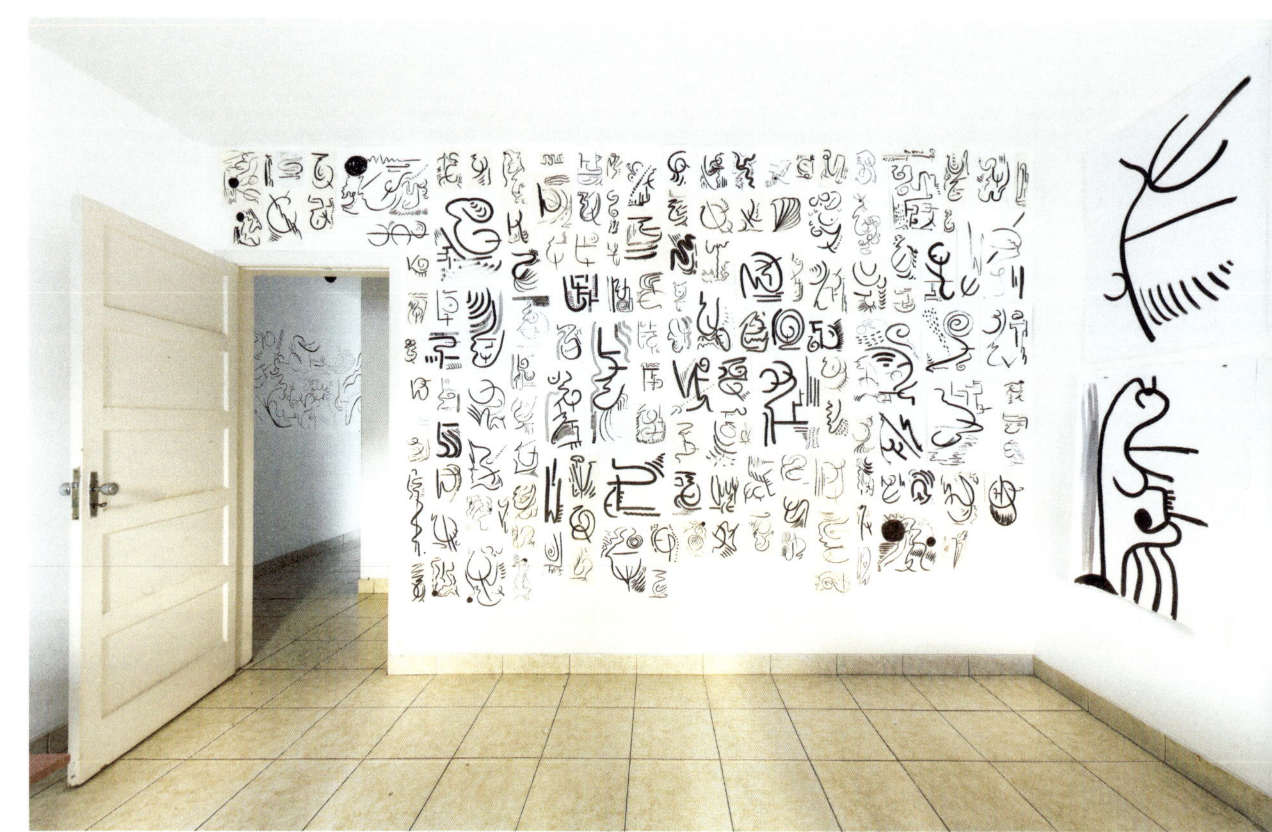

REBECA CARAPIÁ

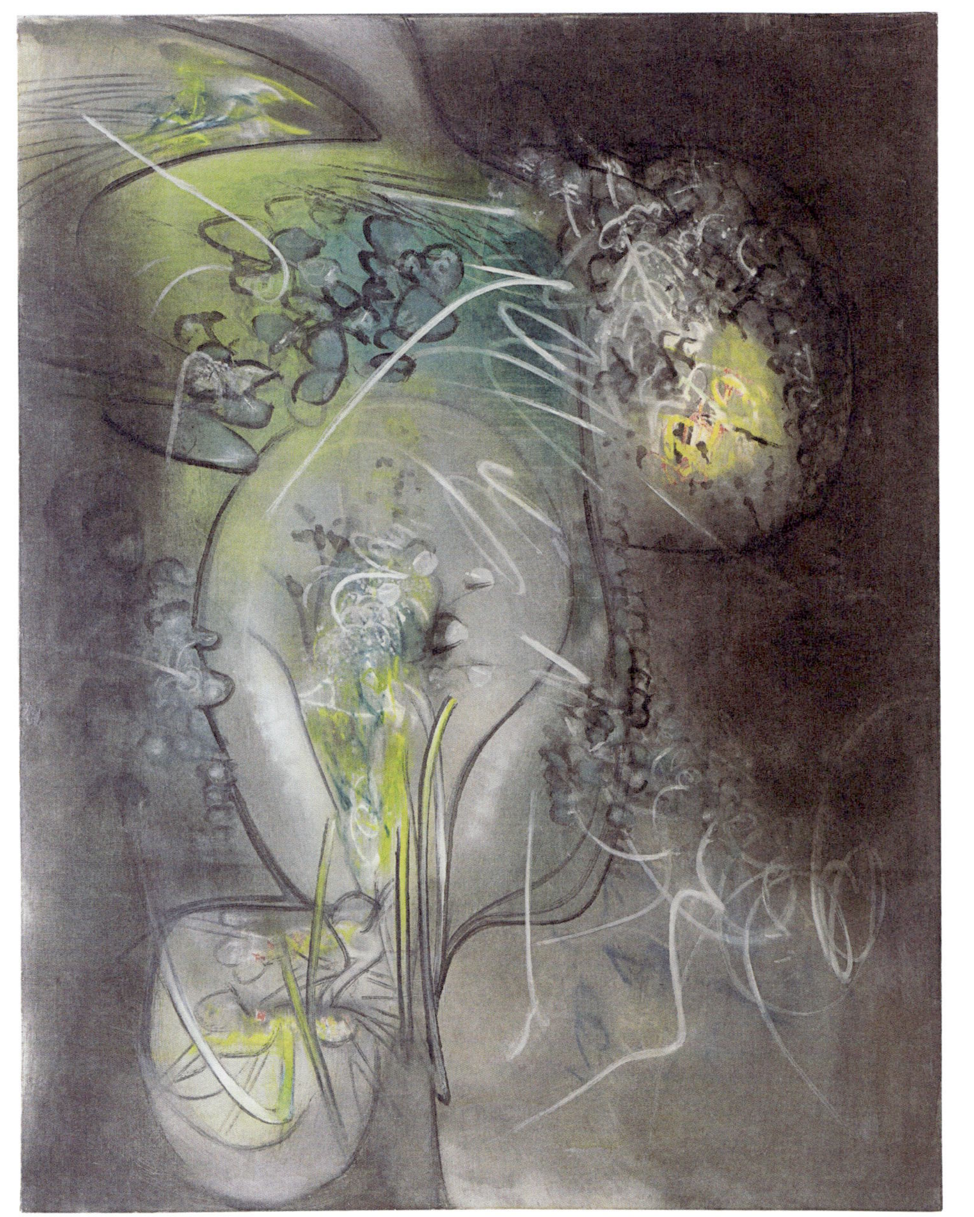

ROBERTO MATTA

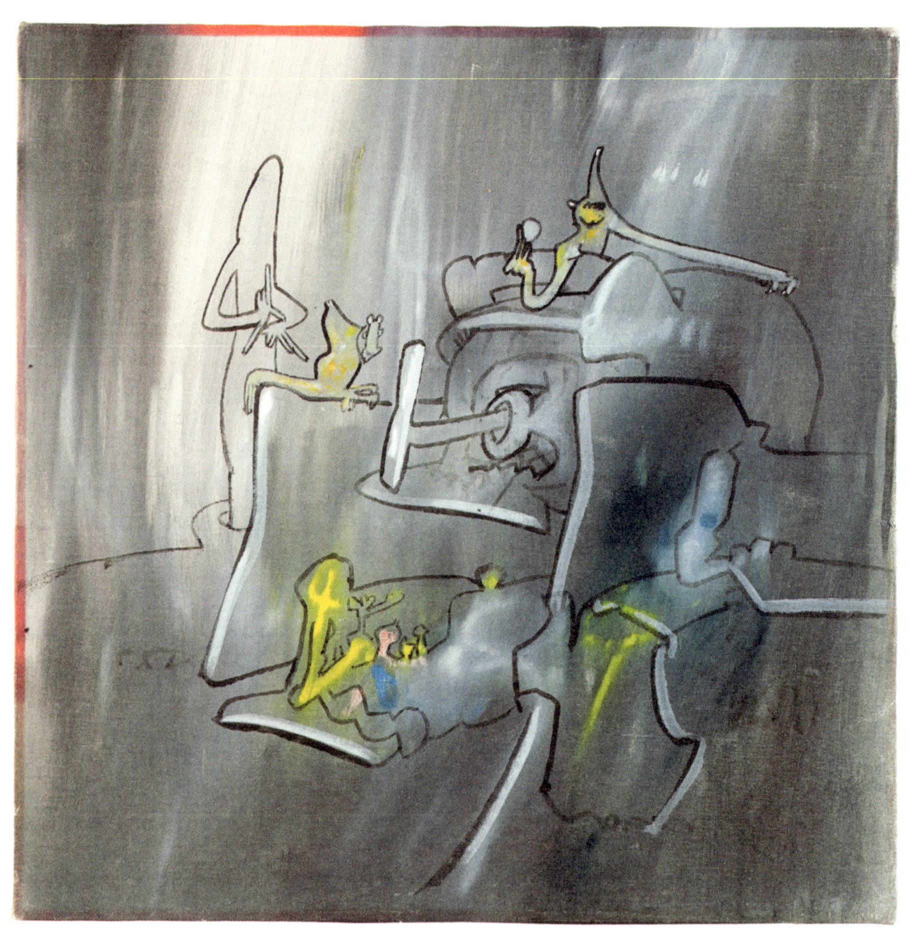

ROBERTO MATTA

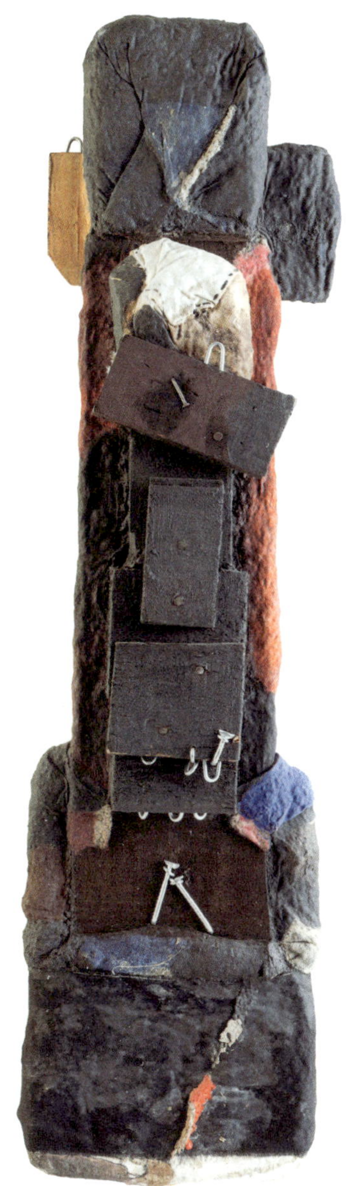

SERGE HÉLÉNON

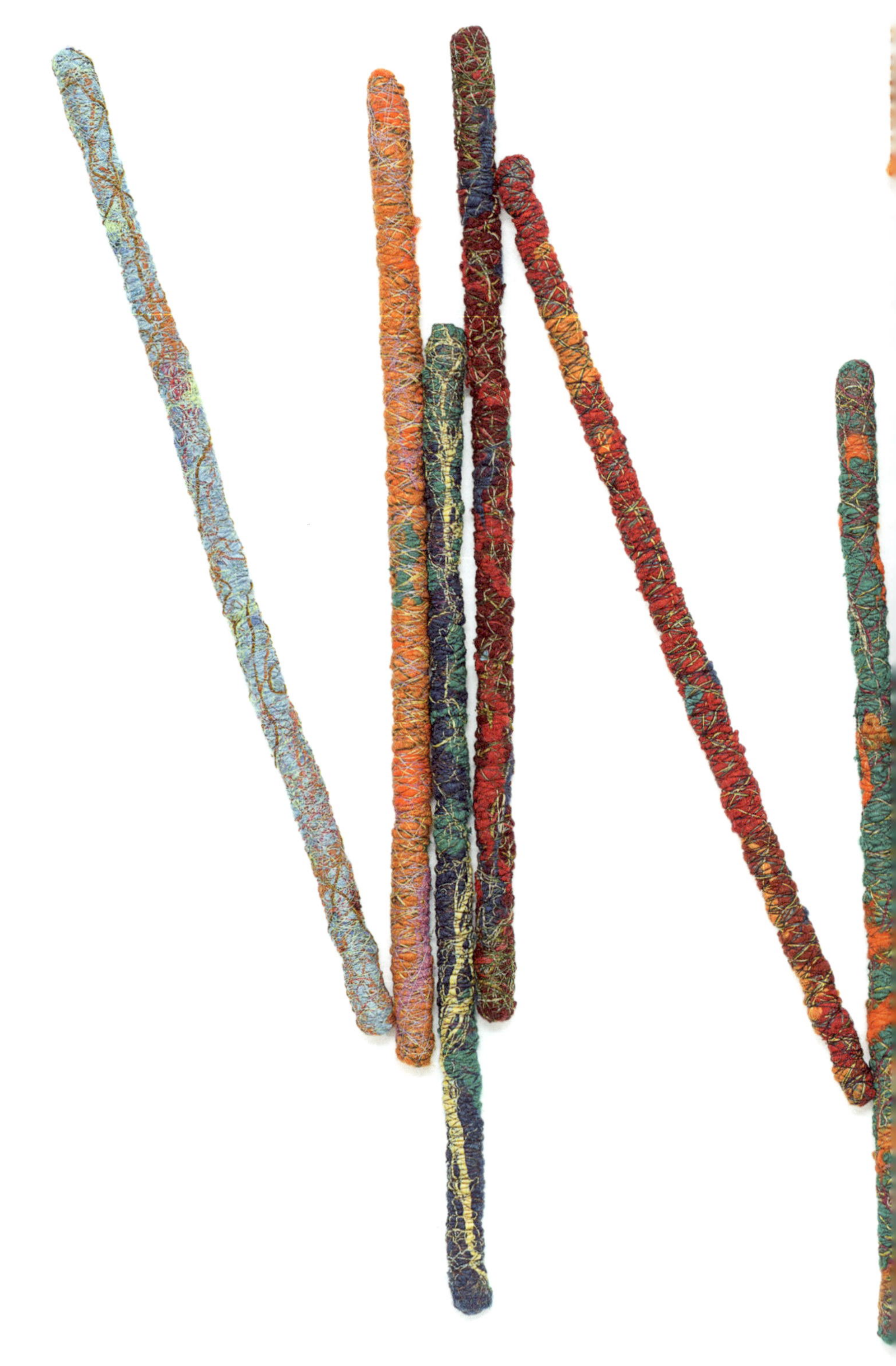

SHEILA HICKS

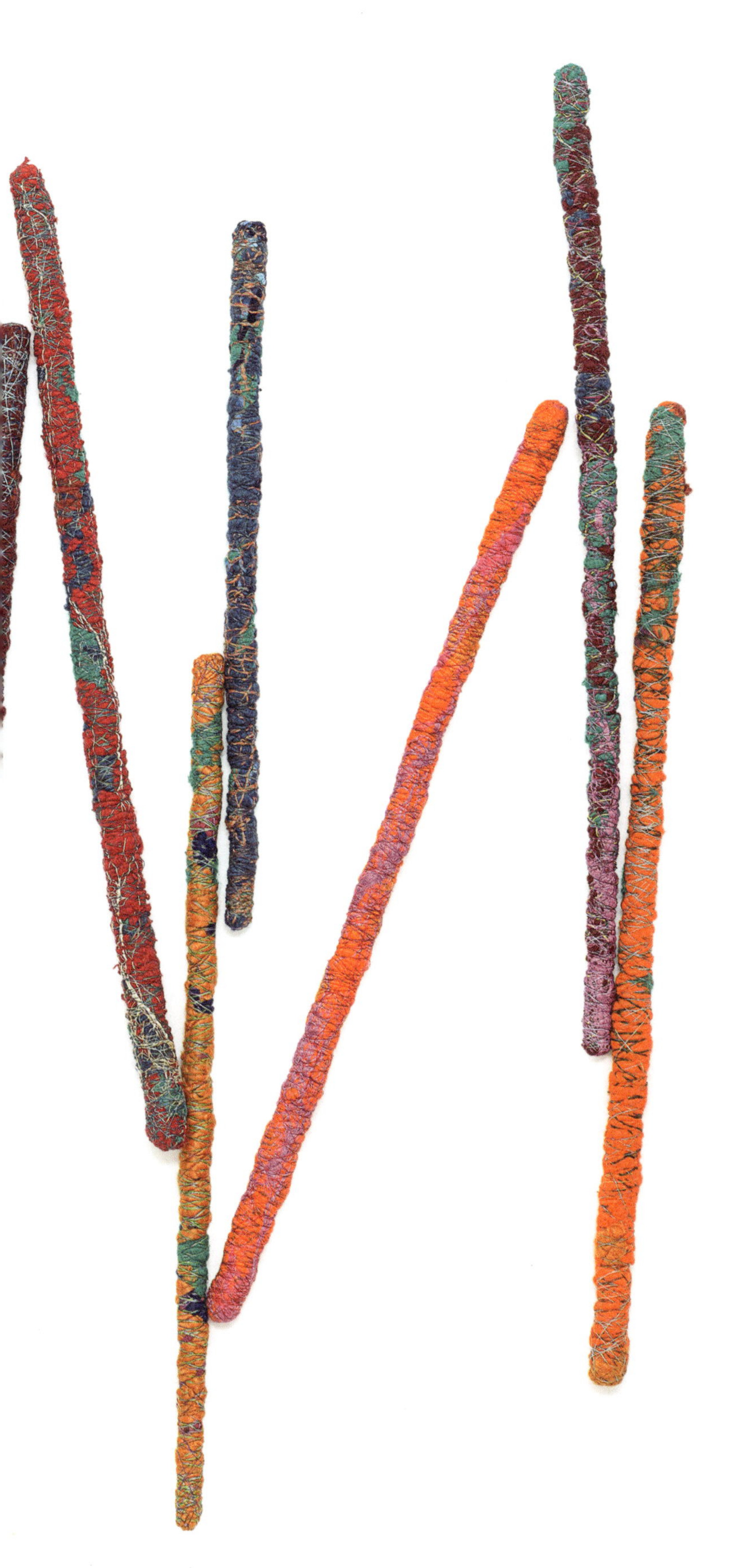

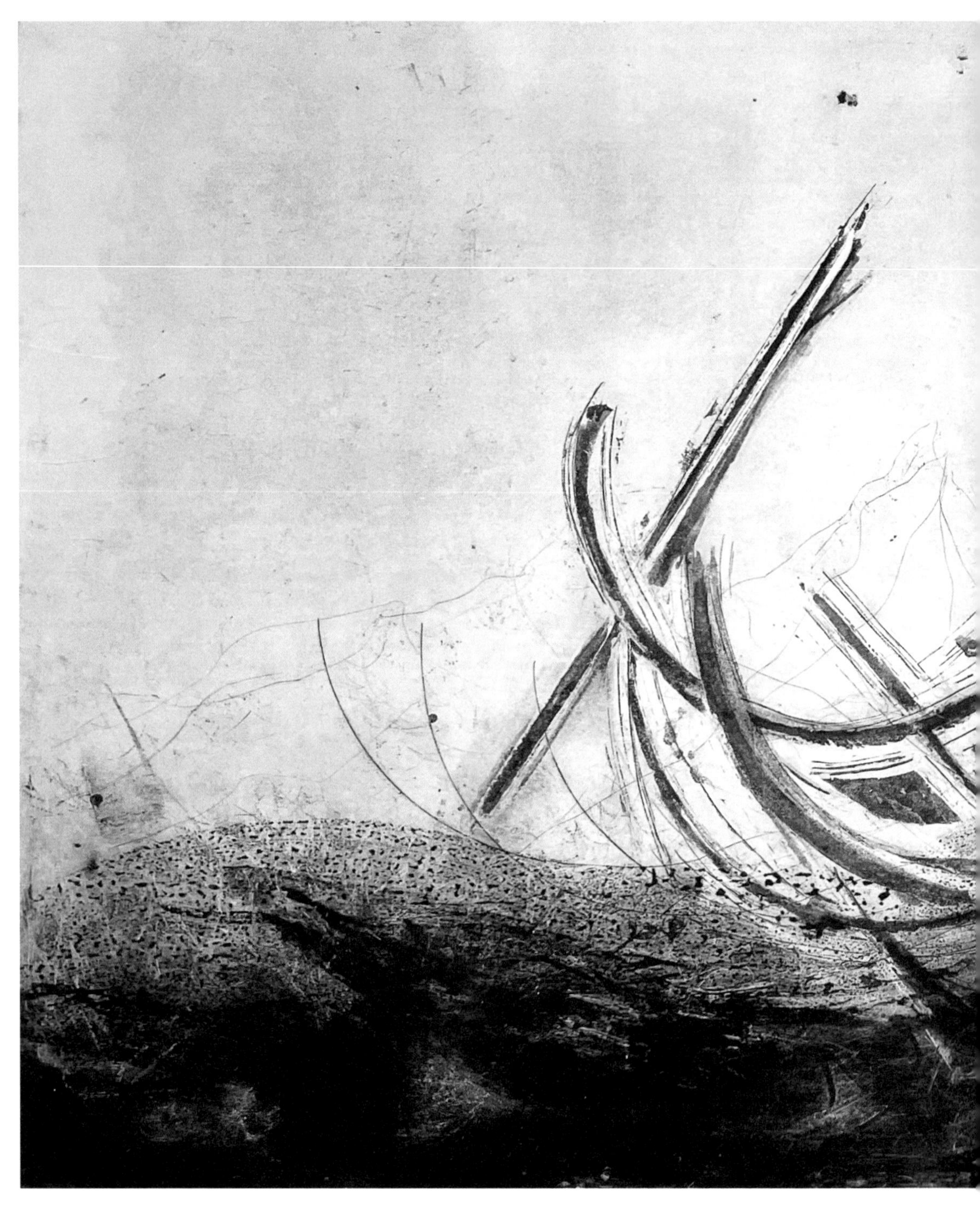

SYLVIE SÉMA GLISSANT

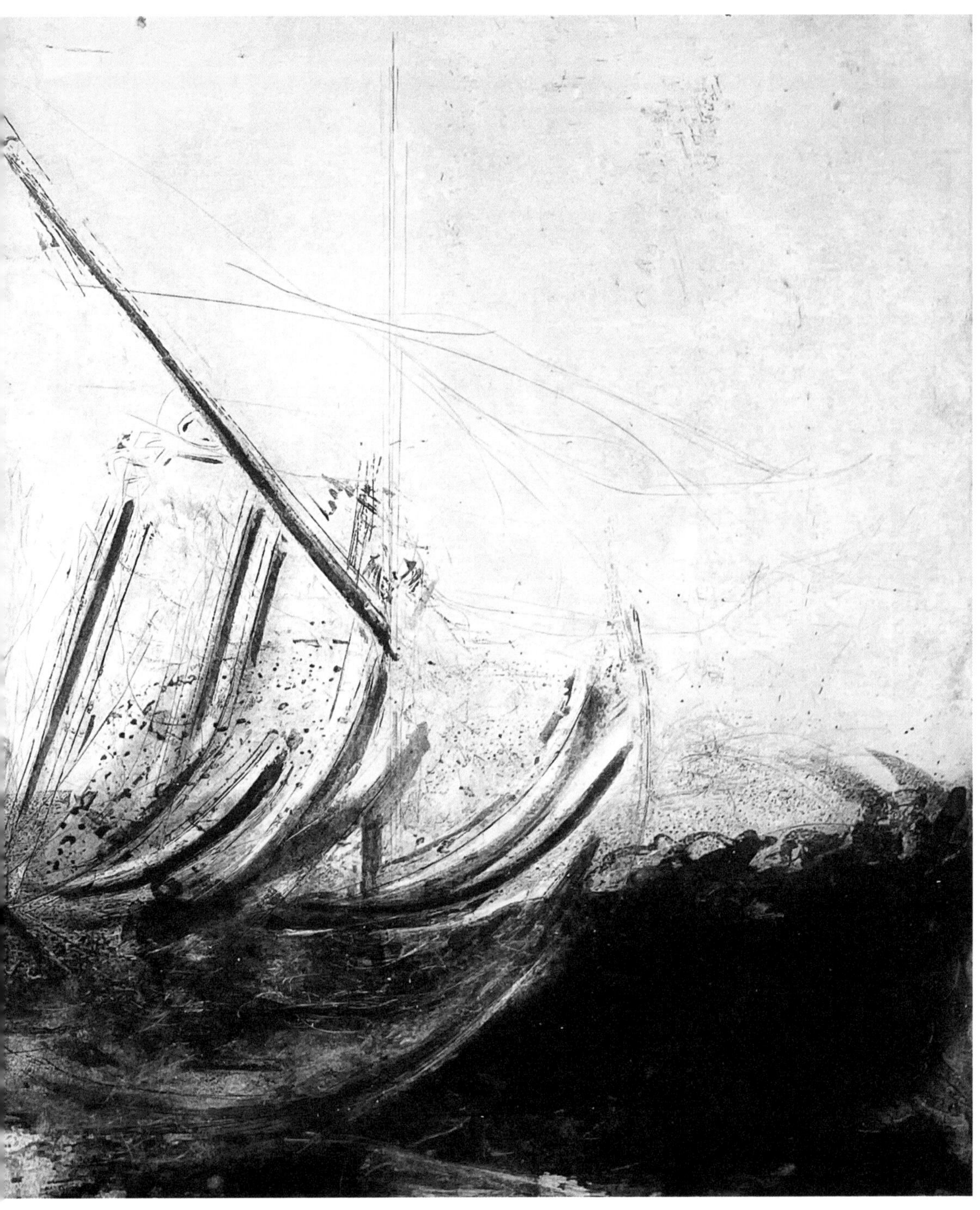

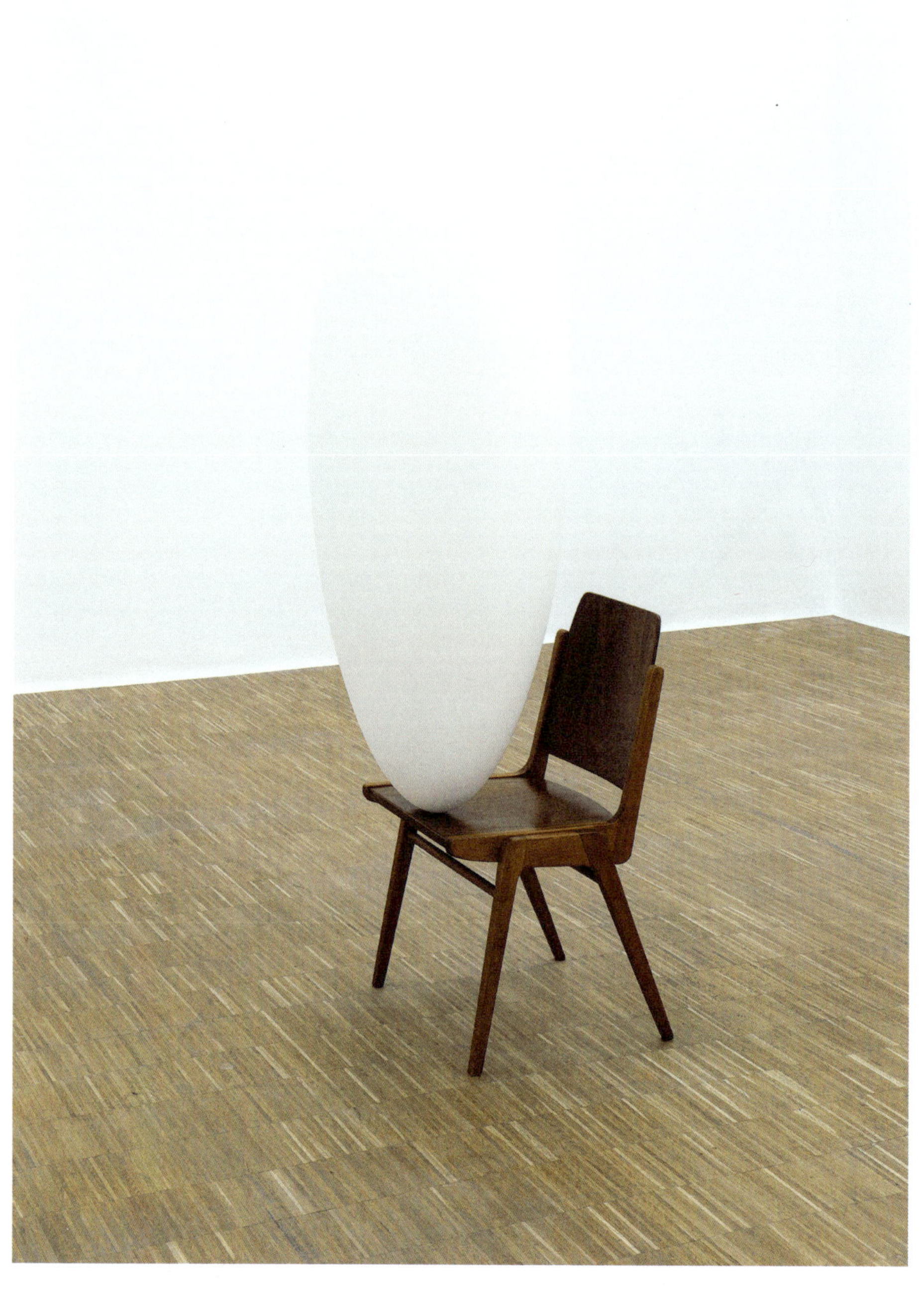

TARIK KISWANSON

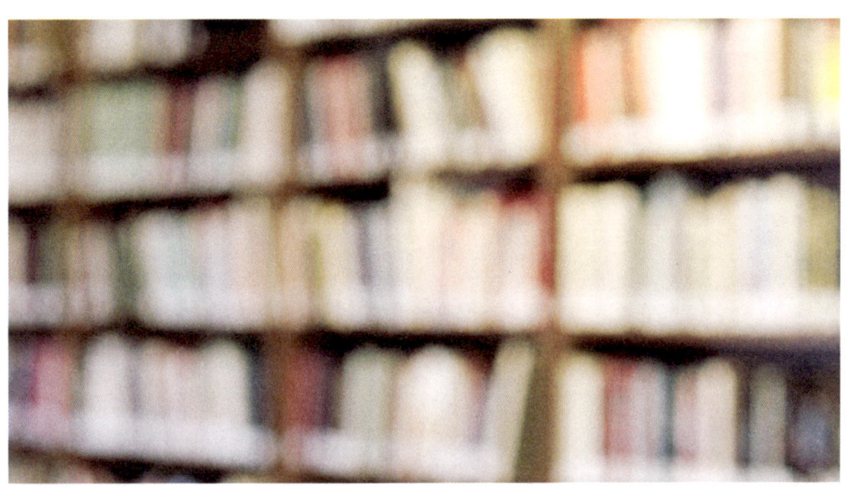

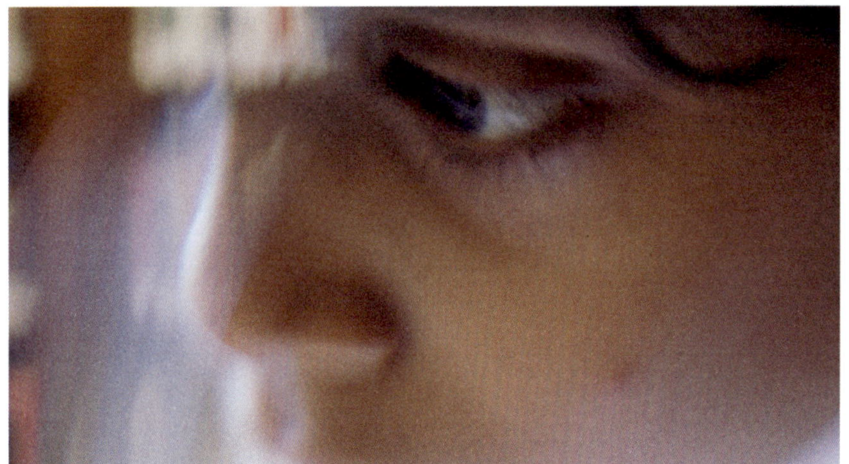

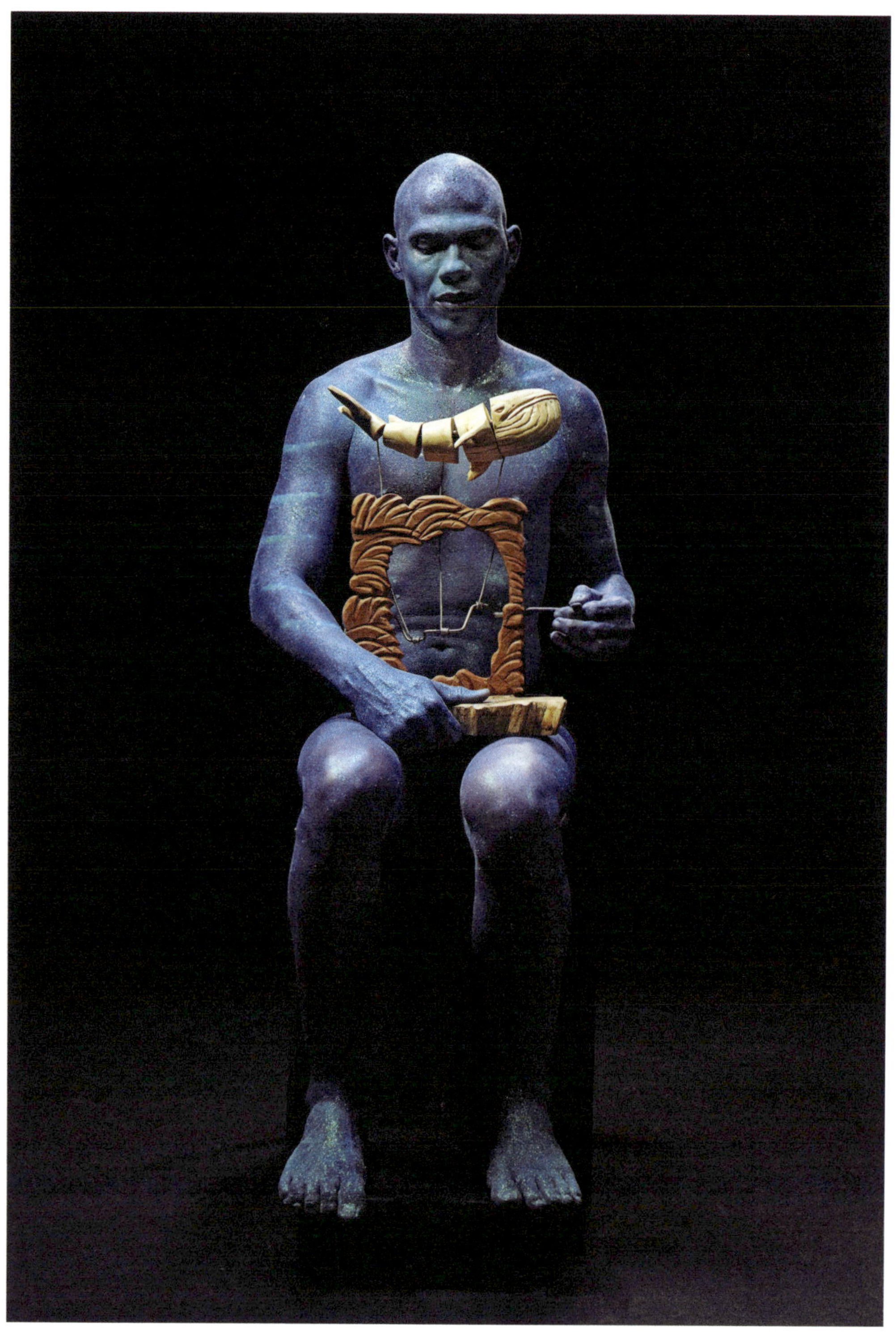

TIAGO SANT'ANA

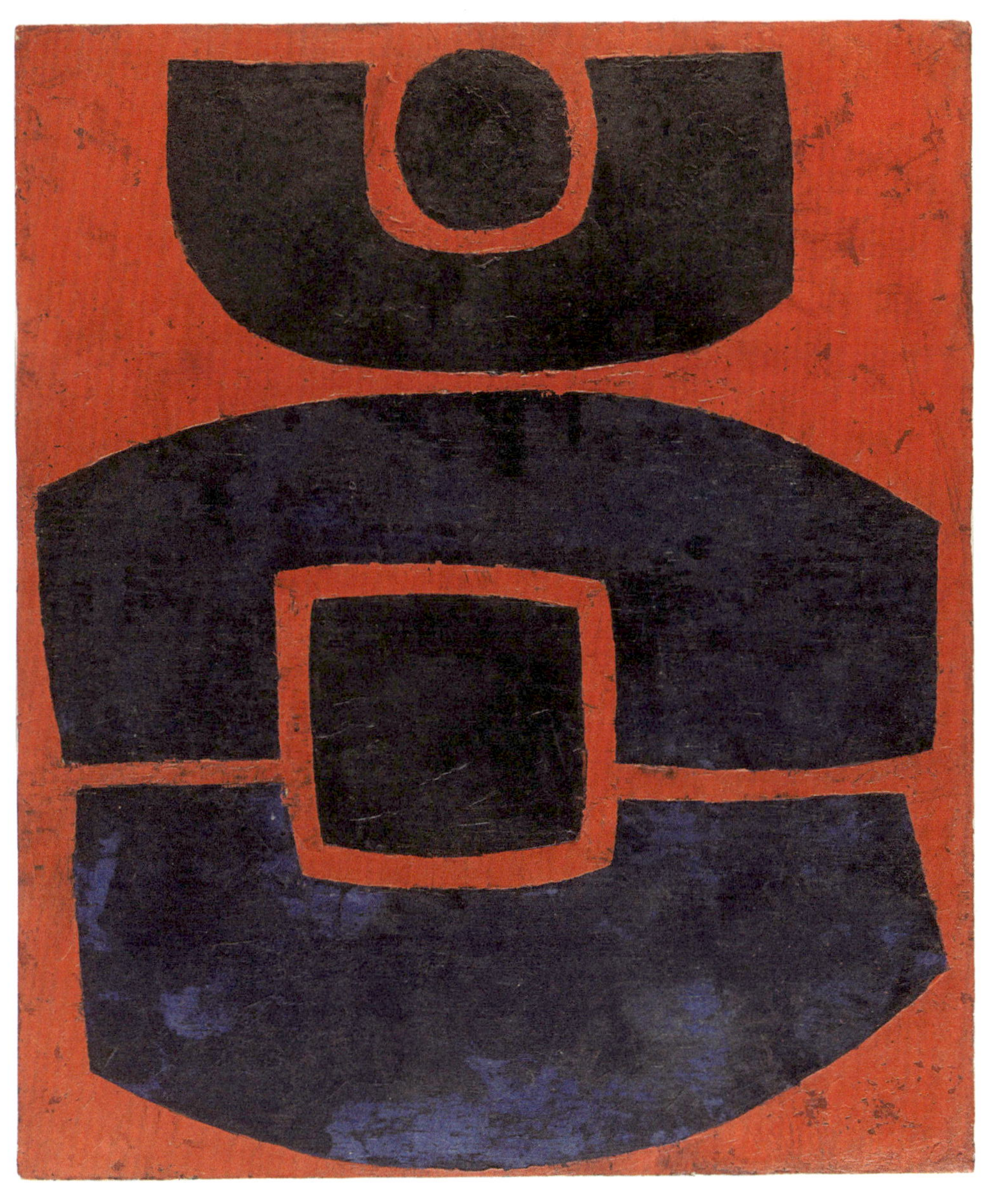

VICTOR ANICET

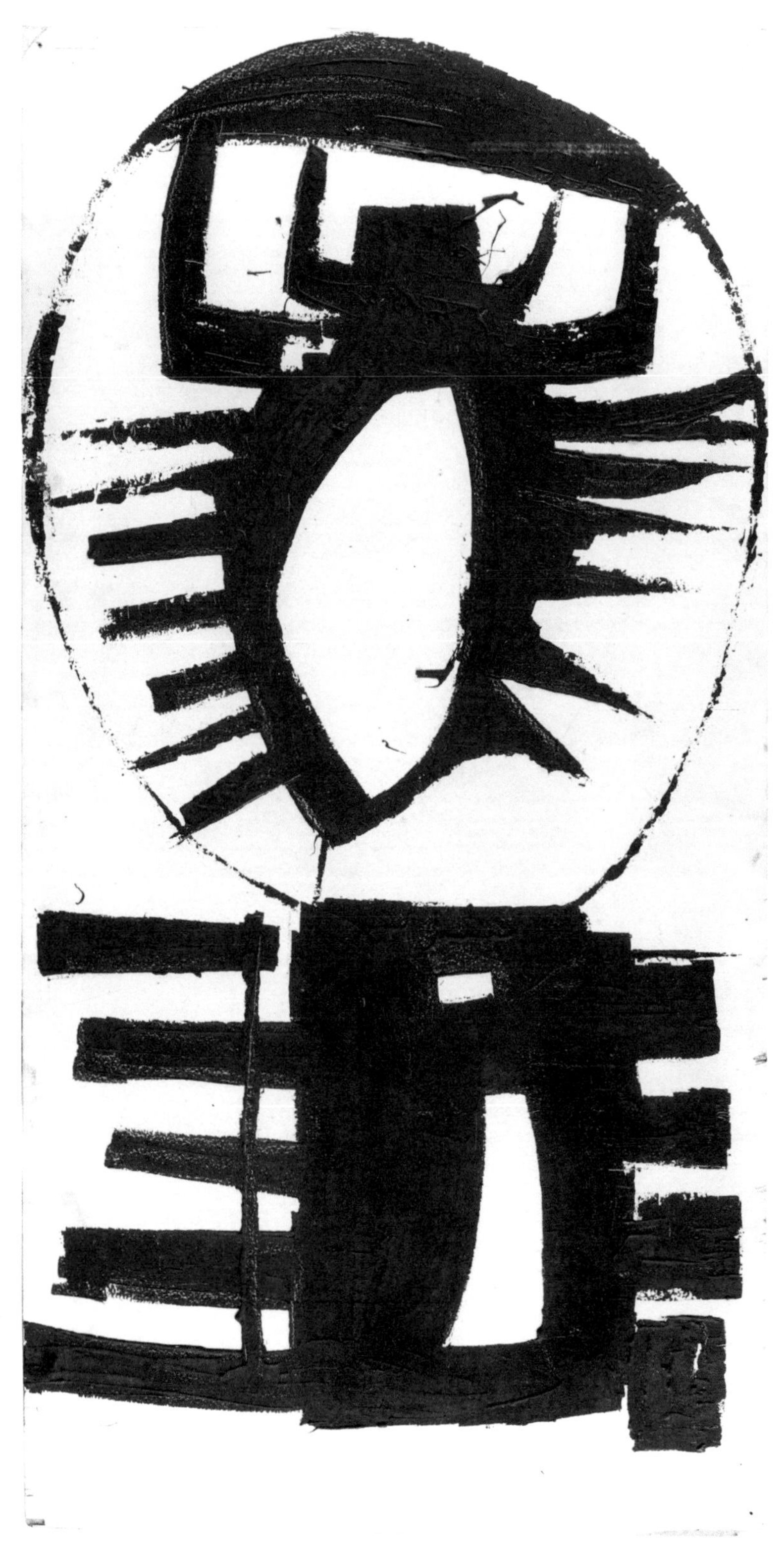

VICTOR ANICET

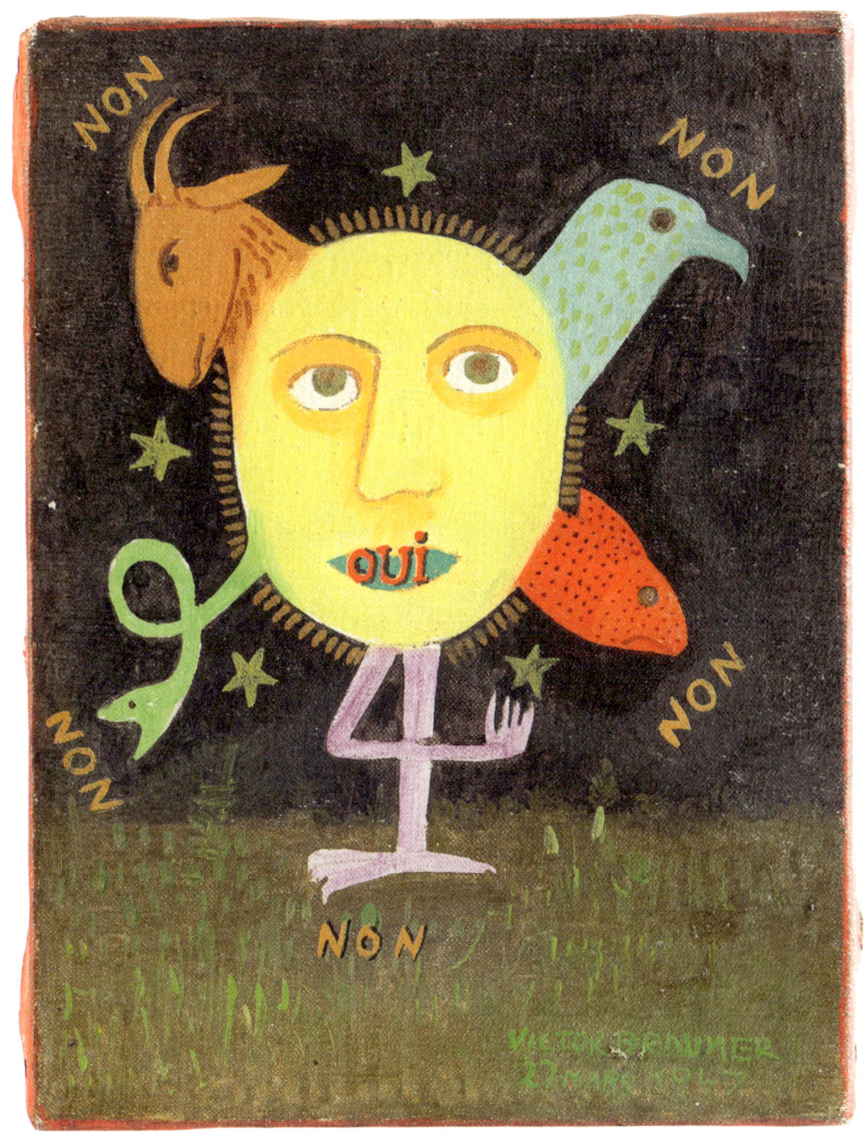

Sim não / Yes No, 1947

VICTOR BRAUNER

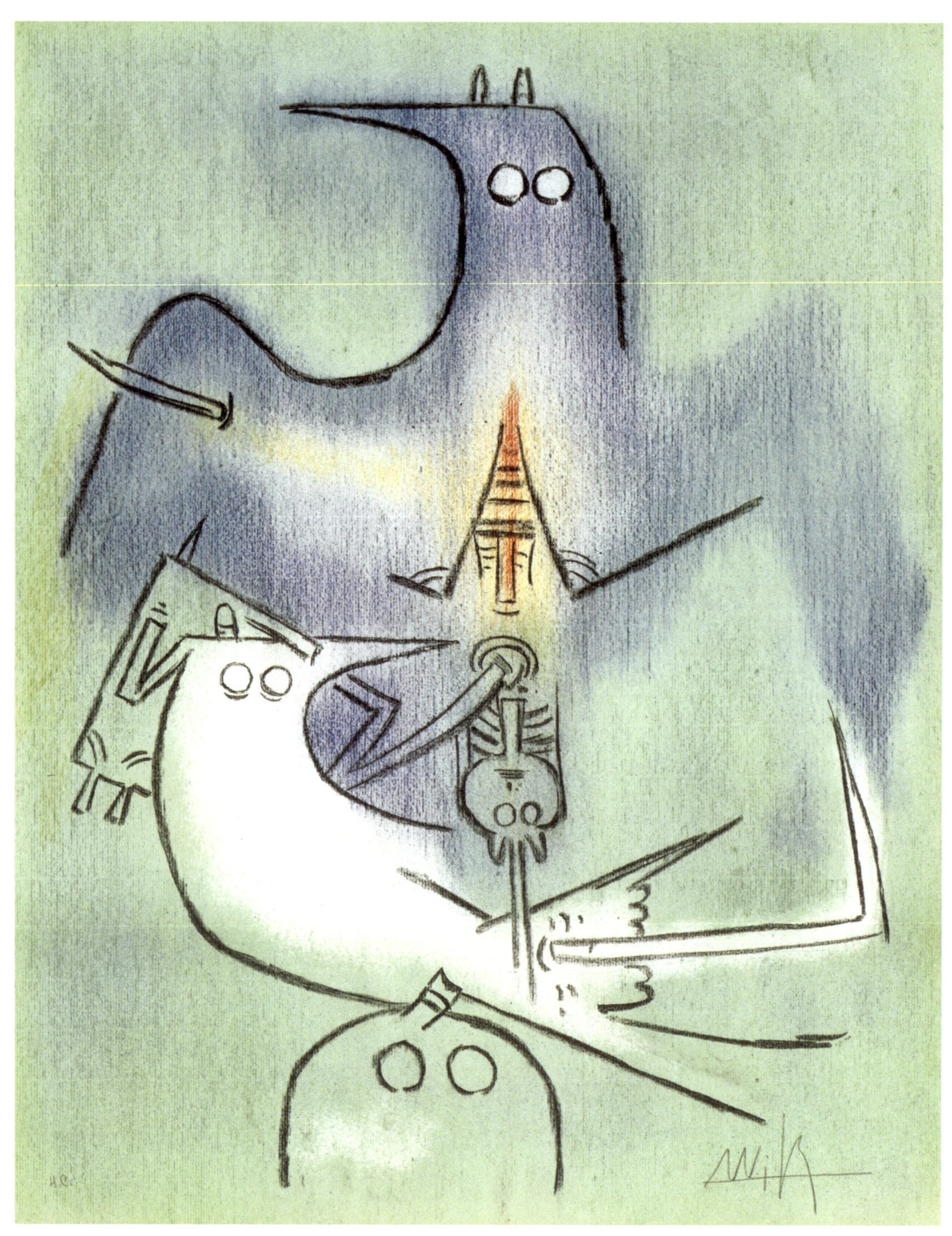

WIFREDO LAM

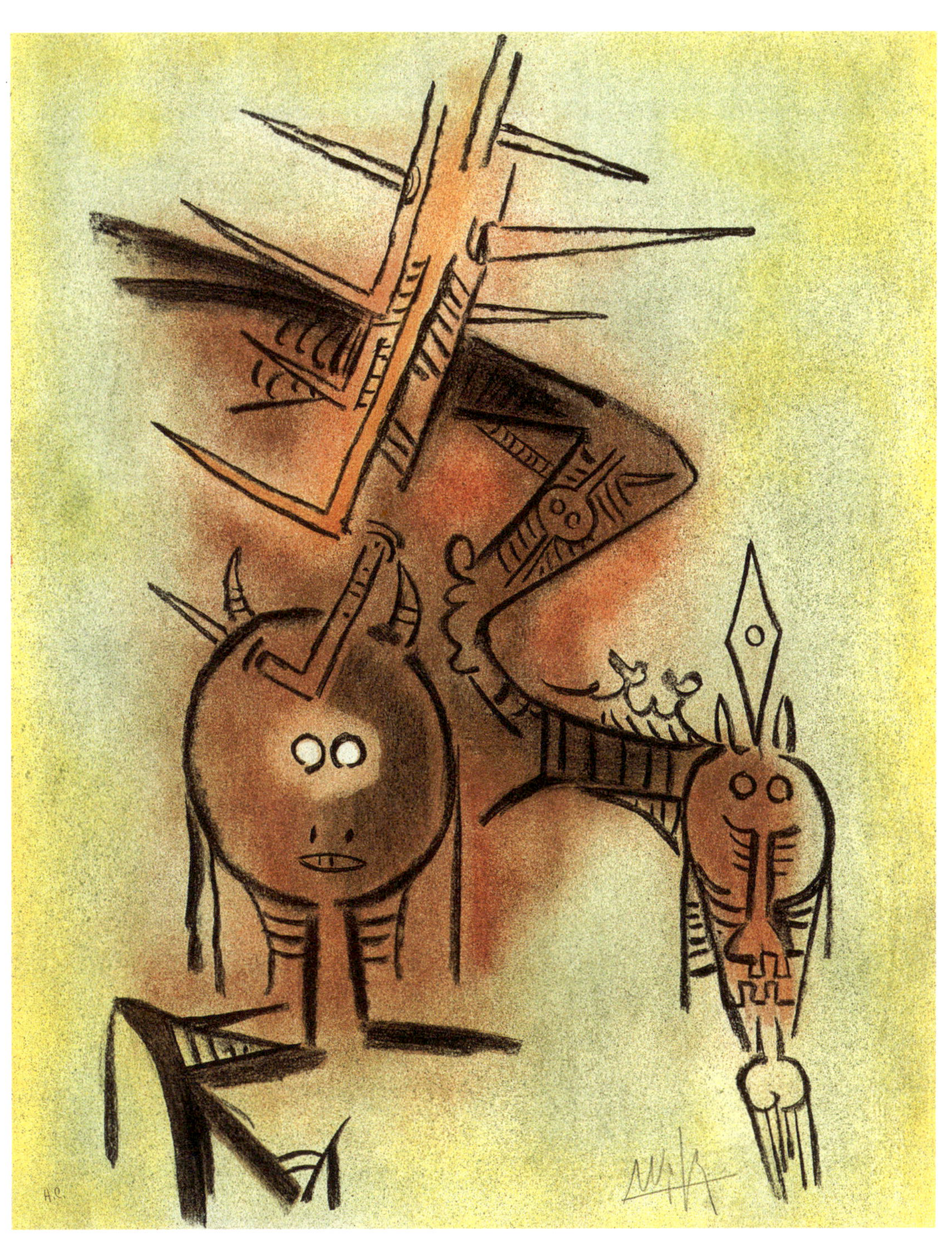

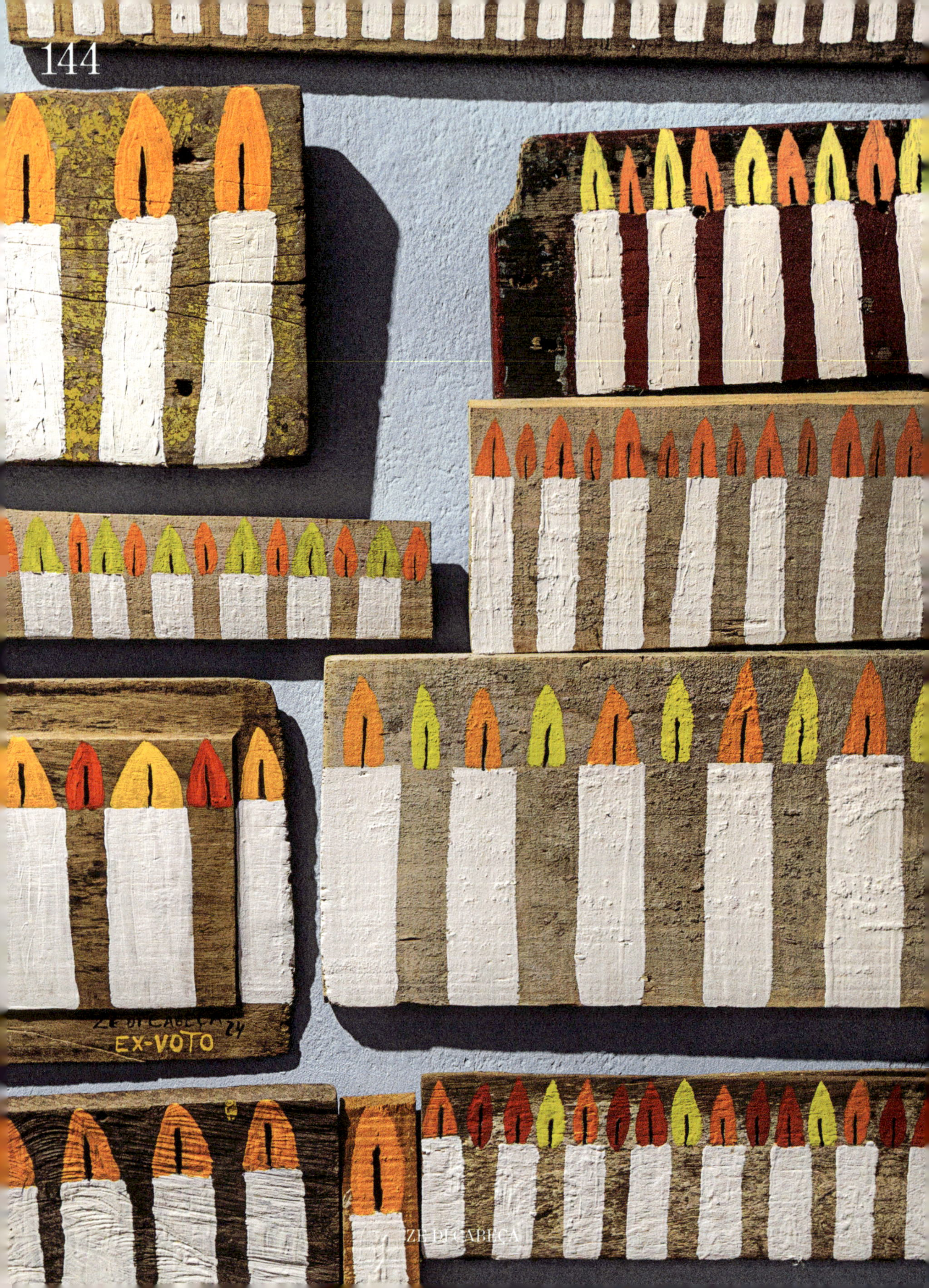
EX-VOTO
ZÉ DI CABEÇA

"The cypress trees gnawed by epiphytes, planted upright in the water of a Louisiana *bayou*; the giant ferns overhanging the sheer cliff of the Route de la Tracée in Martinique; the tide of vegetation, at Tikal in Guatemala, with, rising out of it, the galleons of the temple pyramids, with their flights of steps like so many oars waiting; the pathetic vigil of the palm trees, all over the hills of Santiago in Cuba; the opening of paths between the sugar cane plants, which imprison you in every direction; the hoarse fissures of buried ravines or great canyons open to the sky; the yellowing of the mangroves, bordering the emerald blue of the sea around the town of Pointe-à-Pitre in Guadeloupe; the bottomless barrels of the Guyanan rain that have always marked out the chaos of its forest; the overflowing rivers transporting earth, the Mississippi and the Amazon, and also the little streams drying up under their rocks; and the waterfalls transfixed in their infinite violence, El Salto del Angel, or tiny and secret below the rusts of time: the landscapes of the Americas are openness, immeasurability, a kind of irruption into spaces.

The people's histories cling to them and carve out monuments, which the energy rising from the earth moves and changes infinitely."

Édouard Glissant, *Treatise on the Whole-World*. Translated by Celia Britton. Liverpool: Liverpool University Press, 2020, p. 51.

Matanzas, Cuba, 1927 – Havana, Cuba, 2001

"Our history made visible, that, therefore, is the meaning of the passionate project of Cárdenas's sculpture. His interior landscape is just like ours. From Trinidad and Antigua, man and woman (the *Caribbean couple*) are scattered on windswept paths, in a profusion of transplantation, in the uncertainty of speech; they wait to focus their eyes. With Cárdenas we indeed turn our faces to this wind."

Agustín Cárdenas held his first solo exhibition in 1953 in Havana, where he had been a student of the modernist sculptor, Juan José Sicre, at the Academia Nacional de Bellas Artes San Alejandro, as well as a member of the Los Once group, formed by young artists dedicated to abstract art. Cárdenas, focused on sculpture, laid the foundations for his work using wood and creating shapes with organic curves, whose silhouettes evoke totems and portals. He later transposed this lexicon to marble and bronze.

A context already familiar with the work of Wifredo Lam welcomed Cárdenas upon his 1955 move to Paris; this likely contributed to his immediate acceptance by André Breton, who praised his forms and his connection with Afro-Caribbean ancestry. The artist embraced that perspective, delving deeper into his own roots and emphasizing the symbolic hybridity in his works by fusing elements of West African culture. In the early 1970s, he visited Édouard Glissant at the Institut Martiniquais d'Études in Fort-de-France (IME), where he crafted sculptures in burnt wood—one of them a portrait of the poet: a totem of exceptional sinuosity suggesting the incessant movement of its parts. In 1979, Cárdenas designed engravings for a special edition of Glissant's book of poems titled *Boises* [Woods], a cross-reference between the landscape and the shackles of slavery.

Édouard Glissant, "Seven Landscapes for the sculptures of Cárdenas," *Caribbean Discourse: Selected Essays*. Translated by J. Michael Dash. Charlottesville: University Press of Virginia, 1989, p.238.

AISLAN PANKARARU

Petrolandia, Brazil, 1990. Lives and works in Salvador, Brazil

"I speak to you in your language, and it is in my language that I understand you."

Born in the arid hinterland of Pernambuco, Aislan Pankararu lived in several cities before studying medicine at the University of Brasília, where he took up painting as a way of connecting with the legacy and memory of his Pankararu people. Made of mainly white paint on kraft paper, those works echoed the ancestral practice of body painting by applying clay to the skin. With the repetition and rhythm of their patterns, lines, and dots, they soon drew other associations, evoking features of the Caatinga landscape, silhouettes of plants and seeds, mucous membranes and tissues inspected under microscopes, fragments of the universe magnified by telescope lenses, and other images that elude naming.

Aislan's work bears parallels with the history of his people, with notions such as change and relation becoming resistance tactics. His claim is not for a hypothetical return to a past state, but for exalting the ability to harness memory today. In his commissioned work, Aislan leverages his burgeoning lexicon of signs, interwoven in a vast array of colors cast onto the raw linen fiber, the bare skin of the painting.

Édouard Glissant, *Poetic Intention*. Translated by Nathanaël with Anne Malena. New York: Nightboat Books, 2010, p. 46.

AMOEDAS WANI
& PATRICE ALEXANDRE

"The harmony and, just as persistent, the disharmonies that multilingualism generates in us, this new passion for our most secret voices and rhythms."

Maroon communities–descendants of enslaved Africans who escaped captivity to establish autonomous territories in the Amazon rain forest along the Maroni River, between French Guiana and Suriname–developed Tembé art, designed around a visual system that combines writing, drawing, and cosmology. Featuring wavy lines, spirals, sharp angles, and precise symmetries, those designs are painted or carved onto doors, benches, paddles, or fabrics. Much more than just an ornamental practice, Tembé operates as a relational code signaling protection, friendship, respect, or marking moments of transition.

A testament to diasporic trajectories in the struggle for freedom, this language encompasses multiple temporalities and fosters fields of shared meaning, conveying insights and experiences across generations. The woodcuts signed by Amoedas Wani and Patrice Alexandre, acquired by Sylvie Séma Glissant directly from the Guyana Artists' Association, partake in this tradition as an in-motion sign, suffused with evocations of natural elements. These works bear witness to a virtuous and expressive relationship with the vitality of a collective language that denotes belonging, continuity, and invention.

Édouard Glissant, *Treatise on the Whole-World.* Translated by Celia Britton. Liverpool: Liverpool University Press, 2020, p. 8.

ANTONIO SEGUÍ

Córdoba, Argentina, 1934 – Buenos Aires, Argentina, 2022

"The unexpected thing is thus that in Seguí's work the obstinacy and ruggedness are full of an unfailing charm. This prose is also poetry which navigates in the depths. Seguí paints that which perverts our nature and makes us strangers to our truth, but also everything that carries us away, secretly nourished by an inner sun, in the tango of tenderness."

In his youth, Antonio Seguí visited Africa and Europe, with periods of study in Madrid and Paris, and drove from Argentina to Mexico. His career began in Buenos Aires, where he briefly pursued informal abstraction before definitively shifting to a figurative practice based on critical and ironic chronicles of everyday life. With paintings, prints, drawings, and sculptures, Seguí created a wide-ranging body of work that makes use of simplified lines to relate situations featuring diverse urban types and metaphors for the absurdities of those times.

A pioneer of New Figuration with his combination of the visual repertoire of cartoons and German Expressionism, Seguí moved to Paris in 1963, where he developed most of his work. There he met Édouard Glissant, who invited him to visit Martinique in 1970. During that trip, Seguí produced a series of chalk drawings about the sinking of the Titanic, satirizing the futility of the idea of power embodied and staged by the ship and its passengers. Glissant was impressed by the representation of the luxurious vessel being swallowed up by the abyss of the landscape, and kept those drawings on display in his room.

Édouard Glissant, "Four Artists in Chiaroscuro," *The Unesco Courier*, July 1984, p. 27.

ARÉBÉNOR BASSÉNE

Dakar, Senegal, 1974. Lives and works in Dakar, Senegal

"Oh! to be farther from you than for example air from root, I have no longer leaf or sap. / But I go back up into the fields and the storms which are roads of the country of knowledge, / Pure in the air of myself, and embolden myself with oblivion if the hail comes. / (And what to say of the Ocean, except that it waits?)"

Arébénor Basséne, born in Dakar, focused his studies on African civilizations, harnessing the legacy of teaching and research he had fostered in the wake of his country's independence. Informed by those studies, he has refined a practice that both fables ancestral stories and delves into a wide range of pictorial processes and materials. Combining elements ranging from henna ink to gum arabic, natural pigments and acrylic paint, he crafts laborious works, consistently employing batik, an Indonesian dyeing technique transplanted to West Africa in the 19th century. While many of his paintings feature allegorical figures pertaining to the great empires of Africa and the Mediterranean, others draw on a combination of cartographic elements and evocations of landscapes.

His work, *Méditez-rat-n'est-rien* [untranslatable title] (2023-2024) comprises of 33 paintings referring to crossings, navigations, escapes and diasporas that crossed and still cross the Atlantic Ocean, the Sahara and the Mediterranean Sea. Originally exhibited at the Dakar Biennale in 2024, that work approaches the landscape as a place of wandering in which multiple temporalities, narratives and cultures may intersect.

Édouard Glissant, "The Restless Earth," *The Collected Poems of Édouard Glissant*. Edited by Jeff Humphries. Translated by Jeff Humphries and Melissa Manola. Minneapolis: University of Minnesota Press, 2005, p. 65.

CESARE PEVERELLI

Milan, Italy, 1922 - Paris, France, 2000

"The bursts of light arranged in traced patterns, the fiery blacks and delicate purples, the translucent coils and the hesitations of flesh, all of this ultimately systematized into a foam of time: like a population of crimson vines relentlessly taking root in their future."

Cesare Peverelli attended the Accademia di Belle Arti di Brera. He was among the founders of the journal *Numero - Pittura* in 1946 and, alongside Roberto Crippa, launched the Galleria Pittura, where, in 1949, he held a solo exhibition accompanied by a poem by Aimé Césaire. His approach to the modern avant-gardes' legacy is usually tied to Spatialism, the Italian art movement pioneered by Lucio Fontana. But beyond this affiliation, his body of work illustrates efforts that, without pursuing the path of geometric abstraction, sought to unlock the imaginary of space as something that exceeds the scope of perspective as a form of representation.

The close relationship between Peverelli and Glissant began in Italy, where the Martinican poet visited many times and struck up ties with several Italian artists such as Emilio Tadini, Sandro Somarè, and Valerio Adami, all of whose works are part of his personal collection. In Paris, where Peverelli settled in 1957, this interaction went on within the wider circle formed around the Galerie du Dragon, where he remained in contact with other artists who were rekindling their approach to pictorial space with other repertoires and landscapes.

Cesare Peverelli in *Autour d'Edouard Glissant: Paalen, Lam, Matta, Peverelli, Hultberg, Cardenas, Petlin, Zañartu, Gamarra, Segui, Lutz, Quilici, Somarè, G. Morawetz, Chávez, Eva Ho, Alejandro, Zamora, Chemay, Charasse, Le Maréchal.* Paris: Galerie du Dragon, 1988 - Translated by Sebastião Nascimento.

CHANG YUCHEN

Shanxi, China, 1989. Lives and works in New York

"[…] the famous slogan: '*Traduttore Traditore,*' the treacherous translator, the translation as treason, is no longer true. Because what does translation become? Not rendering a text from one language accessible to another language, but rather: 'rendering a text from the poetics of one language accessible to the poetics of another language.'"

Committed to long-term processes of research and reflection, Chang Yuchen often regards herself as a linguist rather than an artist. Since 2019, an important part of her production involves the Coral Dictionary project, a series of performances, drawings, installations and publications related to the development of a writing system based on fragments of dead coral collected during a residency on a Malaysian island. Yuchen's sensitive listening to the landscape converged with her attention to the inherent flow of the Malay language—which, lacking a distinct alphabet, has adopted different foreign scripts—and prompted an exercise in translation into English and Chinese, turning the coral shapes into signs and vessels.

Within the minute details of this process, we grasp the memory of the languages she fluently speaks (the economical syntax of colloquial English and the bond between image, sound and meaning in Chinese ideograms, for example). We can also sense the impact the memory of the Malaysian landscape has on her treatment of language as a living, open weave, constantly drifting and evolving in its interaction with the other.

Édouard Glissant, *Abécédaire d'Édouard Glissant*, interview by Patrick Chamoiseau, January 2008. Rights: Dorlis / Édouard Glissant Art Fund / Institut du Tout-Monde - Translated by Sebastião Nascimento.

CHICO TABIBUIA

Aldeia Velha, Brazil, 1936 – Casimiro de Abreu, Brazil, 2007

"'The sea we cross is a century.' Yes, a century. And the shore where you land—blind, without soul or voice—is a century. And the forest, preserved in its strength until the day of your escape, simply so that it may open before and close again around you […] is a century. And the land, little by little leveled, laid bare […] is a century."

Having intimate knowledge of trees and forests, Chico Tabibuia, born Francisco Moraes da Silva, first took up sculpting as a child, with no incentive from his family. For decades he worked as a logger, and only became continuously invested in art in the 1970s. His sculptures are primarily carved from whole pieces of wood, without any seams, and provide original depictions of creatures with striking symbolic overtones steeped in remnants of the African diaspora.

As the grandson of a Portuguese man and an enslaved black woman, Tabibuia embraced Umbanda worship as a teenager, and later joined the Assemblies of God, which in no way deprived his practice of a spiritual meaning, as he would often sculpt his figures to capture entities he found embodied in trees or in the woods. Outside the realm of worship, he retained an enchanted understanding of nature and life, expressed in a body of work displaying a remarkable capacity for the invention of archetypes and the synthesis of forms.

Édouard Glissant, *Le Quatrième siècle*. Paris: Seuil, 1964, pp. 268–69. [Free translation]

EDUARDO ZAMORA

Nuevo Laredo, Mexico, 1942 – Paris, France, 2023

> "These charms, these stretches, this parody of gestures, these brutalities of monotonous tasks and silhouettes barely clothed in their meager breath, eventually form structural models, the metaphysical framework of what we believed we saw throughout our days and nights."

Eduardo Zamora studied in Mexico City and Krakow before settling in Paris in 1973. Though Mexican muralism and socialist realism deeply influenced his background, his painting veered toward a representation of everyday life, in sets full of dreamlike figures and absurd scenes, punctuated by comments on social types and reminiscences of Mexican culture. With a palette of opaque, earthy tones highlighted by white hues, he developed a way of painting that is both bleak and fantastical, often revolving around the theater of private life.

Apart from being a regular at the Galerie du Dragon, Zamora was also part of the Magie-Image group, whose first exhibition took place at L'Espace latino-américain in 1983. Active until 1990, the group consisted of young Latin American artists based in Paris, brought together by the context of political violence in their countries of origin and their shared interest in applying to painting an approach that echoed the Surrealist avant-garde and, more specifically, the imagery of Latin American fantastic realism.

Édouard Glissant, "L'absolu incertain," *Artension,* no. 10, 1983, p. 4 - Translated by Sebastião Nascimento.

EMANOEL ARAÚJO

Santo Amaro, Brazil, 1940 – São Paulo, Brazil, 2022

> "I do indeed draw a parallel between the slave ship and the abyss. And not between the slave ship and the heights. Because on the slave ship, even if the cargo rebels against the crew, this is not yet the time of rebellion. It is the time of the abyss. And it is true that rebellion, the heights, is not rebellion either, but rather the permanence of rebellion. It is where we go after rebellion."

As an artist, curator, collector, and cultural manager, Emanoel Araújo has transformed the institutional landscape of art in Brazil and offered far-reaching contributions for a better understanding of the country's African heritage. In his youth, he learned the trades of goldsmithing, carpentry, and lino-typing; skills he brought to bear during his art education in the 1960s in Salvador, where he was soon to become renowned for his paintings and woodcuts, figurative at first and more abstract later on.

The steady development of Araújo's artistic practice saw him move from wood engraving to sculpture and wall reliefs, constantly relying on a compositional language based on surfaces rhythmically arranged through diagonal cuts. His works directly approach the African diaspora, as with the reliefs entitled *Navio* [Vessel] (2011 and 2022)—compositions that synthesize the trauma of transporting enslaved people—but the significance of that subject within Araújo's body of work transcends the thematic scope. His approach to geometry and topology, as well as the constructive framework used in his abstract works, are seminal instances of diasporic black abstraction in Brazil, stemming from the interplay between African repertoires and the local artistic context.

Édouard Glissant, *Abécédaire d'Édouard Glissant*, interview by Patrick Chamoiseau, January 2008. Rights: Dorlis / Édouard Glissant Art Fund / Institut du Tout-Monde - Translated by Sebastião Nascimento.

ENRIQUE ZAÑARTU

Paris, France, 1921–2000

> "When lightning strikes the summit of the Andes, the geological seedlings unravel, supplies fall into abysses, and finally this tremor becomes a woman, who gathers around her reserves of clay and maté."

Enrique Zañartu grew up in Santiago, Chile, where he began painting in 1938. At home in New York between 1944 and 1947, he honed his engraving skills at the renowned Atelier 17, originally founded by William Hayter in Paris and subsequently relocated to the US during the war. After two years in Havana, Zañartu followed in the footsteps of exiled artists and Atelier 17 itself, having returned to Paris in 1949. While in contact with expatriate Latin Americans and with groups affiliated with the surrealist legacy, Zañartu further developed his painting and printmaking work, devoted to shaping atmospheric fields onto which he placed (either in conflict, or at rest, if not in copulation) incomplete fragments of bodies and stretches of landscapes.

Zañartu also produced engravings for publications by poets and writers such as Édouard Glissant, Octavio Paz, and Julio Cortázar. With Glissant, Zañartu published *Les Indes* [*The Indies*], an initiative in which both the artist and the poet explored the intertwined tremors of landscape, body, language, and thought. Zañartu also retained his commitment to supporting political exiles from the Chilean dictatorship, and, from 1982 onwards, was a contributor to the Espacio Latinoamericano.

Rivière-Salée, Martinique, 1945. Lives and works in Fort-de-France, Martinique

"Men with wayward wings, what rush drives you, from the burrows where the first word broods, to the transparencies of this day, when the clamor falls silent and prophecy takes hold?"

In 1984, a year after starting to paint, Ernest Breleur founded, alongside Victor Anicet and some other friends, the Fwomajé group (the Kréyòl name for the monumental tropical tree known as Kapok). As part of that group, whose members explored the diversity of Caribbean identity, Breleur sought inspiration in Africa's rich imaginative heritage and his own memories of Antillean tales. In 1989, however, he broke with Fwomajé and its culturalist aspects and initiated his series of paintings with greater aesthetic density.

Untitled (*Noire* [Black] series, 1990) is a piece with graphic emphasis: brushstrokes in light hues outline turbulent trails on a dark surface. A silhouette body with no head, hands or feet floats while bent over itself, as two inverted houses take off from the horizon. There is no narrative as such, but rather an allusion to a state of instability: Breleur found his way of referring to the turmoil and tensions of his time without resorting to regional iconography or direct commentary on the issues of the day. Restless and prolific, he quit painting in 1992 and continued his experimental work, sometimes intervening on X-rays, sometimes creating assemblages, installations, and drawings.

Paris, France, 1984. Lives and works in Marmeaux, France

> "The idea of the world takes advantage of the imagination of the world, the intertwined poetics that allow me to sense how my place joins up with others, how without moving it ventures elsewhere, and how it carries me along in this immobile movement."

Etienne de France's practice investigates landscape as a territory of imagination, language, and emancipation. In *The Telling of the Stones*, the artist draws on the friendship between Édouard Glissant and Icelandic writer, Thor Vilhjálmsson, to poetically compose a speculative fiction. The video installation stems from the hypothesis of a poem-novel that the duo would have begun to, or dreamed of, writing together; its narrative spans times, geographies, and cosmologies: between Guadeloupe and Iceland, between traces of engraved stones and landscapes with a voice.

In the first canto, a woman from the Kalinago people flees colonial violence in the 17th century, guided by spirit stones toward the volcanic islands of the north. In the second one, two men cross the Icelandic plains of the 19th century, recalling the legend of a foreign woman who left inscriptions on rocks in the central desert. In the two narratives, the stone is both voice and figure: a mask, an archive, a guide. The Garifuna and Icelandic languages pervade the video as music and ruin, conjuring layers of translation, erasure, and survival. References to the novels *Sartorius* by Glissant; *The Magnetic Earth: The Wanderings of Rapa Nui, Easter Island* by Sylvie Séma Glissant and Édouard Glissant; and *Justice Undone* by Vilhjálmsson point to how both authors envisioned landscape as a living language that endures, guiding and preserving the remnants of the world.

Édouard Glissant, *Treatise on the Whole-World*. Translated by Celia Britton. Liverpool: Liverpool University Press, 2020, p. 74.

FEDERICA MATTA

Neuilly-sur-Seine, France, 1955. Lives and works in Paris, France

"The strokes are bold and solid, without hesitation, but it is in their alignment that the unexpected occurs: the drawings and paintings are checkerboards of characters, whose only fixed feature is that of the original great lakes. Their winding paths are the hopscotch of the world. Art of distant myths and the most secret concrete presences: within the rock, the grain of rice, the drop of water that is perpetually startled."

Federica Matta's artistic practice intertwines art, collaboration, education, and fabulation, ranging from educational materials to public works. With her playful and abundant visual language, infused with signs retrieved from a wide spectrum of mythologies, Federica has devoted many drawings, notes, and notebooks to revisiting poetic ideas she reaped from the writings of Glissant, whom she had known since her childhood. At the age of 15, she spent a year studying at the Institut Martiniquais d'Études (IME), founded by Glissant in Fort-de-France in 1967, bearing witness to a time of considerable personal investment by the poet in his country and its people.

One of Federica's most ambitious achievements is the garden of sculpture-games she installed in 1993 at Plaza Brasil in Santiago de Chile. The 22 elements designed by the artist rely on imagination as a tool for social change, providing an exuberant participatory environment for adults and children in a central neighborhood of the city. It soon became an iconic element in the history of Chilean public spaces after a long and brutal dictatorship.

Text for the exhibition *Orage, mirage: Les Perles des dragons* [Storm, Mirage: The Dragons' Pearls]. Chapel of the Incarnate Word, Avignon, summer 2008 - Translated by Sebastião Nascimento.

FLAVIO-SHIRÓ

Sapporo, Japan, 1928. Lives and works between Paris, France and Rio de Janeiro, Brazil

"The whole island was a bird-man, and a boat, and a wandering house, for anyone adrift in the vast Pacific who had lost sight of the path of the currents and the stars. The migratory bird brings the beyond to you, in you it is remade, but soon it departs: the island is ephemeral, and it endures."

Throughout his childhood and youth, Flavio-Shiró lived in Sapporo, Japan; Tomé-Açú, in the Brazilian Amazon region; as well as in the Brazilian state capitals of São Paulo and Rio de Janeiro. Along the way, he experienced not only the zeal for art that his parents had nurtured, but also a deep respect for the nocturnal darkness of the rainforest. Endowed with a remarkable talent for drawing as a key element of painting, his wandering path led him on to Paris in 1953, where he laid down firm roots and became a major contributor to gatherings of Latin American artists.

In that context he also became one of the first Brazilians to explore the pictorial repertoire being developed in France at the time under a multitude of names: Informalism, Art Without Form, Art of Another Kind, and Tachism, among others. Flavio-Shiró embraced the emphasis on gesture, the experimentation with thick layers of paint, the nod to calligraphy, and scribbling as templates for the brushstroke. Nonetheless, he rejected the wholesale dismissal of drawing in favor of abstraction. His works retain drawing as a means of calling forth the world's fear and trembling.

Édouard Glissant and Sylvie Séma Glissant, *La Terre magnétique: Les Errances de Rapa Nui, l'Île de Pâques.* Paris: Seuil, 2007, p. 40. [Free translation]

FLORENCIA RODRÍGUEZ GILES

Buenos Aires, Argentina, 1978. Lives and works in La Plata, Argentina

"Their dialogues are all allegorical. Mad preciosities, unknown science, baroque idioms of these Great Chaoses. Come from everywhere, they decenter the known. Vagrant and offended, they teach. What voices are debating there, announcing every possible language?"

Florencia Rodríguez Giles works with drawing, installation, video, and collaborative practices, articulating art and mental health as fields of aesthetic and political experimentation. She is a member of the Club de Artes y Ocios (CAOs), an autonomous community founded in 2020 focused on collective creation involving artists, people in psychiatric care, and health professionals. Her practice emerges from her experience in psychic suffering, institutional exclusion, and the invention of other ways of life, in a continuous inquiry into the boundaries between reality, delirium, and dream.

She develops a "psychoidal" practice in which listening, delirium, and collective imagination disrupt the logic of diagnosis and reframe the terms of coexistence. Her pencil drawings—mostly large-scale—come across as extensions of shared narratives. They combine eroticism, mutation, and psychic fabulation with a permeable materiality in which the intricate line work hints at secretions. In *Lxs durmientes* [The Sleepers] (2024), bodies pile up in a living mass somewhere between wakefulness and collapse, between shelter and excess. In the background, a landscape suddenly appears, without transition, as though emerging from someone else's dream.

Édouard Glissant, "The Great Chaoses," *The Collected Poems of Édouard Glissant*. Edited by Jeff Humphries. Translated by Jeff Humphries and Melissa Manola. Minneapolis: University of Minnesota Press, 2005, p. 231.

FRANK WALTER

Horsford Hill, Antigua and Barbuda, 1926-2009

"[…] Who is prolonged by waiting / And all the hands in his head / And all splendors in his night / That the earth might be astonished ¶ He accepts the noise of words / More identical than the dread of springs / More uniform than the flesh of plains / Torn into pieces filled with seed ¶ Its clarity is in the ocean / In the patience that is dragged / Toward where no eye may strain / By the flora of oriental islands ¶ That which cradles its song in your eyes / To reach the morning O intimate / Yet unnown one, this is the wild heat / Of Chaos where the eye at least touches […]"

Frank Walter was born in Antigua, a Caribbean island under British colonial rule until 1981. Having multiracial ancestry in a context in which miscegenation was a taboo, Walter became the first black man to work as a manager on the island's sugarcane plantations. He traveled to Europe to finish his education but, when confronted by structural racism, he drifted into a period of wandering marked by poverty and psychiatric institutionalization in major cities such as London, Paris, and Berlin. Upon his return to Antigua in 1961, he tried unsuccessfully to take a leading role in the revival of his homeland.

Over the following decades, he set in motion a wide-ranging cycle of study and production on his own, covering everything from art to science, including ecological sustainability and the history of Europe and its colonialism. He produced his extensive painting output on scrap materials and in small dimensions, such as Polaroid photo negative boxes. With few, decisive strokes of intense color, Walter consistently used landscape as his motif, combining environmental perception, mythical fabulation, analytical thinking, sensory expansion, and the sheltering of subjectivity.

Édouard Glissant, "A Field of Islands," *The Collected Poems of Édouard Glissant*. Edited by Jeff Humphries. Translated by Jeff Humphries and Melissa Manolas. University of Minnesota Press: Minneapolis, 2005, p. 42.

 # GABRIELA MORAWETZ

Rzeszow, Poland, 1952 - Paris, France, 2023

> "All that remains is to occupy the wait, that is, to explore this landscape expanded by its uncertainty, where trees are flames ravaging the route; where bare bodies nevertheless reveal only their inclination toward the dark mirror: the earth with no bottom or reflection."

Gabriela Morawetz graduated from the Academy of Fine Arts in Krakow and subsequently moved to Caracas, Venezuela, where she lived from 1975 to 1983, later settling in Paris. Together with her partner, Pancho Quilici, she constantly moved between Venezuela, France, and Poland throughout her career. Until the 1990s, her paintings explored the clash between the image of the female body-based on her own-and natural landscapes ranging from deserts to forests. Colors and compositional elements in those artworks, with their marked pictorial intensity, push beyond the naturalistic conventions of representation. She underlines states of tension and reciprocity between person and environment, so that subjectivity ceases to be an exclusive feature of the human figure, and the body becomes suffused with landscape attributes.

In more recent decades, Morawetz expanded her practice to embrace sculpture, installation, printmaking, and photography applied to multiple surfaces. Nevertheless, the image of the female body still held sway at the core of her work, serving as a sign that incessantly forms and dissolves itself within the surrounding space.

Édouard Glissant, "Par delà le transparent," *Gabriela Morawetz. Exposition.* Paris: Galerie du Dragon, 1986, pp. 5-6 - Translated by Sebastião Nascimento.

Saint-Martin, France, 1950. Lives and works in Saint-Martin, France

> "Chaos is not devoid of norms, but these neither constitute a goal nor govern a method there. *Chaos-Monde* is neither fusion nor confusion: it acknowledges neither the uniform blend–a ravenous integration– nor muddled nothingness. Chaos is not 'chaotic.'"

Geneviève Gallego grounds her artistic practice in the rugged Pyrenees topography, in a remote village she calls home. Sculpting since 1996, she works mainly with burnt wood such as juniper, oak, boxwood, prunus, heather, and chestnut. Her poetics connects to bodily expression, dance gestures, and living force of words, and she devotes herself to rhythmic forms reacting to the wood's veins and knots, shaping lively curves and volumes that sway between suggesting female bodies and rough topographies.

Gallego was close to Édouard and Sylvie Glissant for over 30 years, having started sculpting in their company. In her words: "Édouard wrote somewhere that in the quivering of the branches he heard the words. I can say that I hear the quivering of Édouard's words, and I use them to carve the wood." Chiseled shortly after a telephone conversation with Glissant as he was planning the Musée Martiniquais des Arts des Amériques, *Géographies du Chaos-Monde* [Geographies of the Chaos-World] (2010) is a direct and intentional response to the fluid nature of his thoughts, while also embodying–with quivering lines and twists and turns–a visceral reaction to the pain of her ailing friend.

Édouard Glissant, "Closed Place, Open World," *Poetics of Relation*. Translated by Betsy Wing. Ann Arbor: University of Michigan Press, 1997, p. 94.

GERARDO CHÁVEZ

Trujillo, Peru, 1937-2025

"The magical leap of the Inca warrior, the spear of the Greek hoplite, the peaceful eye of the agouti, the entangled figures of moon-faced bulls and benevolent gnomes: this world is suspended in a plasma where no body falls, each one balanced at a primal speed, locked in an ancestral embrace, in a battle of budding organs. Recollections of our future lives."

Having studied at the Escuela Nacional Superior Autónoma de Bellas Artes in Lima, Gerardo Chávez moved to Europe in 1960, just in time to evade the encroaching embrace of geometric abstraction across his homeland. An admirer of the Renaissance legacy, he settled in Italy and, in 1962, moved to Paris at the suggestion of Roberto Matta, with whom he held a continuous dialogue, as well as with Wifredo Lam and other Latin American artists of his generation. Such context reinforced his adherence to figurative painting with fantastic, dreamlike, absurd, or surreal tones—depending on the viewer's frame of reference.

Chávez returned to Peru in 1968, on the eve of the rise of the dictatorial regime. Despite this return, his base remained in Paris throughout the 1970s and until the mid-1980s, even as he traveled frequently and gained increasing international recognition. During this period, he managed to keep up his production without long breaks, focusing on groups of humanoid figures engaged in all sorts of activities (from sex to playful games, from rituals to processions) against dark backgrounds that border on monochrome. In his work *Untitled* (1978), figures with spears proliferate in a composition whose spiral movement suggests a battle. The brushstrokes, revealing the color of the wood beneath, lend dynamism to the arms, legs, and weapons that seem to have just subdued a gigantic body.

Édouard Glissant, *La Cohée du Lamentin. Poétique V.* Paris: Gallimard, 2005, p. 61 – Translated by Sebastião Nascimento.

HAMEDINE KANE

Ksar, Mauritania, 1983. Lives and works between Brussels, Belgium;
Paris, France; and Dakar, Senegal

"Understand heat time / Rock heat / wedded sorrow / vaporous cry / vowel by vowel / made concrete."

The artistic practice of Senegalese-Mauritanian artist and filmmaker Hamedine Kane draws on the experience of exile and nomadism to explore the legacies of African independence and the links between literature, politics, and resistance. In this exhibition, Kane showcases twelve prints and one video from the series *Salesman of Revolt*, inspired by the routine of young peddlers selling books in Dakar's markets and streets. Produced with Indian artist Tejswini Narayan Sonawane, these prints are based on the covers of important works of African diasporic literature, such as *Between the World and Me* by Ta-Nehisi Coates, and *C'est le soleil qui m'a brûlée* [*The Sun Hath Looked Upon Me*] by Calixthe Beyala.

The video documents a performance by Kane on the streets of Mumbai, where he replicates the gesture of carrying stacks of books on his head, displacing and re-inscribing those stories onto another territory. As a commissioned work, the artist also presents stitched fabrics, articulating words, symbols and lines inspired by authors such as Édouard Glissant. These fragments compose a poetic cartography of knowledge in transit, somewhere between writing, exile, and imagination.

Édouard Glissant, "Yokes," *The Collected Poems of Édouard Glissant*. Edited by Jeff Humphries. Translated by Jeff Humphries and Melissa Manolas. Minneapolis: University of Minnesota Press, 2005, p. 167.

IRVING PETLIN

Chicago, USA, 1934 - Martha's Vineyard, USA, 2018

> "Petlin's painting begins in the '*inner distance*': in that most remote dwelling, where the movement of our monsters seduces and bewilders us. [...] In Petlin's early canvases, we saw man detach himself from the mud, sprout from the earth—not as a solitary tree nor as a resurrected dead—but as the force that, without faltering, is born of his own effort."

Irving Petlin's work explores landscape as a space of memory, displacement, and historical reverberations. Born in Chicago to Polish Jewish immigrants, he studied at the Art Institute and the Yale School of Art before moving to Paris at the end of the 1950s. There he became associated with artists and intellectuals engaged against the Algerian War, and began experimenting with pastel-a technique that would soon become pivotal in his practice because of its intense and porous chromatic quality, enabling him to combine precision and organicity.

Petlin, between Paris and New York, compiled a body of work steeped in the 20th-century history: wars, exiles, protests, and ghosts permeate his work, where figure and atmosphere merge into what Glissant called the "inner distance." His landscapes are rarely depicted in any literal form: they come across rather as blended masses of saturated colors, from which bodies (human or otherwise) emerge to be dissolved in the atmosphere. He viewed landscapes as surfaces of inscription-not of what can be seen or explained, but of wraiths and fantasies.

Édouard Glissant, "Poétiques," *Le Discours antillais*. Paris: Gallimard, 1997, pp. 445–46. [Free translation]

 # JEAN-CLAUDE GAROUTE
(Tiga)

Jérémie, Haiti, 1935 – Miami, USA, 2006

"He has been made in order to tell the truth about his land."

Jean-Claude Garoute, better known as Tiga, was one of the most influential figures in the 20th-century Haitian art. A visual artist, ceramist, poet, and educator, he founded the Poto Mitan cultural center in Port-au-Prince in 1968, as well as the Saint Soleil school and the Kaytiga center in the 1970s. Committed to art rooted in voodoo teachings and ancestral Haitian practices, and rejecting the separation between high art and popular expression, Tiga conceived and promoted the *rotation artistique* [artistic rotation], a pedagogical and philosophical method that shifts artistic creation from the sphere of individual talent to a process of inner listening, experimentation, and circulation between different media such as painting, sculpture, dance, writing, and music. Rotation implies precisely this continuous passage between media and languages as a way of liberating the gesture from technical impositions.

Tiga's works often evoke hybrid and mutating forms: human figures entangled with natural and spiritual forces. His undulating lines resemble songs or visual prayers; his spiraling, gestural strokes give shape to a living mythology in which landscape, spirit, and matter seem to become intertwined.

Édouard Glissant, *The Ripening*. Translated by Frances Frenaye. New York: George Braziller, 1959, p. 103.

JOSÉ GAMARRA

Tacuarembó, Uruguay, 1934. Lives and works in Paris, France

> "This South American space-time capsule is so living, so organic we cannot distinguish that which was from that which is or will be, or the forest from the plantation, the blood of the beast from the blood of the land, the spurt of water from the cascade of oil, the primeval bird from the helicopter."

Before settling in France–where he formed close ties with Édouard Glissant at the Galerie du Dragon–José Gamarra lived in Rio de Janeiro and São Paulo in the early 1960s, an important stage in his formative years. After moving to Paris in 1963, Gamarra experimented with reconciling the nimble language of New Figuration and imaginary depictions of jungles, thus combining elements of the Brazilian landscape with critical references to traits shared across Latin American countries, ranging from the colonial legacy to the burgeoning state violence in the region.

Blending reality, symbolism, myth, and history, Gamarra's landscapes became progressively more detailed, often emulating the repertoire of European genre painting. *L'inaccessible…* [The Inaccessible…] (1986/1987) renders with meticulous skill a humid, dark tropical environment populated throughout with allegorical figures hinting at both the Amerindian ancestral presence and US imperialism. And the work on paper *Untitled* (1986) revolves around a prowling panther in one of the artist's rare night scenes.

Édouard Glissant, "Four Artists in Chiaroscuro," *The Unesco Courier*, July 1984, p. 27.

JULIEN CREUZET

Le Blanc-Mesnil, France, 1986. Lives and works in Montreuil, France

"Far away the country rang out. In the plowed clearing / Between the high folds of inscrutable trees / This noise, beaten bronze fell in grass / We were two, people of night and people of clearing / First country / That we did not know was first / Any more than the wandering sheep knows the river / That tears him with a water like thorns"

Julien Creuzet's work combines with no hierarchy poetry, moving images, installation, sculpture, sound, and choreography. Raised in Martinique, Creuzet constantly evokes his experience with the Caribbean landscape and culture, as well as the ideas of authors such as Aimé Césaire and Édouard Glissant. As the first artist-in-residence with the Édouard Glissant Art Fund, hosted at the Martinican poet's home, Creuzet developed his own form of "archipelagic thinking," connecting geographies, times, and affections scattered throughout African diasporic history.

In this exhibition, the artist presents a Corten steel sculpture related to the history of the Tietê and Pinheiros rivers in São Paulo, Brazil. The work is part of a larger series he produced for the exhibition *Águas subterrâneas: narrativas de confluência* [Underground Waters: Narratives in Confluence], held in partnership with Frac Poitou-Charentes in connection with the France-Brazil 2025 Season. By visually bridging those distant landscapes, this artwork examines how memory, violence, and time shape and silence the materials that make up the world.

Édouard Glissant, "The Country of Before," *The Collected Poems of Édouard Glissant*. Edited by Jeff Humphries. Translated by Jeff Humphries and Melissa Manolas. Minneapolis: University of Minnesota Press, 2005, p. 185.

KELLY SINNAPAH MARY

Saint-François, Guadeloupe, 1981. Lives and works in Le Gosier, Guadeloupe

"A landscape. What is that, to man? The deliberate series of an always fugitive rapport. The place, stolen off at last, whose formula trembles. [...] What is a country if not the rooted necessity of the relation to the world? [...] Every poetics *of our day* signals its landscape."

Kelly Sinnapah Mary's work spans the historical and ecological layers of the Caribbean. A descendant of Indian workers brought to the island by the French government between 1854 and 1889 to replace enslaved labor, her artistic practice combines African, Asian, Amerindian, and European heritages. In sculptures, tapestries and, above all, paintings, she fancies characters and scenes with echoes to family memories, literary references, and diasporic histories, always with the Caribbean landscape, its forests and mangroves, as her ambience and character.

Sinnapah Mary's choice of colors and the movement of her brushstrokes turn density and temperature into features shared by the environments and protagonists of her works. Through such alignment between people and territories, she conveys playful and domestic references imbricated with issues pertaining to colonialism, forced miscegenation, and displacement. In the series *The Book of Violette* (2025), Mary devises a character inspired by her grandmother, who crosses the canvas in constant metamorphosis—as a girl, an elderly woman, an animal, a deity.

Édouard Glissant, *Poetic Intention.* Translated by Nathanaël with Anne Malena. New York: Nightboat Books, 2010, p. 64.

M. EMILE

"The painted symbol coexists with the oral sign. It is the tightly woven texture of oral expression that is introduced into (and the key to) Haitian painting. The Creole language in Haiti does not suffer the repercussions of the radical ambiguities created by writing, because of an early confrontation with writing and the creation of a dense cultural 'hinterland.' Haitian Creole is practically insulated from *transformation*. The painted symbol is its refuge."

An important Caribbean artistic expression, Haitian folk painting emerged in the 1940s around the Centre d'Art in Port-au-Prince, from which countless artists set out to render depictions of various aspects of daily life in their communities. They depicted celebrations, customs, landscapes, and rituals on the same canvas, intertwining nature, spirituality, everyday life, and politics.

The painting credited to M. Emile—a familiar name in several collections of Haitian folk art—condenses that universe into a complex composition. The artist treats the earth, the trees, and the bodies with the same formal density, dissolving hierarchies between figure and background. The group of people is immersed in the lush environment, which is not only a backdrop but also an agent: a sacred Mapou tree seems to have been uprooted by a storm, triggering multiple actions cascading into a ritual associated with Haitian voodoo. More than a mere description of a social custom, the work blends the visible and the invisible by representing a spiritual, dynamic, and shared landscape.

Édouard Glissant, "On Haitian Painting," *Caribbean Discourse: Selected Essays.* Translated by J. Michael Dash. Charlottesville: University Press of Virgnia, 1992, p. 155.

MANTHIA DIAWARA

Bamako, Mali, 1953. Lives and works in New York, USA;
Abu Dhabi, United Arab Emirates; and Yene, Senegal

"The world trembles, becomes creolized, that is to say, it multiplies, blending its forests and seas, its deserts and ice floes, all of which are threatened, changing and exchanging its customs and cultures and what it had just yesterday called its identities, most of which have now been decimated. Archipelagic thought trembles with this tremor, unsettled by these geological crises, pierced by these human earthquakes, yet it finds rest alongside rivers that are finally calming and moons that languidly linger."

Manthia Diawara was born in Mali, studied in French Guinea and France, moved to the United States, and now lives between New York, Abu Dhabi, and Yene. His journey provided him with a complex and moving perspective on African and African diasporic thought. A critic and professor, writer and filmmaker, Diawara devotes part of his work to documenting and discussing the contributions of thinkers such as Wole Soyinka, Angela Davis, David Hammons, and especially Édouard Glissant, with whom he established a strong bond of friendship that resonates in his ongoing reflections.

A Letter from Yene (2022) is a letter in film form, pieced together from encounters in the Senegalese village where Diawara lives part of the year. As global economic dynamics reshape the region's coastline in the name of purported progress, traditional fishing practices come under strain, and men and women must resort to impoverished survival tactics that risk aggravating the local ecological imbalance. The film takes a close look at the workers, overcoming linguistic and cultural differences to discuss the imbrication of histories and responsibilities in a shared and vulnerable ecosystem. Diawara does not hold back: as both narrator and local resident, he embraces the twists and turns, the silences and the subtle gestures, immersing himself in the contradictions of the landscape he inhabits.

Édouard Glissant, *La Cohée du Lamentin. Poétique V.* Paris: Gallimard, 2005. p. 75 – Translated by Sebastião Nascimento.

MÉLINDA FOURN

Paris, France, 1995. Lives and works between Dakar, Senegal and Kumasi, Ghana

"An act of survival. In the silent universe of the Plantation, oral expression, the only form possible for the slaves, was discontinuously organized. As tales, proverbs, sayings, songs appeared-as much in the Creole-speaking world as elsewhere-they bore the stamp of this discontinuity. [...] As if these texts were striving for disguise beneath the symbol, working to say without saying. This is what 1 have referred to elsewhere as detour [...]."

Mélinda Fourn is a French-Beninese artist whose practice is grounded in direct contact with West African technical skills such as goldsmithing, weaving, ceramics, and metalwork. Having grown up in France and studied at the École des Beaux-Arts in Paris, she moved to Ghana after an exchange program at the Kwame Nkrumah University of Science and Technology in Kumasi, settling between Dakar and Accra. Her research involves learning from master craftsmen resisting the erosion of traditional crafts.

By reshaping everyday objects into new scales and arrangements, Fourn explores the symbolic dimension of craftsmanship.

Her works offer a broader interpretation of landscape: not as a backdrop, but as a surface for inscription. Her installation for the exhibition comprises multiple pieces assembled from scrap metal discarded by metalworking shops in Dakar. The symmetrical arrangements of the fragments refer to the composition of ornaments, while their flat character and their contrast with the wall make them akin to graphic signs of an indecipherable script, somewhere between ideogram and Adinkra. Technical skill and language merge: both depend on transmission, on memory, and on the body.

Édouard Glissant, "Closed Place, Open Word," *Poetics of Relation*. Translated by Betsy Wing. Ann Arbor: University of Michigan Press, 1997, p. 68.

MELVIN EDWARDS

Houston, USA, 1937. Lives and works between New York, USA; and Dakar, Senegal

> "First the slave trade: being snatched away from our original matrix. The journey that has fixed in us the unceasing tug of Africa against which we must paradoxically struggle today in order to take root in our rightful land. The motherland is also for us the inaccessible land."

Melvin Edwards roots his work in the struggle for civil rights in the United States, reflecting tensions between abstract art, historical violence, and black resistance. Since the 1960s, the artist has explored metal welding—chains, tools, nails, hooks—as a sculptural language with the power to condense conflict and memory. His best-known series, *Lynch Fragments* (1963-ongoing), spans several decades and different contexts: originally created in reaction to racial brutality in the US, it has expanded to comment on wars, paying tribute to historical figures and investigating African ancestry. Both the materials used—such as hammers and chisels forged into dense compositions—and the titles of his artworks bring to mind exhausting physical labor and violence done to black bodies.

While rubbing shoulders with Édouard Glissant, Edwards saw similarities between his artistic approach and the ideas of the Martinican philosopher. The notion of tremor, central to Glissant's philosophy, is present in the artist's works as a restrained energy, a vibration between sign and silence. Moreover, his works embody something that greatly interested the poet: the ability to use cries, poetry, and discourse to transform signs usually associated exclusively with trauma.

Édouard Glissant, "Our Relationship with the Context," *Caribbean Discourse: Selected Essays*. Translated by J. Michael Dash. Charlottesville: University Press of Virginia, 1989, pp. 160-61.

MINIA BIABIANY

Basse-Terre, Guadeloupe, 1988. Lives and works in Saint-Claude, Guadeloupe

> "I have already said that this landscape is more powerful in our literature than the physical size of countries would lead us to believe. The fact is that it is not saturated with a single History but effervescent with intermingled histories, spread around, rushing to fuse without destroying or reducing each other."

Minia Biabiany grew up in the shadow of the volcano La Soufrière, in a family with strong interest for the creole garden and the perpetuation of its associated healing knowledges. Her body of work explores the imbrications between bodies, language, and land by questionning the relation with personal stories or landmarks that can help redetermine human and more-than-human narratives within a colonial context. The hanging pieces of burnt wood and banana fiber braids featured in the exhibition were originally part of the show *the sky with root-eyed* (2025), in which the artist matched those materials with pieces of ceramic and water to give shape to a made-up constellation of a frog drawn from existing stars of a night sky of Guadeloupe; the frog chanting pulses at the beginning and end of each day in all the archipelago.

The cuts on the pendants' burnt wood pieces resemble distinctive silhouettes of the volcano, animals, and medicinal plants from the Guadeloupe territory all connected with cyclical rythms, often used as time references from the past and the present. The banana flower, in particular, is fraught with multiple tensions: it evokes uses of its healing properties for the uterus and Biabiany's research on her lineage, while revealing the contamination caused by the pesticide chlordecone, widely used on banana plantations until the mid-1990s, with lingering impacts on soil, water, and bodies.

Édouard Glissant, "Poetics," *Caribbean Discourse: Selected Essays*. Translated by J. Michael Dash. Charlottesville: University Press of Virginia, 1989, p. 154.

 # NOLAN OSWALD DENNIS

Lusaka, Zambia, 1988. Lives and works in Johannesburg, South Africa

"To write is to say: the world."

Nolan Oswald Dennis pursues a practice aimed at unsettling the systems that sustain the colonial world order: its organization of space, time, knowledge, and matter. Through installations, diagrams, and videos, their work investigates the invisible forms of control that shape the limits of political imagination.

In *recurse 4 a late planet* (2024-ongoing), Dennis develops a mural-diagram based on tracking potentially dangerous asteroids orbiting Earth, alongside tracing a history of stone-throwing in protest actions. Together, these cosmic political phenomena provide a social history of rocks as archives of catastrophe, displacement, and reinvention. Between cosmology, geology, and mapping technologies, the artwork explores the forces that sustain the world as we know it—and those that have the potential to unravel it. Dennis's diagrams operate as speculative tools geared toward envisioning forms of life outside dominant models: subterranean, cosmic, deviant. In these diagrams, the combination of information and insights gathered from a variety of contexts is just as important as their distribution in graphic space and their mode of presentation. Research, storytelling, criticism, and visuality come together to set the stage for a reflection on rocks as allegories for justice.

Édouard Glissant, *Treatise on the Whole-World.* Translated by Celia Britton. Liverpool: Liverpool University Press, 2020, p. 73.

ÖYVIND FAHLSTRÖM

São Paulo, Brazil, 1928 - Stockholm, Sweden, 1976

> "Even from the point of view of identity, the scope of the poem results from the search, wandering and often anxious, of conjunctions of forms and structures that allow an idea of the world, expressed in the poem's own place, to meet (or not) other ideas of the world."

The only child of a Swedish mother and a Norwegian father, Öyvind Fahlström was born in São Paulo and traveled to Sweden in 1938 to visit his family. Due to the outbreak of the Second World War, he was prevented from returning to Brazil and remained in Europe. He pursued his studies in Stockholm, where he wrote a pioneering defense of concrete poetry: the manifesto *Hätila ragulpr på fåtskliaben* (1953)—a title borrowed from the Swedish translation of A.A. Milne's *Winnie the Pooh*, in a scene where the character Owl struggles to say "Happy Birthday." The text was published in February 1954 in the magazine *Odysse*.

Inspired by Pierre Schaeffer's *musique concrète,* Fahlström proposed an approach in which language was treated as sonic, graphic, and visual material, breaking with semantic linearity and expanding the expressive potential of vernacular speech. Around the same time, while living in Rome, he began work on *Opera*, his first major visual piece. He continued to write cultural criticism for Stockholm daily newspapers and to produce both concrete poetry and theater works.

In the 1960s, after relocating to New York, Fahlström transposed these principles to the visual field with his so-called "variable works": compositions made of movable elements that could be rearranged by viewers. During this period, he also deepened his engagement with comic books and the language of mass media.

His work includes paintings, drawings, prints, poems, happenings, installations, and films. Alternately associated with Dadaism, New Figuration, or Conceptualism, Fahlström does not fit into categories. In the 1970s, he produced some of his most recognized pieces: diagrammatic compositions of words and signs, visual and poetic systems in which language, image, and landscape drift apart, as a means of contemplating the world in its instability.

Édouard Glissant, *Treatise on the Whole-World.* Translated by Celia Britton. Liverpool: Liverpool University Press, 2020, p. 19.

PANCHO QUILICI

Caracas, Venezuela, 1954. Lives and works in Paris, France

> "What Pancho Quilici reveals here is that the destroyed city is still a forest, that it signifies, on the same level as earth or bark, our shared eternity. This relationship of rediscovered unity, above and beyond the dizzying expanse of space, is what sustains us."

Living in Paris since the early 1980s, Pancho Quilici also remained active in Venezuela, frequently exhibiting at the Galería Minotauro in Caracas, managed by Cecília Ayala, who also ran the Galerie du Dragon in Paris, starting in 1986. Traveling back and forth, he built up a wide network of connections, side by side with his partner, Polish artist, Gabriela Morawetz.

Breaking away from the Venezuelan kinetic-constructivist canon, Quilici based his practice on drawing and on his keen interest in archaeology, topography, architecture, and topology. Landscapes, colonial buildings, Mesoamerican ruins, and invented spaces all converge in works like his collage on paper *Untitled* (1985), featured on the cover of the folio edition of Glissant's novel *Tout-Monde* [Whole-World]. In *Passagem ao centro 2* [Passage to the Center 2] (2000), lines drawn with precision intersect upon a base of fluid emulsions applied somewhat randomly. Quilici's images seem to emerge from a conception of time and space that defies ideas of chronological linearity and territorial division. In Glissant's words, they can be simultaneously perceived as "the boundless memory of the world and the sharp transparency of a new dawn."

Édouard Glissant, "Metamorphoses de la pierre," in *Pancho Quilici*. Paris: Galerie du Dragon, 1985, p. 8 – Translated by Sebastião Nascimento.

PAUL MAYER

Forbach, France, 1922 - Amiens, France, 1998

> "The trace is not an unfinished path where one stumbles helplessly, nor an alley closed on itself, bordering a territory. The trace goes into the land, which will never again be a territory."

Paul Mayer was a poet, linguist, and artist born in Alsace, a region disputed between France and Germany during the Second World War. Drafted into the German army, he endured years of combat and forced displacement until he deliberately surrendered to the Red Army in 1945, and was taken to a labor camp in East Prussia.

After the war, he resumed his studies, moved to Paris, and got involved in the art scene at the Galerie du Dragon, where he met Édouard Glissant. He started painting between 1969 and 1970, and between 1973 and 1974 put out his first poetry-paintings. In these works, Mayer merges paint and words: cut-out poems are applied to surfaces stained by drips and spills of paint. In some pieces, the paper is burned, turning combustion into a poetic and political gesture. These procedures–collage, cutting, the use of language as visual material, and paper burning–place Mayer as the heir to an array of different artistic and linguistic traditions of the early 20th-century and post-war Europe, such as Dadaism, Surrealism, Lettrism, and Situationism.

Édouard Glissant, *Treatise on the Whole-World*. Translated by Celia Britton. Liverpool: Liverpool University Press, 2020, p. 10, italics in the original; presented here in roman by the publisher..

PEDRO FRANÇA

Rio de Janeiro, Brazil, 1984. Lives and works in São Paulo, Brazil

"Everything bursts open, everything sounds and blows in the wind. Everything loses its way and goes down, only to rise again to this wind. It is nothing but assault, vertigo and, drifting, this time. Fields and hill and ravine, mountains and bays! A person who outdoes you in grand passion: a landscape. An imprisoned spring, a muddy delta. And then the cry and the word, in the moment and in duration. Everything to me is seasons and rhythms, that I push towards the single Season."

Over the past thirteen years, the common thread running through Pedro França's artwork has been his interest in allegorical depictions of contemporary society. The images and scenes he creates convey an open narrative meaning, alluding not exclusively to a single fact or episode, but combining and shifting suggestive elements, many of which are drawn from a variety of iconographies from art history and beyond. In his work, there is no single story being told, but rather a bundle of reminiscences and associations that the artist offers to audiences so that they may match their desires, experiences, fears, and traumas.

Resisting the demand for efficiency and clarity, França stands on the side of ambivalence and ambiguity. He has recently committed to crafting landscapes permeated by a sense of absurdity, with environmental elements, figures, and beings gathered in situations of neglect-a kind of desert of expectations. The repetition of scenes and figures across countless drawings, paintings, and frescoes turns them into images at least as pervasive as dreams and prophecies that awaken unconscious fears and desires.

Édouard Glissant, *Treatise on the Whole-World*. Translated by Celia Britton. Liverpool: Liverpool University Press, 2020, p. 45.

POL TABURET

Paris, France, 1997. Lives and works in Paris, France

"Glowing fires scarcely sparked by dizziness. Rainshower motionless. Dwindling echoes. A tree trunk slivers against the rim of the sun, stubbornness, stiff but melting. Call the keepers of silence with their feet in the river. Call the river that used to spill over the rocks."

Pol Taburet works with painting and sculpture, creating hybrid and spectral figures that seem to emerge like revenants. His family roots in Guadeloupe–his grandmother was born on the island–influence his work, permeated by personal and collective mythologies, African diasporic religions such as Quimbois and Voodoo, trap culture, and European painterly tradition. The creatures and scenes he creates–full of traces of dreams, delirium, and ritual–appear to spring from another plane: incandescent eyes, gleaming teeth, bodies in transit between the visible and the shapeless.

Taburet alternates between acrylic paint for airbrushing, resin-based paint, and oil stick to construct dense and unsettling surfaces. His figures are not illustrative: they arise, impose themselves, and contaminate the space. They are born of nocturnal environments–bedrooms, clubs, stages–but also seem to condense something of the landscapes from which they emerge: dense vegetation, heavy atmospheres, silences pierced by invisible presences. The artwork on display in the exhibition, produced in Brazil, reflects on Taburet's journeys through multiple territories around the Atlantic, bringing to light their points of convergence and transformation.

Édouard Glissant, "The Burning Beach," *Poetics of Relation.* Translated by Betsy Wing. Ann Arbor: University of Michigan Press, 1997, p. 209.

Paris, France, 1984. Lives and works in Paris, France

"The story has no clear projection of start, development, or ending. The story projects itself onto beginnings, as much as it projects itself onto endings, but has no logical or metaphysical continuity from start to finish. The story is the origin of Caribbean literary expression."

Raphaël Barontini evokes, through painting, collage, sewing, digital prints, and silkscreen prints on textile elements potential narratives of the African and Caribbean diaspora. His practice–spanning performances as well–threads together colonial archives, popular imagination, and contemporary techniques onto portraits that challenge hegemonic forms of representation and scramble symbols of power, sovereignty, and vitality hailing from myriad origins and temporalities.

In *La clairière du Bois-Caïman* [The Clearing of Bois-Caïman] (2024), the artist draws on the ceremony held in 1791 in the site of Bois-Caïman, in the north of Saint-Domingue, where spiritual leaders such as Dutty Boukman and Cécile Fatiman led a voodoo ritual that preceded and fueled the mass uprising against the French slave system, a turning point for the Haitian Revolution. In this monumental piece, Barontini mixes dyed and embroidered fabrics, screen-printed images, and heraldic displays to create a landscape-territory of symbolic insurrection. His treatment of the material, the intensity of colors, and the mix of symbols conjure up memory and storytelling as meaningful forms of resistance.

RAYANA RAYO

Recife, Brazil, 1989. Lives and works in Recife, Brazil

"To know what within your eyes cradles / A bay of sky a bird / The sea, a devolved caress / The sun returned here / Beauty of space or hostage / Of tentacular future / Every word is lost therefore / In the silence of Waters"

Rayana Rayo's work is steeped in her experience of the climate and the tides, of the mangroves, sandbanks, and islands of her native city of Recife. Her paintings, with thick brushstrokes and colors fine-tuned in their tonal balance, are evocative of humid atmospheres and rounded topographies inhabited by hybrid elements–between plant, animal, and dreamlike beings. Instead of conveying linear narratives, she favors fabulating links between bodies, fragments, and affective atmospheres. Likewise, she doesn't handle the landscape through perspective or description, but rather by bringing all the elements within the composition out of the same material as the painting, thus harnessing their synesthetic properties (their ability to evoke heat and smell, silence and desire, wind and solitude).

For this exhibition, Rayo presents a large-scale commissioned painting; she is also part of a research and residency project at Édouard Glissant's Maison du Diamant, in Martinique, and at the African Art Collection of the Oscar Niemeyer Museum in Curitiba.

Édouard Glissant, "A Field of Islands," *The Collected Poems of Édouard Glissant*. Edited by Jeff Humphries. Translated by Jeff Humphries with Melissa Manolas. Minneapolis: University of Minnesota Press, 2005, p. 37.

REBECA CARAPIÁ

Salvador, Brazil, 1988. Lives and works in São Paulo, Brazil

"Thus, that which protects the Diverse we call opacity."

Rebeca Carapiá's artistic practice encompasses sculpture, installation, printmaking, drawing, and text. Her works foster friction between language, body, and territory, cutting across debates on memory, environmental racism, ancestral technologies, gender dissidence, and economies of precariousness. By bending, cutting, and warping metals such as copper and iron she crafts a kind of calligraphy connected to the peripheral landscapes of Salvador—zones of intersection, erasure, and resistance, which anchor her artwork. Words, often her starting point, are folded, scratched, and distorted until they become a sculptural presence in space, forming a kind of landscape-writing, or writing-landscape.

In this exhibition, Carapiá showcases pieces she developed during an art residency in São Paulo in 2022. The drawings, created on paper, echo the same gestures she performs on metal, but on a different scale and facing another kind of resistance. Between lines, stains, and cuts, the artist sketches a geography of the body in transit, pierced by layers of São Paulo landscape and memories of life in Salvador.

Édouard Glissant, "Expanse and Filiation," *Poetics of Relation*. Translated by Betsy Wing. Ann Arbor: University of Michigan Press, 1997, p. 62.

ROBERTO MATTA

Santiago, Chile, 1911 - Civitavecchia, Italy, 2002

> "From this point on, the non-painter painter will tirelessly combine the universes he creates: the cosmic space, the fractured screens, the radiant characters, the proliferation of near-tropical fertility, the antithetical forces of desire and rejection. These combinations will in turn give rise to new discoveries, never becoming formally fixed or fully finished creations."

Roberto Matta's path is defined by displacement, a constant wandering that led him to declare himself a "resident of the world." His architecture studies in Santiago helped him land a job at Le Corbusier's office in Paris, granting him the opportunity to travel to many European countries in the 1930s. In 1937, he witnessed Picasso's *Guernica* taking shape and, in the same year, met André Breton, who encouraged him to publish the article "Mathématique sensible, architecture du temps" [Sensitive Mathematics–Architecture of Time] (plublished in *Minotaure*, 1938), which marked the beginning of his journey into Surrealism. Matta developed a unique approach to spontaneity, automatism, and the unconscious, broadening the scope of surrealist painting by addressing the pictorial space as an emotional field. His paintings, described by Glissant as "extravagant eruptions," are more spatial than narrative, enacting the visual projection of interior, affective, and multidimensional landscapes.

Matta and Glissant shared a deep and long-lasting dialogue. Their active engagement with the Galerie du Dragon is highlighted by the publication of *Terres Nouvelles* [New Lands] (1956), featuring an essay by the poet and an engraving by the artist. The painting *La Montagne pelée ne fume plus, elle fleurit* [The Pelée Mountain no longer smokes, it blooms] (1958), a reference to the mighty Martinican volcano, Mount Pelée, is a point of convergence for their worldviews, exploring the possibilities both of them saw for approaching landscape through the prism of affections (and vice versa). Glissant's trip to Egypt, recounted in *Journal d'un voyage sur le Nil* [Diary of a Journey on the Nile] (1988), was also undertaken in the company of the artist.

Édouard Glissant, "Préface," in *Matta: dessins 1937-1989*. Nîmes: Carré d'art, Musée d'Art Contemporain, 1990 - Translated by Sebastião Nascimento.

SERGE HÉLÉNON

Fort-de-France, Martinique, 1934. Lives and works in Nice, France

"Shards, debris, ashes. What barely survives of reality when it has been reduced to the liminal or terminal stage of waste or residue. What lurks in forsaken places, oppressed countries, doomed architecture, decaying piles of wood and straw, the immobility of rust and old grease, which must nevertheless be transmuted into ancient novelties, into tremors coming from far away. [...] The seas come trembling before the works that lay here."

Serge Hélénon's work straddles painting, relief, and *assemblage* as an exercise in memory and displacement. He was educated in Martinique and France, and lived for more than two decades in Ivory Coast, where he and other Martinicans founded the École Négro-Caraïbe (1970), a landmark in the alliances of the black diaspora. Hélénon developed a language that breaks with the exoticism of representation while challenging the convention of the flat pictorial surface. Working with scrap materials—wood, fabric, pigments—he crafts compositions in which color, relief, and remnant intertwine. His works operate as rags of history: they condense layers of time and fragments of worlds in collision.

In his stormy compositions, Hélénon gives visual form to the idea of *trace*: vestiges of lost origins that pave the way for the coexistence of times and cultures. Glissant wrote about them: "Then the remnants rise and soar [...]. What grows there is the encounter of differences, the force that breeds [...]." It is about the possibility of recomposing what the world tore apart in its storms and shipwrecks, as in the object *Bwa Mémoire* (2000), whose name in Kréyòl could be translated as "memory tree."

Édouard Glissant, "Un feu secret," preface to Dominique Berthet, *Hélénon. Lieux de peinture*. Paris: HC éditions, 2006, p. 4 – Translated by Sebastião Nascimento.

SHEILA HICKS

Nebraska, USA, 1934. Lives and works in Paris, France

"Is there a language of truth? A discourse? Certainly not, but rather one of those who claim it. Just as there is no language of the living. Yet nothing is alive that does not express itself. The expression of living beings constitutes their speech, whereas the expression of Truth may be its denial or its hidden silence. Nevertheless, if we distinguish between speech and language, we can see that there is no language for what could be Truth."

Sheila Hicks's interest on textiles while studying painting at the Yale School of Art caught the attention of her professor, Josef Albers, who invited her to attend a research and teaching trip to Santiago, Chile, in 1957. She seized that opportunity, turning it into an extensive journey through South America, from Venezuela to Tierra del Fuego, visiting local artisans and researching textile techniques and ancestral cosmogonies. It was the start of a poetic research that continues to this day, in which the artist explores textile thread and fiber with special attention to their structural properties and in dialogue with the repertoire she came across in South American landscapes and communities.

With an output not welcomed in any of the fields of art or crafting, after living and working in Mexico since 1959, Hicks moved to Paris in 1964, where she joined Chilean artists and married Enrique Zañartu, establishing contact with immigrants fleeing Pinochet's dictatorship and with the scene at the Galerie du Dragon and Espacio Latinoamericano (where she held her first exhibition in Paris, in 1968). In *Bâtons de parole* [Talking Sticks] (2024-2025), Hicks connects traditions by weaving multicolored threads around objects that remind us of the right to speak given to those who hold them.

Édouard Glissant, "Rien n'est vrai, tout est vivant," *Francofonia* no.63, Fall 2012, p. 211-26 - Translated by Sebastião Nascimento.

SYLVIE SÉMA GLISSANT

Lives and works in Paris, France

"The wind is expansion and the sea is depth. One must combine both to understand the world."

Both an artist and a clinical psychoanalyst, Sylvie Séma Glissant heads the Institut du Tout-Monde since its founding by Édouard Glissant in 2006. Her early career, in the late 1980s, was influenced by interactions with artists such as Roberto Matta and Augustin Cárdenas, and evolved in parallel with her meaningful dialogue with Glissant. That encounter yielded a rich legacy that includes several drawings combining the strokes and calligraphy of both artists, as well as the symbiotic writing of the book *La Terre magnétique: Les Errances de Rapa Nui, l'Île de Pâques* [The Magnetic Earth: The Wanderings of Rapa Nui, Easter Island] (2007).

In her paintings, drawings, and engravings, Sylvie Séma consistently favors dark tones, spread in expansive gestures, without sketches or contour lines. With the agile movements of her hand, she comes up with suggestions of landscapes: evocations of marks left on the landscape as testimonies of wanderings, migratory routes, diasporas, tides, earthquakes, and other flows, even those invisible to the naked eye. *Dismantling Boats of Disaster* (2023), one of her large-format prints, merges timelines through a combination of engraving and monotyping to convey the simultaneous destruction and reconstruction of a boat amid the restless rhythms of a stormy sea.

Édouard Glissant and Sylvie Séma Glissant, *La Terre magnétique: Les Errances de Rapa Nui, l'Île de Pâques*. Paris: Seuil, 2007, p. 106. [Free translation]

TARIK KISWANSON

Halmstad, Sweden, 1986. Lives and works in Paris, France

"Wandering enables us to moor ourselves to that drift that does not get lost."

Tarik Kiswanson is a visual artist and poet. Born into a Palestinian family that exiled in Jerusalem, by way of Tripoli and Amman, before settling in Halmstad, he now works and lives in Paris. His artistic practice–spanning sculpture, video, performance, and writing–examines how stories of loss, migration, and regeneration are entangled across multiple temporal and spatial dimensions, often through relationships that are invisible or not readily perceptible.

In this exhibition, Kiswanson presents three interrelated works that reflect on displacement, temporality, and the transmission of knowledge across generations. In *The Wait* (2025), a sculptural form–evocative of a seed, pod, or cocoon–rests precariously on the edge of a Móveis Cimo chair, a type of furniture used in the waiting areas of Brazilian immigration offices during the early 1950s. The pale, smooth surface of the object and its delicate balance evoke a suspended temporality, oscillating between anonymity and inscription, regeneration and erasure. In the video *The Reading Room* (2020), a young boy learning to read hesitantly stutters fragments from texts by Édouard Glissant, Gayatri Chakravorty Spivak, and Noam Chomsky–books drawn from the shelves of "The Edward W. Said Reading Room" at Columbia University. Similarly, in *I Tried as Hard as I Could* (2019), a child struggles to transcribe a poem in Arabic, contending with the linguistic estrangement produced by the migration of his Algerian grandparents to France. In both videos, the struggle for articulation becomes a place of converging loss, continuity, re-elaboration, and becoming–revealing the complexities of making meaning within a fractured, diasporic condition.

Édouard Glissant, *Treatise on the Whole-World.* Translated by Celia Britton. Liverpool: Liverpool University Press, 2020, p. 39.

 # TIAGO SANT'ANA

Santo Antônio de Jesus, Brazil, 1990. Lives and works in Salvador, Brazil

"Experience of the abyss lies inside and outside the abyss. The torment of those who never escaped it: straight from the belly of the slave ship into the violet belly of the ocean depths they went. But their ordeal did not die; it quickened into this continuous/discontinuous thing: the panic of the new land, the haunting of the former land, finally the alliance with the imposed land, suffered and redeemed. [...] We cry our cry of poetry. Our boats are open, and we sail them for everyone."

Tiago Sant'Ana's practice makes use of multiple languages–drawing, painting, video, embroidery, sculpture, writing–to articulate a poetics of African diasporic memory rooted in dignity and care. The artist probes the relationships between body, history, and journey, drawing on the Yoruba concept of *itutu* to devise a visual ethic of stillness and contemplation.

In the video *Apneia* [Apnea] (2024), the song of a solitary whale, inspired by the 52-Hertz Whale–a real animal whose vocalization, inaudible to other whales, dooms it to eternal isolation–is the starting point for an allegory of the silenced black voices in the Atlantic crossings. Embedded in a kind of articulated puppet moving in a syncopated manner, the song echoes the immeasurable toll of deaths and also the poetic persistence of diasporic sounds that endured the Atlantic crossing and continue to endlessly reverberate.

Édouard Glissant, "The Open Boat," *Poetics of Relation*. Translated by Betsy Wing. Ann Arbor: University of Michigan Press, 1997, pp. 7, 9.

VICTOR ANICET

Le Marigot, Martinique, 1938. Lives and works in Le Marigot, Martinique

> "Ornaments and masks from the Americas and Africas spring forth in a single blossoming, which we are keen to call hybrid, and whose creolizing development we celebrate. They dwell in the *tray* of memory."

Born to a fisherman father and a sugar mill worker mother, Victor Anicet came into contact with Arawak ceramics as a child while accompanying archaeological excavations in his hometown. In Paris, he visited the Musée de l'Homme and came face to face with the erasure of his culture. Back in Martinique in 1967, he held the exhibition *Soleil noir* [Black Sun] (1970) and co-founded the Fwomajé collective (1984), dedicated to promoting Afro-Caribbean and Amerindian aesthetics. His friendship with Édouard Glissant permeated his career, with decades of dialogue that inspired him to embrace the multiple, unfinished, unassimilable, and opaque nature of the historical experience.

Whether in paintings or ceramics, Anicet designs synthetic forms that reframe multicultural symbolic references, allegories of colonial trauma, and poetic images of the Caribbean archipelago in a vocabulary of his own, a landscape of signs with no words. The work *Carcan* [Shakles] (n.d.), for example, alludes to the iron shackles used to restrain enslaved people, turning their silhouette into a new visual script.

Musée Martiniquais des Arts des Amériques - Maison de l'Amérique Latine, 1999 - Translated by Sebastião Nascimento.

VICTOR BRAUNER

Piatra Neamț, Romania, 1903 – Paris, France, 1966

"To imagine the transparency of Relation is also to justify the opacity of what impels it. The sacred is of us, of this network, of our wandering, our errantry."

Victor Brauner was active in the Bucharest avant-garde before moving to Paris in 1930, where he helped to boost painting within the Surrealist circle. His artistic career was mired in war, exile, and persecution—he was Jewish, and lived underground during the Nazi occupation of France. From an early age, he nurtured an interest in esoteric practices and non-Western cosmologies. The loss of his left eye in 1938—seven years after painting his *Autoportrait à oeil énucléé* [Self-portrait with Enucleated Eye]—became an emblematic episode, and reinforced his interest in images that emphasized inner vision.

During the war years, Brauner, barred from emigrating like other Surrealists had already done, took refuge in southern France, where he developed experimental techniques based on wax and precarious materials. In that period, he was drawn into studies of occultism, alchemy, kabbalah, tarot, and symbolic systems from ancient Egyptian, Mesoamerican, African, and Oceanic civilizations. He thus forged a pictorial vocabulary in which personal mythology and archaic cosmologies intertwine. His painting *Oui Non* [Yes No] (1947), which Édouard Glissant always kept on his desk, arranges numbers, words, geometries, and signs toward a convergence of symbologies regarding the determination of fate.

Édouard Glissant, "Expanse and Filiation," *Poetics of Relation*. Translated by Betsy Wing. Ann Arbor: University of Michigan Press, 1997, p. 56.

WIFREDO LAM

Sagua la Grande, Cuba, 1902 - Paris, France, 1982

> "The work brings together the elements, forms, and sovereign impulses of reconstructed collective memory. It swiftly arranges them into illuminations and *fiestas* that amount to encounters with the other [...]. Native American roots, African cutouts, fiery baroque plumage, and the strident acrobatics of modernity are all stirred up by the same wind that sways the acoma trees of the Caribbean islands, the palm trees of Cuba, and the redwoods of California."

Born in Cuba of Chinese, Spanish, and African descent, Lam shaped his relation with the Caribbean while wandering: first by way of Madrid, where he joined the fight in the Spanish Civil War, and then in Paris after 1938, where he met Picasso and, through him, André Breton, who would ultimately connect him to Surrealism. Within the movement, Lam, whose production was described by Breton as being "in constant change, movement, and connection," nurtured and was nurtured by keen reflections upon the convergence of distinct forms of knowledge that each person can articulate across multiple roots, cultures, and landscapes. With the outbreak of the Second World War, Lam embarked on a dynamic of continuous displacement through Marseille, Martinique, Havana, and New York-a nomadism that persisted beyond the end of the war.

In between, Lam produced a pictorial output based on the creative profusion of drawings, which be decoded by a system of symbols alone. His complex approach to the post-Cubist and Surrealist legacy embraces elements of Afro-Caribbean spiritual iconography, references to a myriad of mythologies, and personal inventions. Édouard Glissant, who grew close to Lam in the 1950s and onwards, admired how traces of memory converged in the artist's work to illustrate the dynamics of imageries among the peoples of the *Tout-Monde* [Whole-World]. Such reading is consistent with Lam's book-montage *Le nouveau Nouveau Monde* [*The New New World*] (1975), unique in its testimony to how Lam perceived the organicity of his migratory flows and the plurality at the core of his identity.

Édouard Glissant, "Lam, l'envol et la réunion," *CARE. Centre Antillais de Recherces et d'Études*, no. 10, April 1983, p.15 - Translated by Sebastião Nascimento.

ZÉ DI CABEÇA

Salvador, Brazil, 1974. Lives and works in Salvador, Brazil

"In this new museum the visit is no longer something that can assimilate to our usual traditional museums because the visitor is not repetitious. They are going to discover something that is unexpected and unpredictable. To put it another way, the contemporary museum—the new museum that corresponds to and reflects our times—is no longer a museum of representation, classification, orientation, explication, of beauty. It is a museum of chance, guesswork, discovery, exploration of unpredictable beauty."

Zé di Cabeça is an educator, holding a master's degree in psychology, a PhD in public health, and is a postdoctoral fellow in contemporary culture. Born and raised in the Subúrbio Ferroviário neighborhood of Salvador, he founded, alongside his wife, Vilma Santos, the Acervo da Laje: an independent cultural space that serves as a home, museum, and school devoted to the preservation and appreciation of artistic and cultural expressions from the outskirts of Salvador.

Since the pandemic, he has been painting as an extension of his research. At the forefront of that practice, he produces numerous pictures of candles, either isolated or grouped together, made onto pieces of discarded wood, many of which have washed up on the beach, carried by the tides. It is a process rooted in his ongoing investigation into votive offerings and explores painting as writing with light. Through repetition, insistence, and variation in approaching a constant structure, the candles arranged in the Acervo da Laje are relit every day at sunset, composing a luminous landscape that becomes a devotional practice and an act of restitution. As stated in a quote by Adélia Prado, displayed in the artist's studio: "a light bathes the world."

Édouard Glissant, "Beauty and the Beautiful and the Orientation Towards the New Museums" (2011), *The Orientation Towards New Museums*, Symposium, Dakar, Senegal, November 9-10, 2024.

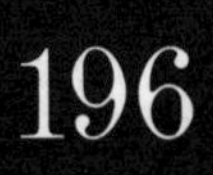

Journal d'un voyage sur le Nile

[Diary of a Journey on the Nile]

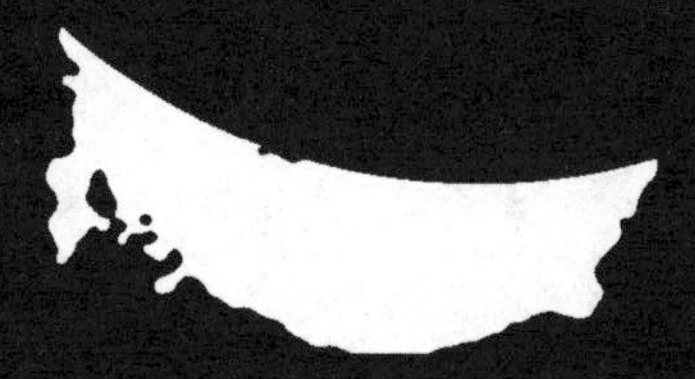

Édouard Glissant

Pages from the manuscript by Édouard Glissant, produced in 1988 during a journey along the Nile River in Egypt.

Édouard Glissant, *Diary of a Journey on the Nile*, 1988. NAF 28894 (67) (NIL), Fonds Édouard Glissant, Bibliothèque nationale de France (BnF). Edited by Instituto Tomie Ohtake / Ana Roman and Paulo Miyada – Translated by Sebastião Nascimento.

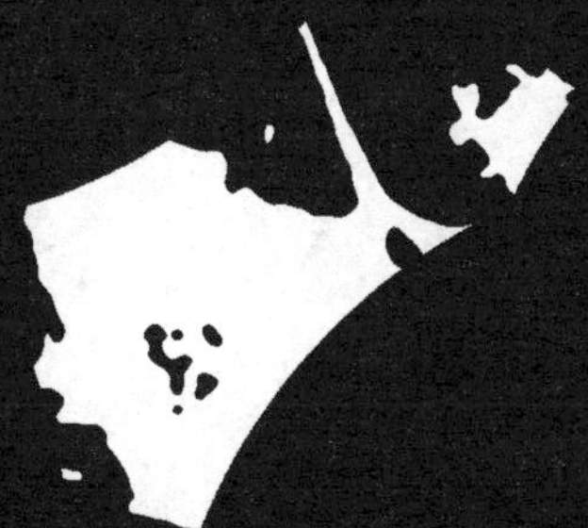

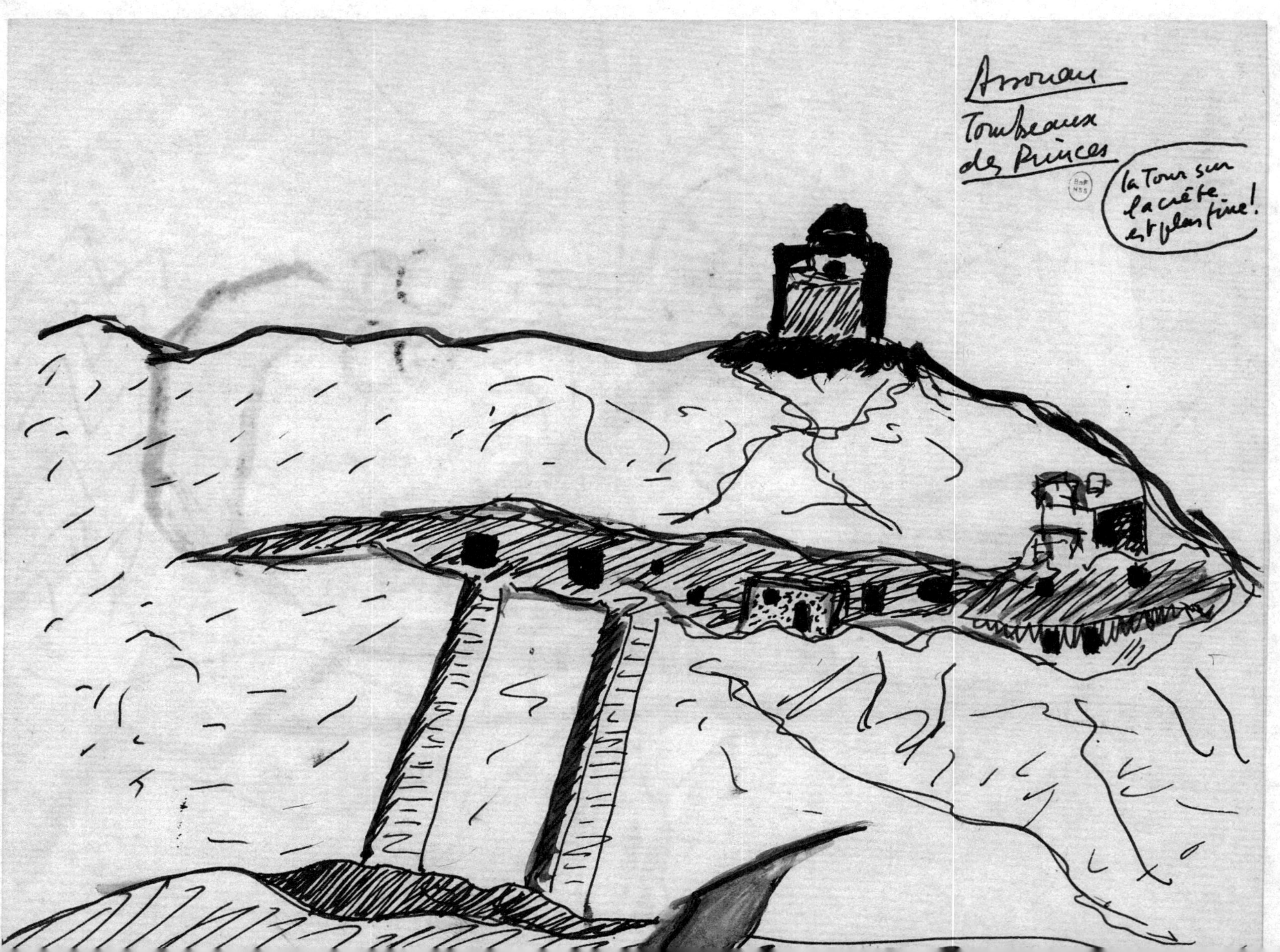

Assouan
Tombeaux des Princes
la Tour sur la crête est plastiquée!

<u>Le Caire</u>.   1.1.88

Cette poussière ne ~~peut~~ pas de sable. ~~Ceux~~ Les ~~us~~ qui ~~s'agitent~~ dans le grouillement ~~n'ont pas conscience~~ ~~ne le savent pas~~. Le grouillement ne frappe que ceux qui, dehors, observent et séparent. Au milieu, il est inutile impossible, aujourd'hui, de tenir un journal de voyage. ~~La~~ notation est immédiatement ~~caduque~~.

Tout comme ces buildings, occupés avant d'être terminés, qui se délabrent ~~sans avoir été neufs~~, au long desquels ~~vous~~ passez, ~~comme~~ ~~à la revue~~ autant de fantômes demi-~~incarnés~~. L'intense pression des villes est la même dans tous nos pays. Comme si se ramassait là ~~le fantasme~~ auquel l'histoire, un jour, nous pousse.

Un des pressentiments que fait naître cette foule à la fois pullulante et tranquille, c'est bien la pensée fugitive que tant de millions d'hommes et de femmes dont les souffrances ~~et~~ la mort furent nécessaires aux merveilles que nous allons ~~admirer~~. Sentiment convenu, dont on se garde comme d'une faiblesse ~~(hors d'usage)~~ comment l'emporte.

Mais, comme toutes les villes du Tiers-Monde, Le Caire a sa logique ~~désarée~~. Comment vivre cet univers urbain qui apparemment ne ~~connaît~~ pas de limites ni de raison? Ici repoussées au rang de ~~petites~~ agglomérations les grandes villes monumentales qui ont accompli l'histoire de l'Occident, comme Paris. Sans doute sont-elles destinées à devenir d'immenses musées, comme d'autres d'immenses ~~lieux~~. Le forcènement urbain conduit à la mort des villes où vivre. Les autostrades qui traversent Le Caire ressemblent, ~~par la~~ poussière ~~qui~~, à ceux qui sillonnent Caracas. Vous pouvez ~~circuler~~, des embouteillages, en ignorant les rues et les maisons ~~qui défilent~~ sous vous. C'est une autre manière de fréquenter ces ~~villes~~: à l'étage vous passez, en bas la vie s'obstine.

Aswan
Tomb of the Nobles
The tower on
the crest
is leaner!

<u>Cairo</u>. January 1, 1988

This dust does not resemble sand. The people passing by
in the bustle do not realize they are part of it, nor do they seem
to. The bustle only impacts those who, from the outside, stand
observant and detached. Trivial observation, clerical detachment.
Likewise, it is pointless and impossible today to keep a travel
journal. Every note is immediately rendered obsolete.

Just like these buildings, occupied before they are finished,
falling into disrepair from being new, along which we pass,
reviewing so many half-embodied ghosts. The intense pressure of
cities is the same in all our countries, as though it were a
distillation of the fantasy[1] to which we are pushed by the history
imposed upon us.

One of the premonitions aroused by this crowd, both teeming
and tranquil, is the fleeting thought of the millions of men and
women whose suffering and death were necessary for the wonders we are
about to see. It is a predictable feeling, which we ward off as an
outdated weakness. The monument prevails.

But, like all Third World cities, Cairo has its own logic
of immeasurability. How can anyone live in this urban universe
that seems to know no bounds or reason? Here, the great monumental
cities that gave birth to Western history, such as Paris, are
demoted to the status of modest settlements. No doubt they
are doomed to become vast museums, like so many other vast slums.
Overcrowding leads to the death of cities as places to live.

The freeways that cut through Cairo resemble those that
crisscross Caracas, only covered in dust. One can soar over the
junctions, stuck in traffic jams, ignoring the streets and houses
stretching out below. It is another way of experiencing these
cities: one drives by above, while life drags on below.

1   Their diagonal run, threatened, draws a line that stuns.

(de vie trop forte ou trop ~~épaisse~~)

←, pour les anciens privilégiés d'Égypte
et pour leurs esclaves,

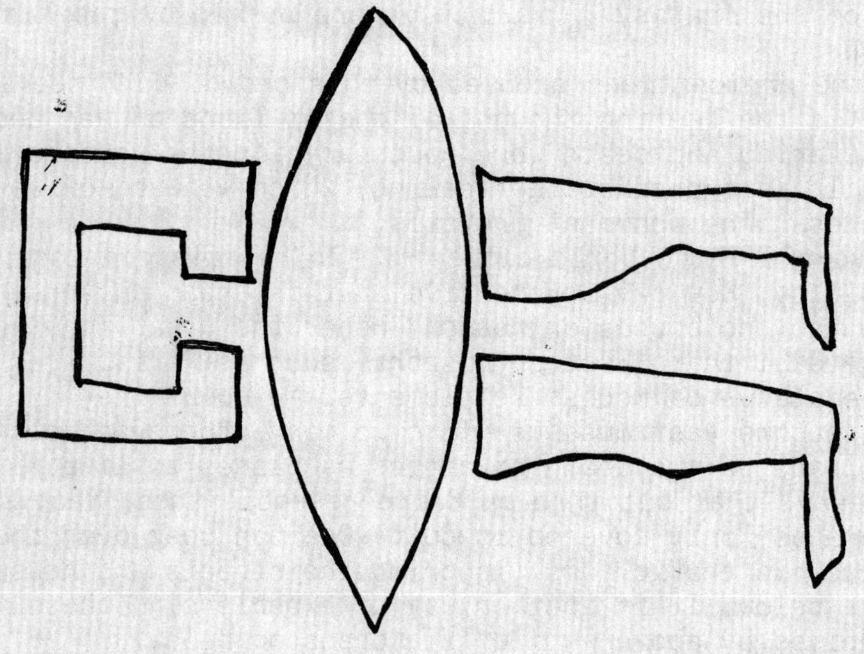

la pulsion de mort ~~[illisible]~~ se fortifie, inséparable d'une satiété
[coll]ective, qui dérive l'individu. Non pas une satiété
[vit]ale, mais ~~de commode~~ un surcroît de malaise. ~~[...]~~ Ce malaise
civilisation est-il à généraliser ? La présence de ~~la~~ mort,
[pr]ivilège d'y être admis pour toujours, écartait-ils l'obsession
[d'u]ne mort impossible ? Était-on plus tranquille, quand on s'y préparait ?
une telle destination ?
[L]a question est ~~[...]~~ la suivante : la pulsion de mort se désavi-
t-elle, quand l'impossibilité de vivre est là ? Dans des pays où
[c']un problème de manger une fois par jour, de soigner la
[moi]ndre des maladies, de s'abriter sous quelque chose qui ne
[n']a pas de paille, de carton ou de mauvaise tôle, d'échapper
[aux] soldats, policiers, fonctionnaires officiels ou non, dans ces pays reste-t-on
[poss]ible, en proie, aux inappréciables pressions du néant
[en]forcénement d'y ~~[...]~~ succomber ?
[Les] civilisations pharaoniques sembleraient en disfonc-
avec toute situation moderne. Elles acclimatient la
t, ~~[...]~~ faisant d'être une présence pour tout privilégié, ~~en~~ y
[mén]ageant un passage long et minutieux. L'appel du néant
[s]inon officialisé, par le fait même qu'il est retenu-
[q]uelques-uns d'y entrer sans enemer.
[n]e pas en parler familièrement. S'efforcer de raidir
[m]ain, de crisper les mots. L'aisance me paraît ici
[d]e manière d'~~affublé~~, la familiarité blessante.

(too tough or too troubled a life), ←

← , for those who were once privileged in Egypt
and for their slaves,

The death drive grows stronger, inseparable from a collective weariness that drifts the individual away. Not a weariness <u>of life</u> (either too tough or too troubled a life), but rather an excess of complacent malaise. Can this discontent with civilization be generalized? Does the presence of death, the privilege of being admitted to it for all eternity, dispel the obsession with the idea of an impossible death? Are we more at peace when we prepare for it with such tenacity?

The question is therefore: does the death drive diminish when the impossibility of living is plain to see? In countries where it is a problem to eat once a day, to treat even the slightest illness, to find shelter under anything other than cardboard or corrugated iron, to evade soldiers, police officers, official or unofficial torturers, in countries like these, do people remain sensitive, tormented by the unfathomable weight of nothingness, of the compulsion to yield to it?

Pharaonic civilizations would seem to be incongruous with any modern situation. They acclimatized death, making it a constant presence for all privileged individuals, and providing for a long and meticulous transition. The call of nothingness is thus formalized by the very fact that entering it without straying was reserved for a select few.

One should not speak lightly of it. Aim to have a firm hand and measured words. Here, the ease of speech might come across as offensive, and familiarity as hurtful.

Vu de Philae, un îlot
à la Ranghphi

Philae   5.1.88 - (Déesse Isis) syncrétisme Isis-Hathor

Production multilingue, enfermée de roches et de déchets,
finesse convenue (et un peu grasse) des dieux de Ptolémée, immédia-
ment prise dans la masse sévère d'un temple de Trajan,
une colonnade d'Hadrien. Celui-ci se méfiait de la sin-
ité des prêtres. Il n'en faisait pas moins offrande. comme partout ailleurs
sur les façades du temple principal, les chrétiens ont consciem-
ment raturé l'image des dieux païens. Mais ces blessures
de la pierre ont tellement respecté les contours d'Horus et
autres dieux qu'elles semblent les souligner, les relever
en vêtement de plume. Ces marques sont le signe d'un
sentiment qui ne s'avoue pas. La religieuse dégradation
une forme de la supplication.
Comme partout, les graffiti insolents des barbares visiteurs,
nous enseignent qu'ils sont de Londres par exemple, et
ils ont passé ici pour y laisser leur misérable trace. Mais
y ne distrait de l'obstination du lieu.
Je veux bien que l'île soit œcuménique. Mais les temples
d'un seul dieu parents ne cessent de m'apparaître comme des
doublés rhétoriques et inutilement impressionnants.
Le nom d'Hadrien est évoqué. Aussitôt se mélange aux
ces colonnes le impeccable de ce style où Marguerite
Yourcenar a voulu le fixer. Je sacrifie au syncrétisme.
visite au souk est traditionnelle. Accroupi devant son échoppe
cordonnier au nez de cuir répare une sandale. Seuls les sans
immobiles dans le mouvement. Malta dit qu'ils méditent
ernité. Sur plus de trois mètres, une colonne de marmites en cuir
me. Relativement peu de bruits. Le souk n'est pas dévoué aux
istes, qui s'y croient en pays prédestiné.
musée d'Éléphantine paresse dans une maison de style colo-
Des vitrines vides témoignent peut-être pour la rapacité
uciens fonctionnaires, coloniaux eux aussi.
jardins de Kitchener, comme un écho arasé de l'énorme prétention
vertir les silences de l'autre en sa propre obstination.
obélisque fêlée, encore prise dans la roche par une de ses
es, géant miné de fièvres dans une glaise aride.

view of Philae, an islet
in the style of ~~Tanguy~~

~~persis[t(s)?]~~
~~who wants to~~
~~stri[ve(s)?]~~

<u>Philae</u> January 5, 1988 - (Goddess Isis) Isis-Hathor syncretism

Multilingual production, surrounded by rocks and waste.

The conventional (and somewhat crude) finesse of Ptolemy's gods, immediately absorbed into the severe mass of Trajan's temple and Augustus's colonnade. During his stay here, Hadrian doubted the sincerity of the priests. And nevertheless made his offerings.

On the facades of the main temple, Christians, as everywhere else, diligently erased the images of pagan gods. But these wounds in the stone so closely followed the contours of Horus and the other gods that they seem to emphasize them, to highlight them with a garment of feathers. These marks are the sign of a consent that is not acknowledged. Religious defacement is a devious form of supplication.

Just like everywhere else, insolent graffiti from barbaric visitors, telling us that they're from London, for example, and that they stopped by to leave their mark. Yet nothing disturbs the obstinacy of this place.

I quite like the idea of the island being ecumenical. But the adjacent temples from the Roman era strike me as rhetorical repetitions and unnecessarily impressive.

The name of Hadrian is still evoked. Immediately, the severe columns blend with the impeccable echo of the style in which Marguerite Yourcenar wanted to capture it. I offer up a sacrifice to syncretism.

A visit to the souk is the traditional thing to do. Crouching in front of his stall, a cobbler with a nose covering made of leather repairs a sandal. Only the donkeys are motionless amid the hustle and bustle. Matta says they are pondering eternity. Over three meters high, a column of tin pots. Relatively little noise. This souk is not catering to tourists, who feel they are in a promised land.

The museum of Elephantine languishes in a colonial-style house. The empty display cases bear witness to the greed of former officials, colonialists themselves.

The Botanical Garden on Kitchener's Island, like a faded echo of the enormous arrogance of converting the silence of others into one's own obstinacy.

The cracked obelisk, still embedded in the rock on one side, resembles a giant consumed by fever and buried in arid clay.

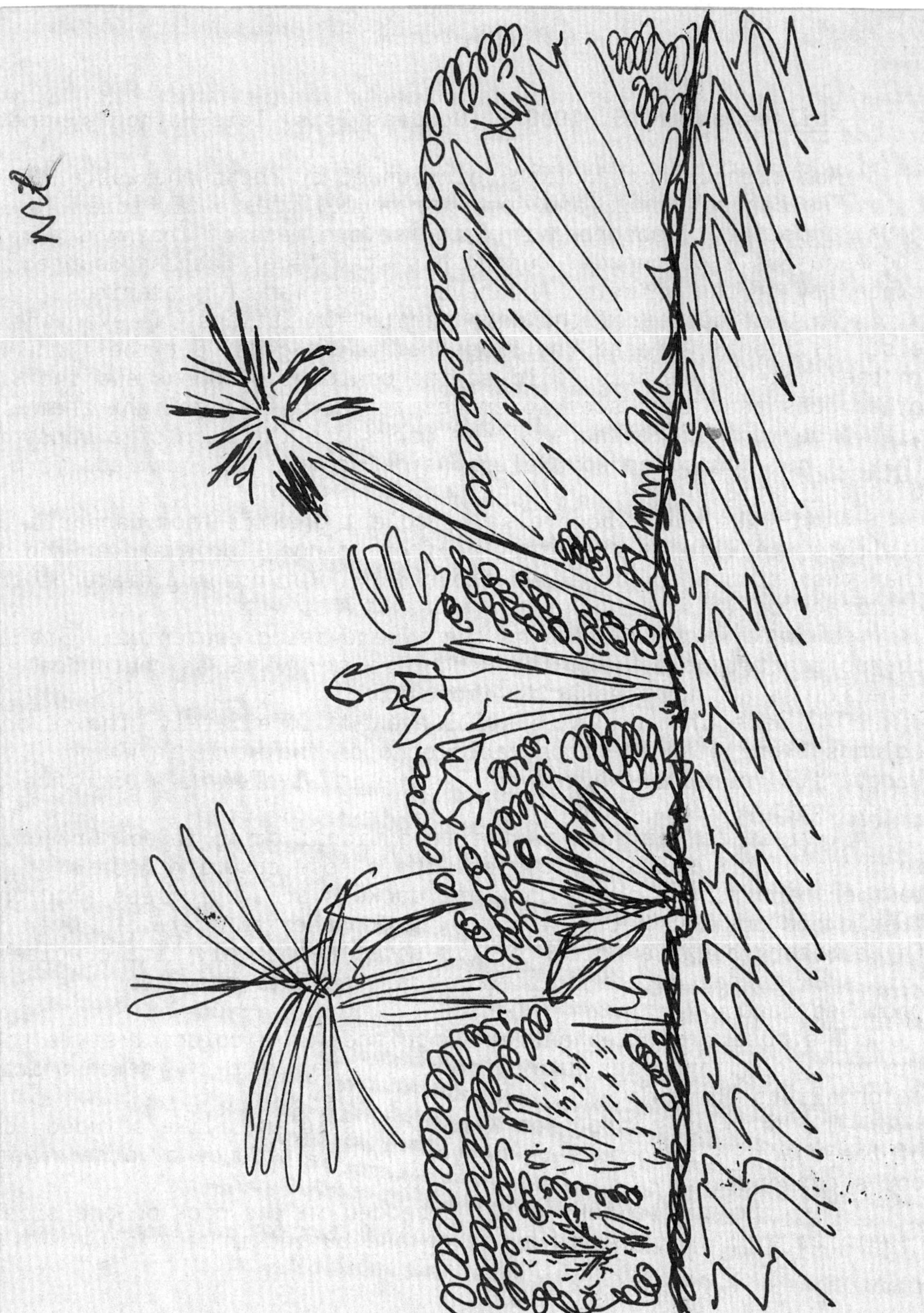

Kom-Ombo 6.1.88.   Haséris (Hathor) — (Horus)
Sobekh — (dieu crocodile)

Temple double. Non pas tant du mal et du bien [que celle de]
un [double] alliance. L'œil dérobé du dieu (par
un autre dieu rituellement énucléé), toute la liturgie
ie ici à le replacer, à retrouver sa lumière. Longue-
nt recensé les instruments chirurgicaux qui y servai-
Ha observe les alignements des nombrils chez les dieux
chez les déesses, celles-ci haut placés. Sylvie ne s'étonne
cunement d'une telle disposition, qu telle ... naturelle
bien entendu, Mme B. nous fait observer la [style] de cette
se époque: le sein des femmes avancé sur le bras,
joues grasses de dieux (Matta prétend qu'ils soufflent
ent, mais c'est le style qui le veut), les chairs rebondies
enrobent ... la silhouette, élancées dans la haute époque.
J'abandonne [tout] le reste: les cobras, les crocodiles,
hiaire sacré qui me repousse.
Nous convenons ... que beaucoup de ces hiéroglyphes,
t présage... les formes de branes. L'œil qui marche,
ui verse une larme en sillage, souligne le rapproche-
t. Il ne faut pourtant pas s'attarder à de tell...
ne font que confirmer une tendance à tout rapporter de
n'on voit à ce qu'on connaît.
a campagne alentour invite irrésistiblement à la ...
amps de ... me parlent. Je vois ... passer ...
gons à ... Ce ... paysage, vu du haut des remblais qui
...ent le temple, semble ne pas finir. Mais de l'autre côté
leuve, une mince traînée de végétation laisse l'espace
e à ... du sable.
aux foulées

**<u>Kom Ombo</u> November 6, 1988.   Haroeris (Hathor) - (Horus)
                                         Sobek - (crocodile god)**

A dual temple. Not so much of good and evil as of their alliance or mutual neutralization. The stolen eye of the god (by another god ritually blinded), the entire liturgy here aims to replace it, to restore its light. Extensive inventory of the surgical instruments used for this purpose. Matta observes the alignment of the navels of the gods and goddesses, the latter being placed high up. Sylvie is not at all surprised by this arrangement, which she considers natural.

Needless to say, Ms. B. draws our attention to the style of this early period: women's breasts protruding from their arms, the plump cheeks of the gods (Matta claims that they are blowing wind, but this is simply a stylistic choice), and the rounded flesh that envelops the figures, in contrast to the slender silhouettes we associate with the later period.

I shall refrain from discussing the rest: snakes, crocodiles, and other sacred animals that I find repulsive.

We agree that many of these hieroglyphs foreshadow Brauner's forms. The walking eye, or the eye shedding a tear, further emphasize the similarity. However, we should not dwell on such digressions, which only confirm a tendency to relate everything we see to what we already know.

The surrounding countryside is irresistibly inviting. The fields of reeds speak to me. In the distance, I see the passing of a train hauling sugarcane. Seen from the top of the embankments that bury the temple, this landscape seems endless. But on the other side of the river, a thin strip of vegetation gives way to sandy plains.

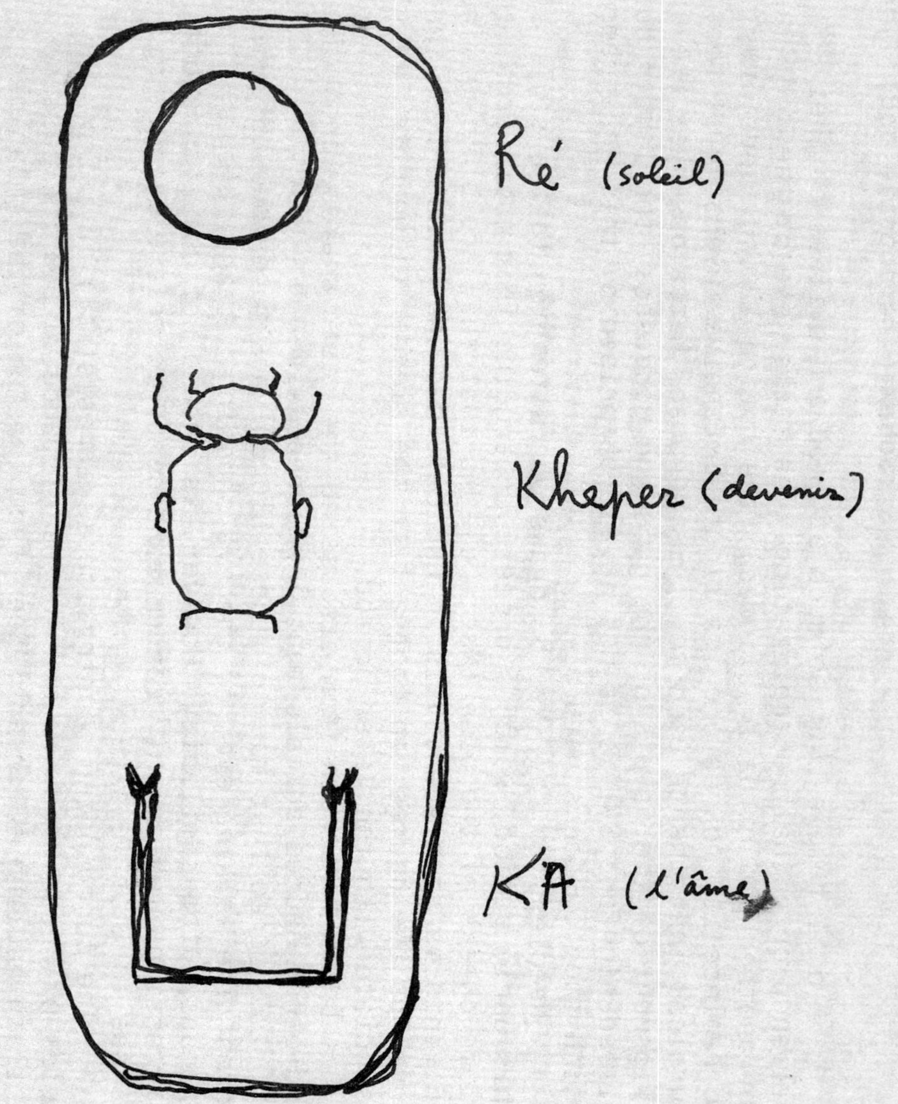

Ré (soleil)
Kheper (devenir)
KA (l'âme)

Temple de Karnac. (1ère visite) – (Amon)

Détournement du cinéma : on ne peut s'empêcher de penser aux scènes [du]
film <u>Mort sur le Nil</u>, tournées ici dans la forêt de colonnes.

La souriante (et inquiète) gentillesse des inspecteurs égyptiens, que je ne puis
m'empêcher de comparer à l'arrogance d'un jeune spécialiste
[fra]nçais, compétent et maître des lieux.
Les prisonniers que le pharaon enchaîne ou qu'il attrape en-
[fra]ppe par les cheveux sont conventionnellement de deux types !
[H]ittites ou les Asyriens à barbe triangulaire venus de l'est, les
[afr]icaines surgis de l'ouest et du sud. (L'Égypte se soucie d'être
un lieu de rencontre. même à cette manière)

Ra (Sun)

Kheper (to come to be)

KA (the soul)

"Your soul becomes Sun"

Karnak Temple. (1st visit) - (Amun)

A cinematic nod: one cannot help but think of scenes from the film *Death on the Nile*, shot here amid the forest of columns.

The smiling and concerned kindness of the Egyptian inspectors, which I cannot help but compare to the arrogance of a young French specialist, who is confident in his abilities and feels he is in control of the situation. The prisoners that the pharaoh chained or grabbed by the hair in handfuls were conventionally of two types: the Hittites or Assyrians with triangular beards from the east, and the Africans who emerged from the west and south. Even in this way, Egypt prided itself on being a crossroads.

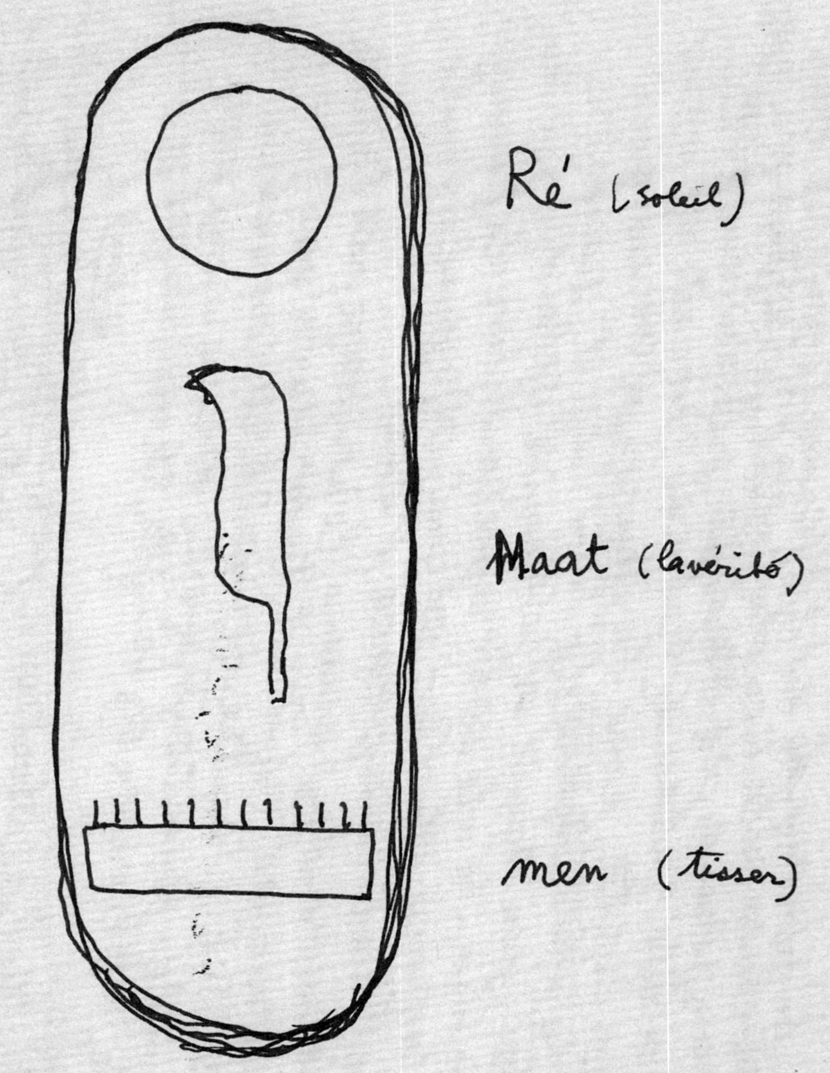

Ré (soleil)
Maat (la vérité)
men (tisser)

Abydos se présente comme le bout d'une route, un barrage
[fon]damental. Sa double structure — une à Sethi, une à Osiris,
en relief dans l'entrée du temple, en creux dans la [pre]-
mière à peine esquissée du profond, marque la pie[rre]
[en] dialogue solennel. Quand on débouche dans cette
[pre]mière que le temple marque ainsi d'un trait définitif
le chemin, on a l'impression d'un ~~à travers~~ ; le senti-
[men]t de naviguer sur une écluse, dont les deux passe-
raient ces deux styles d'inscription dans la pierre.
[P]arallèle entre temple et barrage est accentué par
[l'ex]ploration des alentours de l'édifice : les pierres non
[enc]ore recensées, comme à l'abandon, les échoppes touris-
[t]es, tout rappelle un lieu de passage. On navigue, à l'intérieur
[du] monument, ~~comme~~ porté par les flots incertains d'une
[riv]ière en poussière, çà et là descendue des ouvertures
[s]ur. On ne sait si cette eau de clarté roule dans l'obscu[r]
c'est la demi-ténèbre qui se fraie un lit dans [cet]
[éc]lat mystérieux.
Touchant ce passage, l'oubli.

"Je tisse la vérité à la lumière du soleil "

Ra (Sun)

Maat (truth)

men (to weave)

<u>Abydos</u> - January 11, 1988 - Seti-Osiris

Abydos presents itself as the end of a road, a fundamental barrier. The double structure—one dedicated to Seti, the other to Osiris—emblazoned in relief at the entrance to the temple, hollowed out in the faintly illuminated depths, imbues the stone with a solemn dialogue. When you reach this barrier, which the temple so definitively marks on the path, you get the impression of a crossing, the feeling of navigating a sluice gate, whose two passages are these two different styles of inscription carved into the stone. This parallel between temple and dam is accentuated by exploring the surroundings of the building: the stones that have not yet been catalogued, seemingly abandoned, the tourist shops, everything reminds us of a place of passage. We cruise inside the monument, borne by the uncertain waves of a dusty light, here and there streaming down from the openings in the wall. We do not know whether this water of clarity rolls in the shadows or whether it is the semi-darkness that carves out a bed for itself in this mysterious glow.

Punctuating this passage is oblivion.

"I weave truth in the light of the Sun"

§ j'ai dit l'ibis, viennent les oiseaux bleus d'Ass...
§ j'ai dit le fleuve, où nos bagages gréent d...
sébilles de sables
le chemin qui navigue est un flot o...
des dunes s'enlacent
l'esprit qui veille est un danseur, fou...
ses mains lassées

les nouvelles du monde à peine ont frapp...
la pierre...

passé la puissante colonne, leur lumiè...
s'est mise à nos fronts
l'abeille-aux-pattes-liquides sur...
roseau désenlacé

la langue qui m'enchante ici je la compr...
comme l'acier rauque est noyé d'échos

Une écriture sans projet ni forme, faussement ponctuelle, qui tourne autour de l'objet, comme une felouque en dérive autour des ombres du matin.

I meant the ibis, here come the blue birds of Aswan
I meant the Nile, where our bags hoist sand bowls
the path we sail is a stream where dunes sway
the wary mind is a dancer, mad with tired hands

the news of the world have barely grazed the stone…

past the mighty column, their light shone in our faces
the liquid-legged bee on the untangled reed

the language smokes, soars, strikes, here I pierce it, as the
hoarse steel is drowned in echoes

Writings without a plan or form, deceptively episodic, circling around their subject like a felucca drifting about in the morning shadows.

Les dalots (non nommés) font une structure lisible

L'idée de la relation ne suffit pas à la Relation

L'entassement donne pourtant le sens

Les malheurs du monde n'effraient presque

La théorie du monde n'équivaut pas à un seul poème

Les dalots convergent

le corps de terre en fièvre a quêté sa
essence, il a hélé ses mains de glaise
en l'unité blessée, il échevelle son
étoile, il a pris faille pour pensée, donne volcan pour fleur, et floraison d'é-
pines pour sentier

commence-t-il de labourer ce qui se voit
déboute-t-il tout mot qui surgit en cactée
son espace-pensée

les nouvelles d'îles au front
naufrages de soleil, bouquets rouges de
laves
nous y laçons nos mots si faciles
à découdre
sombres courant, le fleuve où nous me-
nons nos rades

comme écume comme racine

The gutters (unnamed) form a legible structure

The idea of relationship is not enough for the Relationship

Yet the accumulation gives meaning

The misfortunes of the world hardly frighten us.

The theory of the world is not equivalent to a single poem

The gutters converge

    the earthen body in fever struck its beat, hailed its clay
hands in bruised unity, tattered its star,
    took flaw for thought, offered volcano for flower, and thorn
thicket for path

    as he plows through what meets the eye
    as he throws out all words like cacti sprout
    his space of thought

    news from the island gripped to the front
    sunwrecks and lavish crimson lava feasts
    where we lace our words too frail to unravel
    dark ones drifting the river where we steer our rafts

    like froth like root

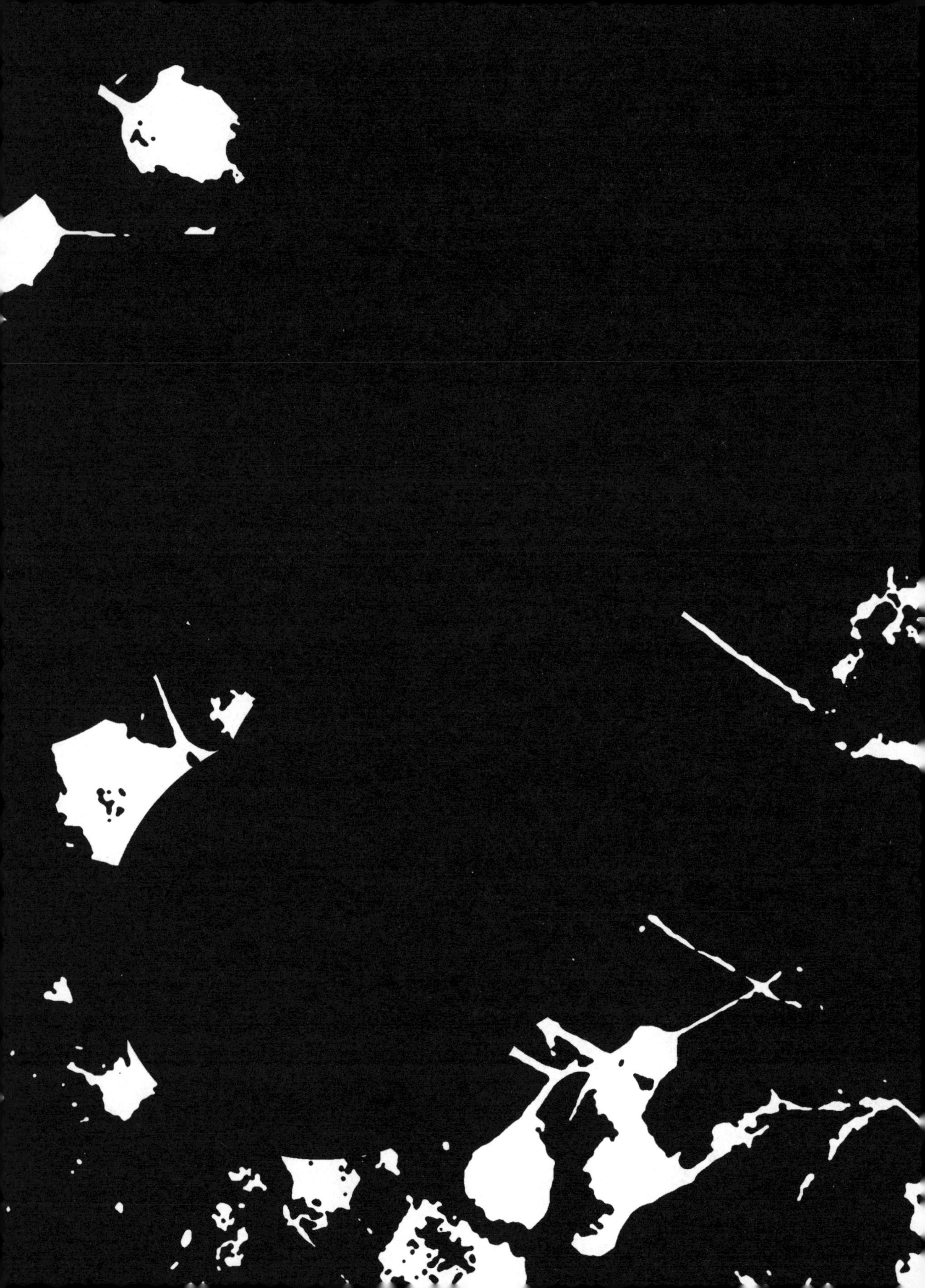

LIST
OF
IMAGES

**AGUSTÍN
CÁRDENAS**

Édouard Glissant, 1970s
Charred wood,
216 × 50 × 32 cm
Édouard Glissant personal
collection. Collection
Mémorial ACTe, fonds
Région Guadeloupe.
© Cárdenas, Agustín /
AUTVIS, Brazil, 2025

Untitled [Illustration
of Édouard Glissant's
Caribbean Discourse], 1980
Pen and wash on paper,
40 × 32.4 cm
Édouard Glissant personal
collection. Collection
Mémorial ACTe, fonds
Région Guadeloupe.
© Cárdenas, Agustín /
AUTVIS, Brazil, 2025

Untitled, 1979
Watercolor and ground
black stone on paper,
51 × 65.5 cm
Édouard Glissant personal
collection. Collection
Mémorial ACTe, fonds
Région Guadeloupe.
© Cárdenas, Agustín /
AUTVIS, Brazil, 2025

**AISLAN
PANKARARU**

Antiestático e teu silêncio
[Anti-static and Your
Silence], 2025
Acrylic paint on raw linen
canvas, 280 × 300 cm
Artist's collection.
Photo: EstudioEmObra

**AMOEDAS
WANI &
PATRICE
ALEXANDRE**

Untitled, 1997
Tembé woodprint,
62 × 70 cm
Sylvie Glissant
collection. Musée
Martiniquais des Arts
des Amériques (M2A2)
collection, France. Photo:
Raphaela Cinquepalmi

Untitled, 1997
Tembé woodprint,
62 × 32 cm
Sylvie Glissant collection
Musée Martiniquais des
Arts des Amériques (M2A2)
collection, France. Photo:
Raphaela Cinquepalmi

**ANTONIO
SEGUÍ**

Titanic series, 1970s
Soft pastel on paper,
50 × 65 cm
Édouard Glissant personal
collection. Collection
Mémorial ACTe, fonds
Région Guadeloupe.
Courtesy Mémorial ACTe

Titanic series, 1970s
Soft pastel on paper,
65.2 × 50.2 cm
Édouard Glissant personal
collection. Collection
Mémorial ACTe, fonds
Région Guadeloupe.
Courtesy Mémorial ACTe

**ARÉBÉNOR
BASSÉNE**

*Fu Munda After
Bermuda*, 2025
Mixed media on batik,
242 × 127.5 × 4 cm
Instituto Paz collection,
Brazil. Photo: Aicha
Tamsir Niane

**CESARE
PEVERELLI**

Untitled, n.d.
Oil on canvas, 33 × 41 cm
Édouard Glissant personal
collection. Collection
Mémorial ACTe, fonds
Région Guadeloupe.
Courtesy Mémorial ACTe

**CHANG
YUCHEN**

*Coral Dictionary
(That Girl is Braiding
her Hair)*, 2024
Pencil on paper,
35.6 × 43.2 cm
Courtesy of the artist and
the Beijing Commune

CHICO TABIBUIA

Exú hermafrodita [Hermaphrodite Exú], 1980s

Wood, 100 × 60 × 60 cm

Rafael Moraes collection, São Paulo, Brazil. Photo: Ricardo Miyada

EDOUARDO ZAMORA

Los Amantes 2 [The Lovers 2], 1987

Oil on canvas, 73 × 60 cm

Édouard Glissant personal collection. Collection Mémorial ACTe, fonds Région Guadeloupe. Courtesy Mémorial ACTe

EMANOEL ARAÚJO

Untitled, n.d.

Iron, 130 × 95 × 95 cm

James Acacio Lobo Lisboa collection, Brazil. Photo: Luan Torres, courtesy Galeria Frente

Navio [Vessel], 2011

Polychrome wood, metal, and beads, 221 × 80.5 × 18 cm

Courtesy of Simões de Assis, Brazil. Photo: EstudioEmObra, courtesy of Simões de Assis

ENRIQUE ZAÑARTU

Untitled, 1956

Etching and mixed media on paper, 23.5 × 28 cm

Édouard Glissant personal collection. Collection Mémorial ACTe, fonds Région Guadeloupe. Courtesy Mémorial ACTe

Untitled, 1956

Etching and mixed media on paper, 23.5 × 28 cm

Édouard Glissant personal collection. Collection Mémorial ACTe, fonds Région Guadeloupe. Courtesy Mémorial ACTe

ERNEST BRELEUR

Untitled, from the *Black* series, 1990

Acrylic on canvas, 131.5 × 144.5 × 3.5 cm

Private collection. Musée Martiniquais des Arts des Amériques (M2A2) collection, France. Photo: Raphaela Cinquepalmi

ETIENNE DE FRANCE

The Telling of the Stones, 2025

Film still

© de France, Etienne / AUTVIS, Brazil, 2025

FEDERICA MATTA

Federica Matta's record, *Cerro Santa-Lucia*, public installation in Plaza Brazil, Santiago, Chile, 1993

Photo: Courtesy of the artist

Federica Matta's record, *El Iceberg*, public installation in Plaza Brazil, Santiago, Chile, 1993

Photo: Courtesy of the artist

FLAVIO-SHIRÓ

Cocoon, 1999–2000

Oil on canvas, 61 × 186 cm

Artist's collection. Photo: Jaime Acioli

FLORENCIA RODRÍGUEZ GILLES

Lxs durmientes [The Sleepers], 2024

Pencil on paper mounting on canvas and double-edged axe, 250 × 450 × 7 cm

Artist's collection. Photo: Ignacio Iasparra

FRANK WALTER

Untitled (Views of Trees with Green Fields), n.d.

Oil on single ply cardboard, 23 × 20 cm

Paulo Vieira collection, Brazil. Photo: Eduardo Ortega. © Courtesy of Frank Walter's family

GABRIELA MORAWETZ

Untitled, 1985

Oil on canvas, 73 × 60 cm

Édouard Glissant personal collection. Collection Mémorial ACTe, fonds Région Guadeloupe. Courtesy Mémorial ACTe

GENEVIÈVE GALLEGO

Geographies of the Chaos-World, 2010

Relief on red-dyed charred wood, 90 × 180 cm

Private collection. Photo: Raphaela Cinquepalmi

GERARDO CHÁVEZ

Untitled, 1978

Oil on wood, 38 × 46 cm

Édouard Glissant personal collection. Collection Mémorial ACTe, fonds Région Guadeloupe. Courtesy Mémorial ACTe

HAMEDINE KANE [IN COLABORATION WITH TEJSWINI SONAWANE]

Salesman of Revolt, 2018–ongoing

Woodcuts, 54 × 39.5 cm each

Ronan Grossiat collection, France. Photo: Nikolas Brasseur

IRVING PETLIN

Untitled, 1990
Oil on canvas,
30.5 × 23 cm
Édouard Glissant personal collection. Collection Mémorial ACTe, fonds Région Guadeloupe. Courtesy Mémorial ACTe

Untitled, 1990
Oil on canvas,
30.5 × 23 cm
Édouard Glissant personal collection. Collection Mémorial ACTe, fonds Région Guadeloupe. Courtesy Mémorial ACTe

JEAN-CLAUDE GAROUTE (TIGA)

Untitled, 1994
Acrylic on canvas,
122 × 61 cm
Private collection. Musée Martiniquais des Arts des Amériques (M2A2) collection, France. Photo: Raphaela Cinquepalmi

JOSÉ GAMARRA

The inaccessible…, 1986-87
Oil on canvas,
73.5 × 100 cm
Édouard Glissant personal collection. Collection Mémorial ACTe, fonds Région Guadeloupe. Courtesy Mémorial ACTe

Untitled, 1986
Watercolor and ink on paper, 17.3 × 22.5 cm
Édouard Glissant personal collection. Collection Mémorial ACTe, fonds Région Guadeloupe. Courtesy Mémorial ACTe

JULIEN CREUZET

Exhibition view, *Eaux souterraines: récits en confluence*, Frac Poitou-Charentes, Angoulême, France, 2025

Photo: Aurélien Mole

KELLY SINNAPAH MARY

The Book of Violette: La Ballade, 2025
Acrylic on canvas,
162 × 130 cm
© Kelly Sinnapah Mary 2025, courtesy of the artist and James Cohan, New York. Photo: Dan Bradica, courtesy of the artist and James Cohan, New York

The Book of Violette: The Great Camouflage, 2025
Acrylic on canvas,
198.1 × 340.4 cm
© Kelly Sinnapah Mary 2025, courtesy of the artist and James Cohan, New York. Photo: Dan Bradica, courtesy of the artist and James Cohan, New York

M. EMILE

Untitled, n.d.
Oil on canvas,
92 × 61.2 cm
Édouard Glissant personal collection. Collection Mémorial ACTe, fonds Région Guadeloupe. Courtesy Mémorial ACTe

MANTHIA DIAWARA

A Letter from Yene, 2022
Film still
Commissioned by Serpentine, MUBI, and PCAI Polygreen Culture & Art Initiative, as part of Serpentine's Back to Earth project. Courtesy of the artist and Lumiar Cité / Maumaus, Portugal

MÉLINDA FOURN

Alphabet #2, 2024
Steel, dimensions variable
Courtesy of Selebe Yoon, Dakar. Photo: Courtesy of the artist

MELVIN EDWARDS

Labor (Then and Now), from the *Lynch Fragments* series, 1986
Steel, 38 × 16 × 19 cm
Ricardo Ortiz Kugelmas collection, Brazil. Photo: Ding Musa

Chains Variations in Color, 1974
Watercolor on paper,
58 × 89 cm
Ricardo Ortiz Kugelmas collection, Brazil. Photo: Ding Musa

MINIA BIABIANY

Exhibition view, *the sky with root-eyed*, Imane Farès, Paris, France, 2025
Courtesy of the artist and Imane Farès Gallery, France. Photo: Tadzio

NOLAN OSWALD DENNIS

recurse 4 a late planet, 2024–ongoing
Annotated wallpaper, archival images, notes, wall mount, dimensions variable
Courtesy of the artist. Photo: Dan Weill Gasworks, London

ÖYVIND FAHLSTRÖM

Notes 7 ("Gook" masks), 1971
Etching, gouache, ink, and dip pen, 66 × 50.2 cm
Édouard Glissant personal collection. Collection Mémorial ACTe, fonds Région Guadeloupe. Courtesy Mémorial ACTe

PANCHO QUILICI

Untitled, 1985
Collage, gouache, acrylic, graphite, colored pencil, ink, and scraping on paper, 49 × 60.5 cm
Édouard Glissant personal collection. Collection Mémorial ACTe, fonds Région Guadeloupe. Courtesy Mémorial ACTe

PAUL MAYER

Untitled, n.d.
Burned wallpaper and glass
Édouard Glissant personal collection. Collection Mémorial ACTe, fonds Région Guadeloupe. Courtesy Mémorial ACTe

PEDRO FRANÇA

Potosí, 2024–2025
Oil and tempera on linen mounted on wood,
22.5 × 30.5 cm
Artist's collection. Photo: Julia Thompson

POL TABURET

Dad was Incandescent that Night, 2025
Acrylics, alcohol-based paint and oil pastel on canvas, 220 × 220 cm
Courtesy of the artist and Mendes Wood DM, São Paulo, Brussels, Paris, New York. Photo: Pauline Assathiany

RAPHAËL BARONTINI

Exhibition view, *Somewhere in the Night, the People Dance*, Palais de Tokyo, Paris, France, 2025
Courtesy of Raphaël Barontini and Mariane Ibrahim (Chicago, Paris, Mexico City).
© Barontini, Raphaël / AUTVIS, Brazil, 2025

**RAYANA
RAYO**

As the Hours Go By, 2025
Oil on canvas,
74 × 64 × 3.5 cm each
Courtesy of the artist and
Mendes Wood DM, São Paulo,
Brussels, Paris, New York.
Photo: EstudioEmObra

**REBECA
CARAPIÁ**

Two Months of Stay, 2022
Ink on paper,
48 × 35.8 cm cada
Courtesy of the artist.
Photo: Ding Musa

**ROBERTO
MATTA**

*The Pelée Mountain
no Longer Smokes,
it Blooms*, 1958
Oil on canvas,
116 × 150 cm
Édouard Glissant personal
collection. Collection
Mémorial ACTe, fonds
Région Guadeloupe.
© Echaurren, Roberto
Sebastián Antonio Matta /
AUTVIS, Brazil, 2025

*Witnesses of the
Impossible*, 1987
Oil on canvas, 50 × 50 cm
Édouard Glissant personal
collection. Collection
Mémorial ACTe, fonds
Région Guadeloupe.
© Echaurren, Roberto
Sebastián Antonio Matta /
AUTVIS, Brazil, 2025

**SERGE
HÉLÉNON**

Memory Tree, 2000
Mixed media and collage
on an assemblage of
stretched wood and nails,
81 × 21 × 12.5 cm
Édouard Glissant personal
collection. Collection
Mémorial ACTe, fonds
Région Guadeloupe

**SHEILA
HICKS**

Talking Sticks,
2024–ongoing
Synthetic fiber, cotton,
and bamboo,
140 × 160 × 5 cm
Courtesy of the artist
and Nara Roesler.
Photo: Flavio Freire

**SYLVIE
SÉMA GLISSANT**

*Dismantling Boats
of Disaster*, 2023
Monotype engraving on
canvas, 220 × 140 cm
Courtesy Collection
agnès b. Courtesy
of the artist

**TARIK
KISWANSON**

*The Wait (Cimo
Furniture, 1953)*, 2025
Resin, fiberglass, paint
and Brazilian rosewood,
185 × 55 × 65 cm
Work comissioned by
Instituto Tomie Ohtake.
Courtesy of the artist

The Reading Room, 2019
Film still
Courtesy of the artist
and Carré d'Art - Musée
d'art contemporain

**TIAGO
SANT'ANA**

Apnea, 2024
Film still
Courtesy of the artist
and Leme Gallery

**VICTOR
ANICET**

Carcan, n.d.
Oil on wood, 60 × 60 cm
Édouard Glissant personal
collection. Collection
Mémorial ACTe, fonds
Région Guadeloupe.
Courtesy Mémorial ACTe

Cockroach, from *Major
Projections from Martinican
History* series, 1970
Oil on wood,
122 × 60.7 cm
Édouard Glissant personal
collection. Collection
Mémorial ACTe, fonds
Région Guadeloupe.
Courtesy Mémorial ACTe

**VICTOR
BRAUNER**

Yes No, 1947
Oil on canvas, 22 × 16 cm
Édouard Glissant personal
collection. Collection
Mémorial ACTe, fonds
Région Guadeloupe.
© Brauner, Victor /
AUTVIS, Brazil, 2025

**WIFREDO
LAM**

Pleni Luna series, 1974
*Feather Tree
Beautiful Thorn*
Lithograph in colors,
65 × 49.8 cm
Private collection,
France. Photo: Christophe
Laurentin. © Wifredo Lam
Estate, France

**ZÉ DI
CABEÇA**

Ex-votos, 2025
Acrylic on reclaimed
demolition wood found
in discarded materials,
dimensions variable
Acervo da Laje collection.
Photo: Rafael Martin

Instituto Tomie Ohtake

ARTISTIC DIRECTORSHIP

Paulo Miyada
Artistic Director
Ana Roman
Artistic Superintendent

CURATORSHIP

Catalina Bergues
Sabrina Fontenele

PRODUCTION

Carolina Pasinato
Production Manager
Rodolfo Borbel Pitarello
Assembly Coordinator

PRODUCERS

André Luiz Bella
**Maria Fernanda
   Bonfante Rosalem**
Pedro Lemme
Victor Constantino
Tamara da Silva Pereira
Apprentice

EDUCATION

Lilian L'Abbate Kelian
Education Superintendent
Mariana Per
Education Manager
Giselle Vitor da Rocha
Specialist in Integral
   Education and Territories
Mariana Galender
Research and Systematization
   Advisor
Thamata Barbosa
Producer
Maria Trindade
Natália Dias da Mota Sá
Educators

**FINANCE AND
   OPERATIONS BOARD**

Fábio Santiago
CFO and Operations Director

PLANNING

Fernanda de Lima Beraldi
Planning and Process Manager

FINANCIAL

Yasmin Tavares Lima
Financial Coordinator
Tarcísio Barbosa
Junior Financial Analyst

HUMAN RESOURCES

Tatiane Romani
Human Resources Analyst
Vitória Gomes
Intern

IT SUPPORT

Wesley Silva
IT Analyst

LEGAL

Escritório BS&A
Mei Jou
Attorney
Sofia Cavalcante
Attorney

OPERATIONS

Marcos Sutani
Coordinator
Samuel Luiz Costa Sena
Supervisor
**Alessandro Nóbrega
   de Oliveira**
Administrative Assistant

CUSTOMER SUPPORT

Cristian Mariano Moreira
Subcontract
**Cristiane Aparecida
   Santos**
**Darc Kenylce
   Rebouças Paiva**
Subcontract
Edson José Dias
Subcontract
Elza Martins Santos
Fábio Antonio de Araújo
Gilliard Gabriel da Silva
Subcontract
Giovanna Conceição
Apprentice
Jonas Pires Gomes Costa
**Marcelo Mariano
   de Oliveira**
Margarete Oliveira
Marleide Soares da Costa
Subcontract
Tainara de Jesus Veloso

CLEANING

Ana Paula da Silva
Subcontract
Ivanilda Pereira Santos
Subcontract
Jairo do Nascimento
Sebastião Alves Silva

MAINTENANCE

Adilson Oliveira
Jacildo Antonio de Paula

Manuela Moscoso
Executive and Artistic
   Director

Maya Piergies
Deputy Director

Emmy Catedral
Director of Bookstore

Rachel Valinsky
Director of Publications

Agustin Schang
Head of Production

Sam Riehl
Head of Communications

Marian Chudnovsky
Curatorial Assistant

Mia Weathers-Fowler
Advancement Associate

**Omololu Refilwe
   Babatunde**
Bookstore and Visitor
   Services Associate

Jane Hait
Founder and Board President

Exhibition

THE EARTH, THE FIRE,
THE WATER, AND THE
WINDS: FOR A MUSEUM
OF ERRANTRY WITH
ÉDOUARD GLISSANT

Conceived and Produced by
Instituto Tomie Ohtake

Curated by
Ana Roman
Paulo Miyada

Exhibition Design
Ligia Zilbersztejn
Rian Tito

Graphic Design
Catê Bloise
Paula Lobato
Tie Ito
Vitor Cesar

Contributors
Ana Roman
Catalina Bergues
Cecília Vilela
Paulo Miyada
Sabrina Fontenele

Proofreading
Ana Elisa Camasmie
Divina Prado
Fabiana Pino
Felipe Carnevalli

Translators
John Norman
Sebastião Nascimento

Artists
**Aislan Pankararu,
Amoedas Wani &
Patrice Alexandre,
Antonio Seguí,
Arébénor Basséne,
Agustín Cárdenas,
Cesare Peverelli, Chang
Yuchen, Chico Tabibuia,
Eduardo Zamora,
Emanoel Araújo,
Enrique Zañartu,
Ernest Breleur, Etienne
de France, Federica
Matta, Flavio-Shiró,
Florencia Rodríguez
Giles, Frank Walter,
Gabriela Morawetz,
Geneviève Gallego,
Gerardo Chávez,
Hamedine Kane, Irving
Petlin, Jean-Claude
Garoute, José Gamarra,
Julien Creuzet, Kelly
Sinnapah Mary,
M. Emile, Manthia
Diawara, Mélinda
Fourn, Melvin Edwards,
Minia Biabiany,
Nolan Oswald Dennis,
Öyvind Fahlström,
Pancho Quilici, Paul
Mayer, Pedro França,
Pol Taburet, Raphaël
Barontini, Rayana
Rayo, Rebeca Carapiá,
Roberto Matta, Serge
Hélénon, Sheila Hicks,
Sylvie Séma Glissant,
Tarik Kiswanson, Tiago
Sant'Ana, Victor Anicet,
Victor Brauner, Wifredo
Lam, Zé di Cabeça.**

THE EARTH, THE FIRE,
THE WATER, AND THE
WINDS: FOR A MUSEUM
OF ERRANTRY WITH
ÉDOUARD GLISSANT

Publication

Produced by
Instituto Tomie Ohtake

Co-published by
Center for Art, Research and Alliances (CARA)

Editors
Ana Roman
Paulo Miyada

Texts
Ana Roman
Catalina Bergues
Cecília Vilela
Édouard Glissant
Patrick Chamoiseau
Paulo Miyada
Sabrina Fontenele

Graphic Design
Catê Bloise
Paula Lobato
Tie Ito
Vitor Cesar

Editorial Coordination
Ana Roman
Divina Prado
Felipe Carnevalli

Proofreading
Ana Elisa Camasmie
Divina Prado
Fabiana Pino
Felipe Carnevalli
Rachel Valinsky

Translators
Ana Roman
Ivan Rocha
John Norman
Sebastião Nascimento

Images Licensing
Carolina Pasinato
Maria Fernanda Rosalem

Photos
Aicha Tamsir Niane, Aurélien Mole, Christophe Laurentin, Dan Bradica, Dan Weill, Ding Musa, Eduardo Ortega, EstudioEmObra, Flavio Freire, Ignacio Iasparra, Jaime Acioli, Julia Thompson, Luan Torres, Nikolas Brasseur, Pauline Assalthiany, Rafael Martins, Raphaela Cinquepalmi, Ricardo Miyada, Tadzio

Printer
Ipsis

ISBN
978-65-89342-59-5

LCCN
2025945173

Distributed worldwide by
ARTBOOK | D.A.P.
75 Broad Street, Suite 630
New York, NY 10004
orders@dapinc.com
www.artbook.com

Acknowledgments
Ministério da Cultura, Nubank, SKY, Fundação Norma y Leo Werthein, 2025 France–Brazil Season, Institut Français, Instituto Guimarães Rosa (Itamaraty), Ministério das Relações Exteriores, Engie, LVMH, ADEO, JCDecaux, Sanofi, Airbus, CMA CGM, CNP Seguradora, L'Oréal, TotalEnergies, Vinci, BNP Paribas, Carrefour, VICAT, SCOR, Mémorial ACTe, Édouard Glissant Art Fund, Institut du Tout-Monde, CARA, Alexandra Mollof, Cleusa Garfinkel, Coleção Ivani e Jorge Yunes, Laura Ning, Sarina Tang, Sylvie Séma Glissant, Mathieu Glissant, Ronan Grossiat

Technical Specifications

Cover
Paperback flexibound, 18 × 24 cm closed, 72 × 24 cm open (including book spine and flaps)
Masterblank Lino 270g
4/1 colors
36 × 24 cm embossing

Bookblock
240 pages
160 pages in Munken Print Cream 80g, b&w
80 pages in Munken Linx Rough 120g, 4/4 color
Illustrations: 80 color, 4 b&w

Print run
2,500 copies

Printer
Ipsis

Type
EK Roumald
Transcript Mono Pro
Plantin MT Pro

Publisher information
Published by Instituto Tomie Ohtake and the Center for Art, Research and Alliances (CARA) on the occasion of the traveling exhibition, *The Earth, the Fire, the Water, and the Winds: For a Museum of Errantry with Édouard Glissant*, organized by the Instituto Tomie Ohtake

Instituto Tomie Ohtake,
São Paulo, Brazil
September 3rd, 2025
to January 25th, 2026

Center for Art,
Research and Alliances
(CARA), New York, USA
February 21
to May 10, 2026

INSTITUTO
TOMIE OHTAKE
Complexo Aché Cultural
Rua Coropés 88   05426-010
Pinheiros – São Paulo
(11) 2245-1900
www.institutotomieohtake.
   org.br
instituto@
   institutotomieohtake.
   org.br

CENTER FOR ART,
RESEARCH AND
ALLIANCES (CARA)
225 West 13th Street
New York, NY 10011
www.cara-nyc.org

Dados Internacionais de Catalogação na Publicação (CIP)
(Câmara Brasileira do Livro, SP, Brasil)

The Earth, the Fire, the Water, and the Winds : For a Museum of
Errantry with Édouard Glissant / [organização Instituto Tomie
Ohtake ; tradução John Norman, Sebastião Nascimento, Ana Roman].
-- 1. ed. -- São Paulo : Instituto Tomie Ohtake, 2025.

Vários colaboradores.
Título original: A terra, o fogo, a água e os
ventos: Por um Museu da Errância com Édouard
Glissant.

ISBN 978-65-89342-59-5

1. Artes visuais - Exposições - Catálogos
I. Instituto Tomie Ohtake.

25-286601   CDD-700

Índices para catálogo sistemático:
1. Artes visuais 700
Aline Graziele Benitez - Bibliotecária - CRB-1/3129

Instituto Tomie Ohtake is a cultural institute dedicated to the visual arts and their intersections with education, architecture, and design, always open to dialogue with other languages and contemporary themes. Our approach is grounded in research, experimentation, and the development of exhibitions and educational experiences that bring together multiple voices and consider access in its many dimensions. Founded in São Paulo (SP) in 2001, the Institute operates throughout Brazil through its awards, educational programs, and dissemination of knowledge. In addition, we foster connections and work in partnership with national and international institutions. The Institute preserves and nurtures the legacy of Tomie Ohtake and her sons, Ruy and Ricardo, and remains committed to the memory and continuity of the knowledge it produces.

CARA is an arts nonprofit, research center, and publisher that aims to expand public discourses and historical records to reflect art's abundant pasts, presents, and futures.Through initiatives including publishing, exhibitions, public programs, and fellowships, we seek to challenge dominant narratives and amplify the breadth of arts and culture.